SHAPE UP!

The Infinite
Possibilities
of Shapes
in Design

SANDU

SHAPE UP!

The Infinite Possibilities of Shapes in Design

First Published in the USA in 2024 by

GINGKO PRESS

Gingko Press, Inc.
217 W Richmond Ave, Suite B
Richmond, CA 94801
Tel: (510) 898 1195
Fax: (510) 898 1196
Email: books@gingkopress.com
www.gingkopress.com

ISBN 978-1-58423-798-3

By arrangement with
Sandu Publishing Co., Ltd.

SANDU ⊜
PUBLISHING

Edited and produced by Sandu Publishing Co., Ltd.
Executive Editor: Liz Yao, Joann Chung
Designer: Wu Yanting
Cover Design by Wu Yanting
Shapes in the cover concepts provided by Brand
Brothers, Lina Forsgren, Ilab design ltd.,
Paprika Design, Loukas Chondros

info@sandupublishing.com
sales@sandupublishing.com
www.sandupublishing.com

Printed and bound in China

Contents

Preface

" The origin of graphics comes with the emergence of human beings. When our ancestors painted the caves and murals in which they lived, shaps became a medium for communication, expressing feelings and consciousness. "

Graphic design is a way of conveying information and expressing meaning through visual elements. As the most basic factor in visual communication, shapes are composed of points, lines, and plane. They are images with a certain form and style. They can be abstract or concrete, static or dynamic, appear alone or in combination. At the design level, it can enhance visual effects, create atmosphere, express emotions, shape images, and allow the design to carry the brand values and ideas of the creators.

The origin of graphics comes with the emergence of human beings. When our ancestors painted the caves and murals in which they lived, shapes became a medium for communication, expressing feelings and consciousness. With the advancement of civilization, shapes are not only used to depict animals and humans. It is no longer a single communication tool. It is also a carrier for people to understand and convey information related to life, culture, art, etc. In the modern civilization era, shapes started to enter the fields of design and architecture. The various theories of ancient architecture, mathematics, and art that we have studied and used so far are all closely related to graphics. From a specific aspect, its role in graphic design is self-evident. As we know, shapes have a variety of styles, and the use of shapes in different designs also has their own emphasis. Apple's logo, which is an apple with a bite, is impressive. Abstract-style illustrations, which fully express the creator's intention, are done with flexible use of shapes and a large number of overlapping and combinations of shapes. It can be said that shapes are an essential source of inspiration for creators from all fields.

Looking back at the history of shapes, Bauhaus is an important node that must be mentioned. Its three important elements are "primary colors, geometry and minimalism". Compared with other design theories, Bauhaus used graphics as a design element to the extreme. Wassily Kandinsky transformed "points, lines, and plane" into notes in his creation, and made many wonderful works. The reason why Bauhaus can influence so many people is that while it pays attention to the color of form, it also emphasizes the relationship between points, lines, and plane, which has guiding significance for the use of geometric shapes, so we decided to base on the "geometric figures" elements of Bauhaus, to launch this book and lead readers into this "world of shapes".

At the opening chapter, this book shows readers the shapes in the grottoes and Mesopotamian civilization, the use of graphics by art schools such as Bauhaus and De Stijl, combined with contemporary creativity around the world, presenting a variety of design works using geometric, abstract and figurative graphics. This book brings together 75 outstanding design agencies and designers from around the world, with more than 100 works, from various fields, such as brand design, packaging design, logo design, layout design, etc. In order to gain an in-depth understanding of the design concepts behind the works, this book also invites interviews with design agencies and designers to present to readers the importance of shapes in gra-phic design. Designers from different countries and regions have different understandings and answers to the same question, but due to the commonality of graphics, some of the answers also make us feel that design has "the same goal through different paths." In the book, we divide shape into geometric shapes, abstract shapes and figurative shapes, but in fact, no matter whether the graphics are complex or not, the purpose and method of design are the same. As a question mentioned in the book, "What will be your focus when creating shapes?" One agency's answer is "Always emotion and function." The values of the brand, the emotion of the viewer, the design's function are crucial in any design.

Finally, we would like to thank all the design agencies and designers who helped us in the invitation and editing of this book. One person's view may be one-sided, but when we look at one thing from many angles, we can see the beauty in more levels and angles. Shapes themselves are also a kind of beauty. They have a long history, and people are still working hard to show their beauty in various places until now. The designers' idea is "for a better life", and shapes play an indelible role in this.

How Graphics Develop

The Development of Graphics Throughout History

I. Definition of Graphics

As the name graphic design implies, graphics, also known as shapes, are fundamental in design. Throughout human history, shapes have been used since the beginning of civilization as a way of communication, artistic representation, and design. Shapes have played a vital role in visual, from the simple geometric patterns in cave paintings to the detailed and abstract forms of contemporary art. In this article, we will take a look at the history of shapes and their evolution across different areas.

II. Prehistoric and Ancient Shapes

A. Patterns in Cave Paintings

Lascaux Painting
©Wikicommons

The earliest form of human expression, shapes, serve as the primary language of visual communication. Throughout ancient times, people left their mark through cave paintings, revealing a fascination with basic shapes. Cave artists utilized various techniques, including finger tracing, clay modeling, engravings, and hand stencils, to create their remarkable artworks.

While motifs may vary in cave paintings around the world, certain similarities can be observed across regions. Cave artists predominantly depict wildlife such as bison, deer, and hunting scenes. This preference can be attributed to the close relationship between early humans and animals, as well as the artists' ability to closely observe these creatures.

An exemplary case is the Lascaux Cave Paintings from the Magdalenian cultures, dating back to 15,000 BCE. It was discovered by an 18-year-old teenager, Marcel Ravidat, in 1940. Located in the caves of Lascaux in France, most of the images on the wall have been painted with red, yellow, and black colors from mineral pigments. Lines, dots, and shapes were likely used to depict animals, human figures, or abstract concepts.

B. Symbolic Shapes in Ancient Cultures and Civilizations

Ancient Egyptian Hieroglyphs
©Wikicommons

Symbolic meanings are embedded in shapes in ancient cultures, which serve as a visual language to deliver concepts, beliefs, and cultural identities.

In ancient Egyptian art, shapes played a significant role in religious and funerary contexts. Egyptian hieroglyphic writing was composed of pictures. They are visually figurative because they represent real-life objects or abstract elements. The use of squares, rectangles, and triangles in hieroglyphics depicted objects, deities, or abstract ideas. Either stylized or simplified, the symbols are easy to be recognized.

For example, a circle with a dot inside represents the sun, a rectangle with a vacancy at the bottom represents the house, and a half-missing semicircle represents a mountain. Some of these logograms are identical to Oracle. They can be used alone or combined with phonetic complements and determinatives to deliver meanings.

In ancient Mesopotamian civilizations of Sumer, Babylon, and Assyria, cuneiform writing, which consisted of wedge-shaped symbols, was impressed onto clay tablets. Though not strictly geometric, these symbols conveyed abstract concepts, marking an early use of shapes for communication.

Cuneiform emerged at the end of the fourth millennium BC and was originally a proto-cuneiform script consisting of cuneiform hieroglyphs printed on clay tablets. During the early Dynastic period, writing evolved from purely hieroglyphic to a combination of pictograms and early syllabic symbols, expanding the range of expression.

During the Sumerian cuneiform period (2350—2000 BCE), the dominance of Sumerians brought about a major change. The system shifted to representing syllables and sounds and offered greater flexibility and precision. When Akkadian (a Semitic language) replaced Sumerian, cuneiform was further simplified and standardized. Logographic symbols were reduced to make way for phonetic symbols.

In the Old Babylonian period (2000—1600 BCE), cuneiform writing reached its peak. Writing became more standardized. Cuneiform was used for administrative records, legal texts, literature, and correspondence.

In later periods, such as the Assyrian and Neo-Babylonian, cuneiform evolved into a more sloppy and streamlined script. Symbols and abbreviations were introduced to simplify the writing process. With the conquest of Mesopotamia by the Persian Empire, cuneiform gradually deteriorated, and by the 1st century AD, it was no longer used.

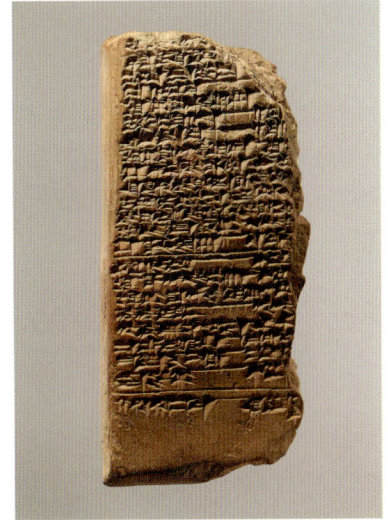

Cuneiform tablet: Old Babylonian balag to the mother goddess Aruru ©Wikicommons

III. Classical and Renaissance Geometry

A. The principles of Geometric Shapes in Euclid's *Elements* and Their Impact on Greek and Roman Architecture

Ancient Greek is vital in promoting the study of geometry. Euclid, an Ancient Greek Mathematician, is considered the "father of geometry." His *Elements* introduces principles of geometric shapes and their properties. The concepts of points, lines, angles, and shapes allow architects to understand and manipulate geometric forms. Heavily influenced by the ideals of symmetry and proportion, the architecture in ancient Greece and Rome use geometric forms in the design.

Symmetry is a fundamental concept of Euclidean geometry and was widely used in ancient Greek and Roman architecture. The Greeks were known for their pursuit of visual harmony and balance. The Parthenon, a masterpiece of classical Greek architecture in Athens, is a clear example of this. The facade displays remarkable symmetry with rows of evenly spaced columns and a perfectly balanced triangular portico. This symmetry is achieved through precise calculation and careful placement of architectural elements, resulting in a visually appealing and aesthetically balanced structure.

The Parthenon in Athens, photograph by Steve Swayne

The Colosseum in Rome, Photograph by DAVID ILIFF

Inspired by the architectural achievements of the Greeks, the Romans further extended the Euclidean principle of symmetry in their monumental architecture. The Roman Pantheon is an example of their mastery of symmetrical design. The iconic dome, supported by a circular colonnade, creates a perfectly symmetrical interior. The balance achieved by the symmetrical composition contributes to the structural stability and visual grandeur of the building.

Proportion, another important aspect of Euclid's influence, was intricately incorporated into architectural designs in Greek and Roman times. Euclid's mathematical concept of proportion provided architects with guidelines for creating harmonious relationships between different architectural elements. The ancient Greeks recognized the importance of proportion in their architectural achievements and often used the "golden ratio" as a guide. The Temple of Apollo in Didyma, Turkey, is a remarkable example of Greek architecture that embodies a sense of proportion and balance. The elongated floor plan and column construction conform to mathematical proportions, creating a visually appealing proportional structure.

Roman architects also embraced the principles of Euclid's proportions in their monumental buildings. The Colosseum is one of the most iconic architectural achievements of ancient Rome and demonstrates a meticulous application of proportions. The amphitheater's elliptical shape and tiered seating show a precise understanding of proportions and provide visual harmony and balance to the design.

B. The Renewed Geometry in Renaissance

Leonardo da Vinci and Filippo Brunelleschi, two visionary figures of the Renaissance, played instrumental roles in the renewed interest in mathematical proportions and geometric symmetry in design. Both artists and thinkers recognized the profound impact that mathematics and geometry could have on the aesthetics and functionality of architectural and artistic creations.

Leonardo da Vinci, renowned for his mastery in various fields, including painting, sculpture, and engineering, had an insatiable curiosity about the natural world. His deep understanding of mathematics and geometry allowed him to infuse his artworks with a sense of harmony and balance. Leonardo da Vinci's exploration of proportion can be seen in his iconic painting, *The Vitruvian Man*. Inspired by ancient Roman architect Vitruvius, this famous work illustrates a male figure with his arms and legs extended in different positions and inscribed within both a circle and a square. Commentators note that Leonardo da Vinci created an artistic depiction of a male figure, instead of a simple portrayal of the human body. His use of intricate lines and explicit presentation of details "weaves together the human and the divine." This work represents a meticulous study of human proportions and exemplifies Leonardo da Vinci's fascination with mathematical harmony in the human form.

Filippo Brunelleschi, an early Renaissance architect, and engineer, also revolutionized architectural design through his innovative use of geometry and mathematical relationships. Brunelleschi used his profound knowledge of geometric and engineering principles in his most famous architectural work, the dome of Florence Cathedral (Duomo). The dome's harmonious proportions and elegant design were achieved through precise calculations and meticulous attention to symmetry. Brunelleschi's use of geometric principles not only resulted in a visually stunning structure but also ensured structural stability and longevity.

Both Leonardo da Vinci and Filippo Brunelleschi were inspired by the ancient world, and in particular by the work of Greek mathematicians and architects such as Euclid and Vitruvius. Mathematics and geometry

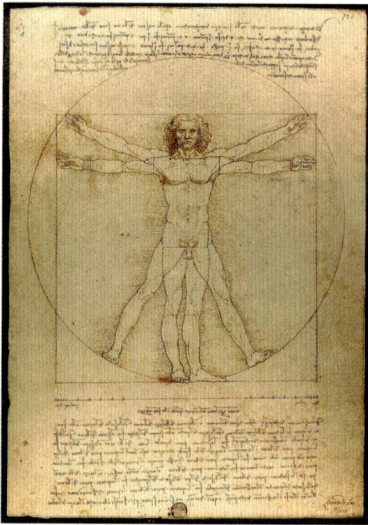

The Vitruvian Man
by Leonardo da Vinci
©Wikicommons

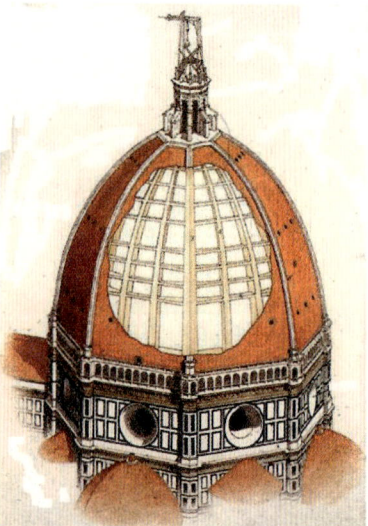

Cutaway of the Dome of Florence
Cathedral ©Wikicommons

were the keys to unraveling the secrets of beauty and order in art and architecture.

Their renewed interest in mathematical relationships and geometric symmetry influenced not only their work but also the broader artistic and architectural movements of the time. Their ideas and techniques spread through the Renaissance and formed the aesthetic and intellectual foundations of that period.

Bauhaus Building in Dessau
©Wikicommons

IV. Modernist Abstraction and Geometric Exploration

A. The Bauhaus Movement

The 20th century witnessed a revolution in the exploration of forms, fueled by the rise of influential modernist movements such as Bauhaus and De Stijl.

Founded in 1919 in Weimar, Germany, by Walter Gropius, the Bauhaus movement sought to unify all forms of art and promote functional design in which form and function merged seamlessly. With a vision to integrate the disciplines of art, sculpture, technology, and architecture, Gropius founded a school that embodied these ideals. In 1925, the Bauhaus school moved to Dessau, marking a crucial period when the distinctive Bauhaus style began to take shape. The work of the Bauhaus Design School employs abstract and modernist principles, reflecting a conscious removal of excessive detail and emphasizing simplicity and purity of form.

Wassily Kandinsky, a Russian painter and art theorist, was born in Moscow on Dec. 16, 1866. His personal history has followed a fascinating path, intertwined with the development of modern art and the influential Bauhaus movement. Kandinsky was a pioneer of abstraction in Western art.

His artistic style went through a long period of development. In his art, Kandinsky placed a strong emphasis on the relationship between shapes and their ability to convey emotion and spirituality. This became particularly evident when he was back in Germany and the Bauhaus after 1922. He developed forms study based on points and line forms and further applied his geometric approach to painting.

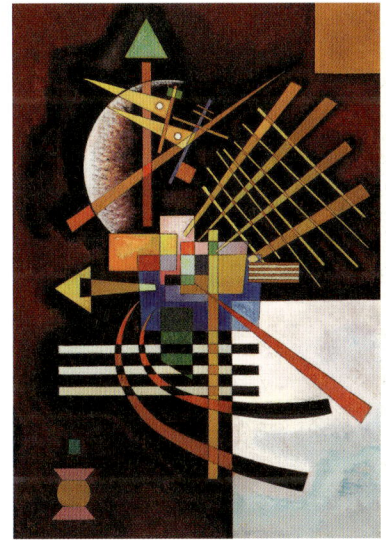

Oben und links by Wassily Kandinsky
©Wikicommons

Kandinsky believes in the spiritual and emotional power of geometric shapes. The interplay between circles, squares, triangles, and arcs invites the viewer to consider the symbolism and meaning inherent in each shape. He also believes that shapes have a language of their own, capable of conveying profound truths and evoking specific emotions.

One of his notable works, *Im lockeren Schwarz* (In Loose Black), exemplifies his mastery of shapes and their transformative qualities. *Im lockeren Schwarz*, created in 1927, is a piece of work Kandinsky created in memory of his time in the Bavarian town of Murnau. He distilled the elements from the natural landscape, like mountains and trees, into shapes, including squares, triangles, and circles. The captivating composition is characterized by a variety of geometric shapes, block colors, and textured surface effects. This painting showcases Kandinsky's fascination with geometric forms and their expressive potential.

The triangle and the circle are the two primary plane figures, Kandinsky. A triangle signifies aggression, a circle delivers a sense of deepening and a square demonstrates calmness. The pointed and linear forms create a dynamic visual rhythm, building up "worlds" through abstract shapes. The use of black, contrasted with hints of vibrant colors, adds depth and intensity to the composition.

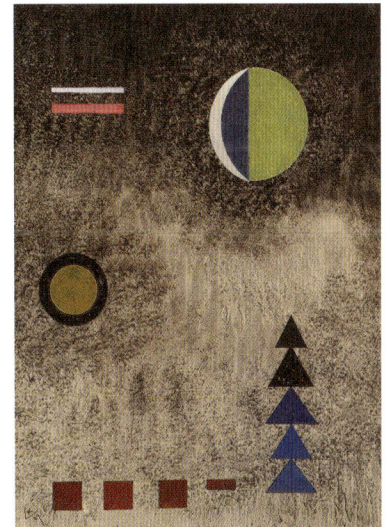

Im lockeren Schwarz
by Wassily Kandinsky
©Wikicommons

B. De Stijl

De Stijl, also known as Neoplasticism, is a Dutch artistic movement founded in 1917 and holds a prominent place in the history of modern art. The movement advocated pure abstraction and the return to the essence of form and color. The visual composition is either vertical or horizontal, and only primary colors, black and white are used.

At the forefront of this influential movement stood Piet Mondrian, a visionary artist who played a leading role in shaping its principles and aesthetics. He is the figure synonymous with De Stijl through his distinctive art style.

As a leading figure, Mondrian not only exemplified the movement's principles in his art but also contributed to its theoretical discourse. He published essays and manifestos outlining the ideas of De Stijl, emphasizing the importance of abstraction, simplicity, and the integration of art with daily life.

He set the boundaries of De Stijl in his essay, "This new plastic idea will ignore the particulars of appearance, that is to say, natural form and color. On the contrary, it should find its expression in the abstraction of form and color, that is to say, in the straight line and the clearly defined primary color." He aimed to create a universal visual language that transcended individualistic expression and embraced a harmonious order.

Mondrian's approach to art is characterized by deep simplicity and a focus on basic elements such as geometric shapes, primary colors, and straight lines. Mondrian's artistic style reflects his belief in the power of abstraction and the inherent harmony of geometric forms, as he once stated, "As a pure representation of human thought, art will express itself in aesthetic purification, that is, in abstraction. Therefore, the new idea of form could not take the form of natural or concrete expression."

He tried to strip away all superfluous elements and reduce his compositions to their purest essence. Using only horizontal and vertical lines, Mondrian created grids and planes that he filled with primary colors such as red, yellow, and blue, as well as black, white, and gray. These elements are carefully balanced to evoke a sense of balance and rhythm.

Mondrian's compositions, such as his iconic *Composition with Red, Yellow, and Blue*, exemplify his revolutionary approach to art. The use of straight lines and primary colors created a visual language that conveyed a universal order and balance. The large red block at the upper right, which dominates the composition, is balanced by the blue block at the bottom left. To create a harmony of contrasts, he also used shades of slightly lighter or darker colors and different textures. Through this reduction of form and color to their essential elements, Mondrian created a direct connection with the spiritual and transcendental.

The influence of De Stijl and Mondrian's artistic style extends beyond the visual arts. Their principles influenced architecture, design, and even urban planning. The emphasis on clean lines, geometric shapes, and a sense of harmony is reflected in the design of buildings, furniture, and everyday objects.

Mondrian's legacy as a pioneer of abstraction and a leading figure in De Stijl remains profound. His art continues to inspire artists and designers around the world, and his vision of a harmonious and universal visual language continues to resonate in the art world and beyond. Through his exploration of geometric shapes, primary colors, and his quest for balanced order, Mondrian created a timeless aesthetic that revolutionized the art world and left an indelible mark on the history of modern art.

Composition with Yellow, Red, Black, Blue, and Gray by Piet Mondrian
©Wikicommons

Composition with Red, Yellow, and Blue by Piet Mondrian
©Wikicommons

V. The Application of Shapes in Modern Graphic Design

The use of shapes in modern graphic design consists of a wide variety of forms, including geometric, abstract, and figurative shapes. Each type of shape has a unique quality and visual impact, allowing designers to create striking and dynamic images that attract attention and convey meaning.

Geometric shapes, characterized by precise lines and defined angles, are essential elements of graphic design. Squares, triangles, circles, and rectangles are common geometric shapes used to create structure, symmetry, and order in designs. They give the viewer a sense of stability, balance, and precision. Geometric shapes are often used in logo design, branding, and minimalist aesthetics, where clean lines and simplicity are desired.

Abstract forms that deviate from direct visual perception mainly refer to the organic forms presented in this book. On the other hand, they deviate from representational forms and include non-referential and subjective designs. These forms allow designers to convey emotions, concepts, or feelings through a non-literal visual language. Abstract forms can evoke a sense of movement, energy, and ambiguity and provide a more interpretive and open visual experience.

Figurative forms, also called expressive forms, come from recognizable objects or shapes in the real world. They include images of people, animals, objects, and scenes. Figurative shapes are widely used in storytelling, advertising, and branding because they provide direct visual communication and are easily and immediately recognizable. These shapes allow designers to convey a specific message, evoke emotion and build a connection with the viewer.

The combination and interaction of these three shapes allow designers to create visually dynamic and impactful designs. By using geometric shapes strategically, designers can create structure, organization, and visual hierarchy. Abstract shapes add depth, creativity, and a touch of personality to designs, stimulating the imagination and creating curiosity. Figurative shapes provide direct representation and connection, allowing for effective communication and instant recognition.

For example, a technology company's logo could include geometric shapes to convey a sense of precision and innovation. Abstract shapes can be used to evoke a sense of futurism and energy, while figurative shapes can represent concepts such as connectivity or progress. Combining these shapes produces a visually appealing and conceptually meaningful logo that resonates with the brand and its target audience.

The use of shapes in contemporary graphic design has been further expanded by digital tools and techniques. Designers can easily manipulate and transform shapes and experiment with scale, color, and texture to create visually stunning and interactive designs. The versatility of digital platforms enables the seamless integration of geometric, abstract, and figurative forms, providing endless opportunities for creative expression and engaging user experiences.

In short, modern graphic design includes the use of geometric, abstract, and figurative forms. Each category offers a unique visual quality and plays a specific role in design. Geometric shapes provide structure and order, abstract shapes evoke emotion and creativity, and figurative shapes promote direct expression and recognition. By making clever use of these shapes, designers can create visually striking, conceptually rich, and engaging designs that have a lasting impact on the viewer.

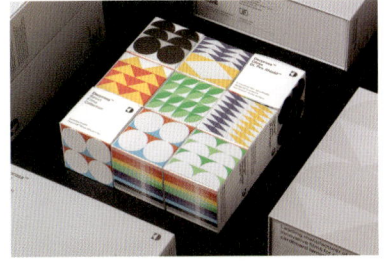
Derprosa by Plácida

Buds by Sakaria Studio

Mushroom Compadres by Ochodias Studio

Geometric

Shapes

In graphic design, geometric patterns use shapes and lines
repeatedly to create eye-catching, original designs.

01. From your perspective, what meaning do geometric shapes carry in visual communication?

Geometric shapes are part of visual communication from an early age. One of the first things that children learn to draw is a circle as a head for stick puppets. For me, that's the point! Everyone is capable of perceiving a geometric shape. In other situations, too. For example, video game joysticks that were created with triangle, circle and square buttons. Geometric shapes are everywhere.

● **Anselmi Comunicação**

They mean everything. In fact, visual communication is impossible without geometric shapes because they are everywhere, directly or indirectly: in illustrations, in typography, in any image or composition… Everything is built from geometric shapes. Thanks to that, we can modulate the communicative intention with more minimalist designs (less geometric shapes) or more ornate (more geometric shapes).

● **errorerror.studio®**

Geometric shapes, because of their simplicity and universality, allow the creation of new forms of language, understandable by everyone. They reassure, they are malleable, and convey a panel of very vast notions, which can revolve around the organization, the rigor, the structure, but also the play and the inventiveness. It is an infinite playground, these forms being at the base of all the most complex structures.

● **Brand Brothers**

For me, geometric shapes represent a clear order and pureness of beauty. It is interesting that every geometric shape can be represented by mathematical equations, so they are the hidden order in natural beauty, a universal language that people of different ages and cultural backgrounds could understand.

● **for&st**

Geometric shapes serve as a fundamental component of visual communication. The level of significance they hold within the design hierarchy determine the prominence of other elements, such as typography, illustrations, and photography. In other words, the use and placement of geometric shapes can define the visual importance of a design and how it communicates its intended message.

● **Studio Herrström (Erik Herrström, Creative Director)**

They are, together with dots and lines, the simplest forms you can use in graphic design. Basic elements — like fire, water, earth, and air. But the number of ways how you use them and combine them can be infinite. Thanks to the constraints, they bring to the design you can easily create a visual system that is in some way unique.

● **Jakub Konvica and Martin Egrt**

Geometric shapes are a powerful graphic asset that can appeal to many people regardless of where they live, education, age, ethnicity, etc. Why is that? Because they are primarily familiar to us, remember that we played with them before learning about letters. Culturally, we build conventions regarding some of them. For example, if we see a yellow circle, we can easily relate that image to the sun, and if the circle is white over a black colored background, we can see a moon. So imagine how effective the geometric shapes (also the usage of color) are in visual communication to captivate our audience simply and straightforwardly.

● **MAKEBARDO**

We think that geometry is a visual communication method that can easily convey messages to people through modern graphics.

When there is something with a clear motif in the design, the design of the decorative elements may not be good. Minimize decorative elements and leverage shapes to deliver messages.

● **maum studio**

The fundamental components of any design are simple geometric shapes. These shapes can serve different functions in any work, such as being the foundation on which the product image is built or being used to add flourishes. However, each shape must serve a specific purpose, whether it's to express a particular idea or concept, draw attention to a specific element of the design, improve the overall aesthetic appeal, or conceal any imperfections. Therefore, it's crucial to consider the role of each geometric shape in a design carefully.

● **PG Brand Reforming
(Dzianis Valianski, Creative Director)**

Geometric shapes are a universal visual language, a set of graphic lines or a set of logical arrangements that carry a diversity of ideas and lead the viewer to receive the information through visual expression.

● **nomo®creative**

The methodology we use in every project of any kind is always the same: analysis, concept, and form.

We use graphic synthesis in project, which we understand as a more direct and effective way of communication, as well as a way to reach less obsolete solutions.

The use of geometric shapes helps us to simplify each project. Graphic synthesis is the ability to simplify forms or concepts, giving them greater expressive force and a clearer presentation of the message.

● **Plácida**

Geometric shapes play a big role in visual communication as they can convey meaning, and communicate ideas and concepts in a powerful way. Each shape has its own unique properties and can be used to convey different messages. For example, circles and curves are often associated with softness and unity, while sharp angles and straight lines can represent stability, balance, and order.

Geometric shapes can also be used to create patterns and designs that can be both aesthetically pleasing and functional. They can be used to organize information and create visual hierarchy in design, making it easier for the viewer to navigate and understand the content.

Overall, geometric shapes are a versatile and powerful tool in visual communication, and their use can greatly impact the message and effectiveness of a design.

● **Tobias van der Valk**

02. Under what circumstances would you choose geometric shapes as the main visual for your creation?

Well, we can use geometric shapes in a lot of creations. You can use them in logotypes for a construction company or a real estate, for example, and you may surprise your customer. I like using geometric shapes, too, in projects that I need everyone to be capable of perceiving my job easier, because that's simple. Actually, geometric shapes are powerful tools in the hand of great designers. The basic stuff works!

● **Anselmi Comunicação**

There is no typical project that is destined to be worked around geometric shapes; it is a feeling, linked more to the temperament of the client, the state of mind, to what he/she wishes to convey, while obviously being open to this type of graphic design, which is often abstract and metaphorical. Nevertheless, most of the time, when ideas emerge around simplicity, assembly, construction or modularity, geometric shapes are a very suitable research vector.

● **Brand Brothers**

In design, geometric shapes have the power to communicate complex concepts in a simple way. Whenever the project to be communicated requires or has the potential to use them for this purpose, it should be valued as a creative path to explore. This applies to projects in any field, but especially in sectors where the "intellect" plays a main role such as philosophy, education, science, and technology.

● **errorerror.studio®**

When it comes to choosing geometric shapes as the primary visual for a visual communication or brand identity, I consider various factors. However, I find that geometric shapes work exceptionally well when creating brand identities. This is because they provide a solid foundation that defines the overall look and feel of the brand.

One of the main advantages of using geometric shapes in this context is that they can be employed without the need for a third party to create other assets such as photography or illustration. This means that they can be easily reproduced and scaled, making them ideal for various communications.

● **Studio Herrström**
  (Erik Herrström, Creative Director)

I usually start my project with geometric shapes, as it gives greater flexibility in helping me to get a quick preview of whether the design concept is workable. I believe a solid and valid concept will tell you how the execution should be.

Geometric shapes help to draw and allows the audience to stay focused on the elements you want to emphasize, so when there are design projects that need to convey complicated information structure, it is a reliable tool for me to direct the reader's reading flow.

● **for&st**

In case we want to be very simple and direct.

● **Jakub Konvica and Martin Egrt**

If we had to define it briefly, our design is conceptual, minimalist, playful and with sensibility. So under these parameters, geometry is usually closely linked to our creations. We feel comfortable facing the blank sheet if we have geometric shapes to play with. They are usually the basis of everything we design. Sometimes they last as such, and other times they transform into other things. And that's the magic we love about them; they can change and evolve.

● **MAKEBARDO**

Geometrical shapes are used in graphics in the work of projects that require clear representation of the message they want to convey.

● **maum studio**

Geometric shapes are our primary visual component of choice for situations where quick focus and reading are particularly important.

● **nomo®creative**

Our approach to designing varies depending on the specific task. In most cases, we start with basic geometric shapes, which serve as the foundation for our design. If our objective is to create a minimalist design, we use these shapes and colors to convey our vision using simple tools. This helps us achieve a clean and sleek look, while the choice of colors adds depth and character to the design.

● **PG Brand Reforming**
(Dzianis Valianski, Creative Director)

The graphic proposal of the visual identity made for Derprosa is based on two fundamental principles of the Bauhaus. Under these principles, a brand architecture is generated, ranging from the brand symbol, the result of the union of square, circular and triangular shapes, to the new graphic application that will define each Derprosa product.

The system is created based on the main finishes and the different ranges available. Under this approach and for the first axis of classification, four different geometric grids are proposed; three of them represent the characteristics of basic optical appearances, transversal to all products, gloss, matte and semi-matte. The fourth grid is dedicated exclusively to DL Soft Touch®, Derprosa's flagship product. For the second axis, six color combinations are reserved to identify each of the six ranges into which the product catalog can be divided.

● **Plácida**

Geometric shapes can be used in a variety of contexts to create effective and visually appealing designs. It can be used to create interesting and abstract compositions, as well as creating a pattern or texture or in a logo or brand identity.

In the visual identity of Bureau Buitendienst, the geometric shapes visualize the interventions in public space. Bureau Buitendienst is a placemaking agency. They help governments, urban planners and project developers to think about and act upon the livable environment of the future. These visions are visualized through the geometric shapes in the logo. Combined with the straightforward typography which highlights the rational side of their approach, colorful shapes the creative side.

● **Tobias van der Valk**

03. Geometric shapes, as classic elements, are never outdated. Could you share the works, creators, or schools that influenced you?

When I was a child, I liked to drawing organic shapes. Whereas in the university, I studied hard about Bauhaus. In the real market, I learned to make the right choice, between using organic or geometric shapes. Nowadays, I think my job can be influenced by everything! I think every day I find a way to be my own reference. The best reference bench is our own mind, with the projects that we have already created or searched in a customer immersion.

● **Anselmi Comunicação**

As a self-taught designer, I find inspiration for geometric designs from a variety of sources, including architecture and nature. While I recognize the contributions of influential schools of design such as the Bauhaus movement and Swiss Style, I don't have specific references that have influenced me personally. Overall, I believe in keeping an open mind and drawing inspiration from a wide range of sources to create unique and compelling designs.

● **Studio Herrström**
   (Erik Herrström, Creative Director)

I fell in love with graphic design when I came face to face with the modernist logos and symbols of the 1960s and 1970s. It is, for me, of unspeakable beauty and intelligence. It is the ultimate intellectual exercise, the noblest design because it reduces all unnecessary noise to something pure. They are also objects that last, that leave a mark, that make the environment more beautiful and that help to clarify information in a statutory way, far from any visual frenzy. My references are therefore a few decades old!

● **Brand Brothers**

Like most designers, the work of great master Yusaku Kamekura has a great impact on my vision towards design. The legendary design for the Tokyo Olympic 1964, the big bright red circle with precise proportion, is truly unforgettable.

● **for&st**

We are influenced by the cultures that communicated with symbols, by the geometric logos of the Scandinavian school, by Cubism and, of course, by the Bauhaus (and who wouldn't be!). As for studios or designers, we feel very influenced by the use of the geometric shapes by Cruz Novillo, Mario Eskenazi, Hey Studio, De_Form, Studio Carreras, Brand Brothers or Ceci Erlich among others.

● **errorerror.studio®**

Bauhaus is of course the obvious matador of geometric shapes. But if we could name some contemporary examples, we really like the work of an illustrator Marco Oggian. Or Spotify Wrapped 2022 by agency Hornet and motion designer Vucko.

● **Jakub Konvica and Martin Egrt**

The first that comes to our mind is the Bauhaus because we feel inspired by it and use it as a reference in our design. Without a doubt, its legacy in using geometry in different disciplines was revolutionary. Its minimalism and rationalism still influence contemporary design. On the other hand, we cannot leave out Pre-Columbian cultures and their immense beauty regarding geometric use. More near in history, we could name Ellsworth Kelly or Yayoi Kusama, but naming someone is always unfair because one is made up of many references, and all are valuable.

● MAKEBARDO

Growing up in Eastern Europe, we were surrounded by expressive geometry in the environment, particularly in the form of constructivist posters. This tradition has influenced our perception of art and design from a young age, including brutal architecture, graphic design, and illustration. Notable names include Roman Duszek, Bruno Munari and avant-garde poster designers from the early 20th century also left a lasting impact in our works.

● PG Brand Reforming
   (Dzianis Valianski, Creative Director)

The inspiration of the work is mainly derived from daily observations.
   The patterns used in the "Team Korea" package graphics are all derived from actual sports stadiums such as track and field, tennis courts, and swimming pools.
   Graphics in "Bongja Festival" were designed based on the actual flower shape, and "I am Ground" was also designed in consideration of the human shape.
   Through investigation and observation, we used molding elements that can express the characteristics most clearly.
   We were influenced by the Bauhaus, which deeply influenced the development of art, architecture, graphic design, interior design, industrial design, and typography.

● maum studio

There is a great influence by geometry, basic forms and the reduced use of elements in all our work. In general, everything that originated at the Bauhaus and the Ulm Design School later on has a great impact on us.
   During the 1940s the Swiss, from their eternal neutrality, had been shaping what was later called "international style". An exercise in synthesis inherited from the Bauhaus and architectural rationalism. The Ulm Design School took the baton from them in the mid-1950s, when a group of designers led by Max Bill and Otl Aicher decided to give a scientific and objective sense to design. Understanding design as a scientific discipline meant the way to mathematics, geometry, technique... and above all to a concept of continuous experimentation and methodological research.

● Plácida

When it comes to geometric works that have never gone out of fashion, one of the most influential is the European typeface Futura by German designer Paul Renner, which is definitely on our font list whenever we need to use geometry as a design vocabulary.

● nomo®creative

Being a designer from the Netherlands, I frequently draw inspiration from the Dutch style which includes the works of renowned artists like Piet Mondrian, Gerrit Thomas Rietveld, and Wim Crouwel. However, I also find inspiration in styles such as Bauhaus because of the way they combine simple geometric forms with powerful typography.

● Tobias van der Valk

04. How to make better use of geometric shapes in design?

The key is the concept! Beautiful shapes you can see in every part of the world. But, shapes with concept, explanation, strengthen the brand, bring result for your client — everything making sense. This is the real point! I think it's not about "how to use geometric shapes", but "how to make a great design".

● **Anselmi Comunicação**

A lot of things have been done around these forms, especially via modular systems. In my opinion, the pitfalls to avoid are to fall into simplism and déjà vu. Today, assembling rounds and squares is not enough! It's a wonderful framework for research, but you have to keep pushing the boundaries of geometry, to reinvent the language and surprise your audience. And, despite the simplicity of this working base, it is always possible to find new graphic forms...

● **Brand Brothers**

To me, the key is to find a reason for everything. Whatever shape you use needs to connect back to the brand, its strategy and values at the same time as you solve the given brief. To me, when it comes to making better use of geometric shapes in design, the key is to have a purpose for the shapes that are being used. It's essential to ensure that the shapes chosen align with the brand, its values, and the overall design strategy while also meeting the requirements of the design brief.

● **Studio Herrström**
   (Erik Herrström, Creative Director)

There's no correct answer to this question, because it depends on several variables. What is considered a "misuse" can sometimes be a success depending on each case. The "good" cannot be the enemy of the "new". But if we had to say something about it, we would invite visual communication professionals to ask us the right questions, such as: Does the project really need it? What would happen if you didn't use it? Does it help the audience to understand the message better or does it fulfill an aesthetic role? Am I using this resource or abusing it?

● **errorerror.studio®**

Executions with geometric shapes never get old. In the past, it usually presented in a 2D graphic form, but with the help of 3D modelling and animation, it greatly expanded the possibility of using geometric shapes, is exciting to see how a solid geometric form being simulated as a real object and react to the law of physics.

● **for&st**

For the very reason they are still used pretty often we need to constantly think how to reinvent them. How to use them the new way, how to emphasize their strengths — being so elemental and simple but at the same time in combination they can form more complex structures.

● **Jakub Konvica and Martin Egrt**

We would be unable to answer if there is a way to make "better" use of geometric shapes. Because our method when it comes to creating evolves as the projects follow one another, so what today turns out to be the "best way" will surely change tomorrow.

● MAKEBARDO

We think it is important to include "wit" based on certain rules in the design. Geometric shapes must have certain rules because shapes without rules can be rather confusing. However, it is hard to like a design with only rules, so we consider the sensibility as much as possible.

● maum studio

Before discussing the "better" use of geometry, it is important to return to the concept of design and to consider the role that geometry plays in the concept as language, grid, or logic, just like the title of the book *Less but better* by designer Dieter Rams.

● nomo®creative

Creating geometric shapes for a project may seem easy, but it requires a lot of attention to detail. The challenge is to view familiar shapes freshly, considering factors such as angle, color, and space between shapes to create something unique and appropriate for the project. While there are countless circles and combinations of circles in the world, the Mastercard logo stands out among them due to its meaningful design. The difficulty lies in transforming simple shapes into something significant.

● PG Brand Reforming
(Dzianis Valianski, Creative Director)

We do not make good use of geometry if we use it only for aesthetic purposes. A good project must be functional and forms must always be the result of a good conceptualization. "Form follows function".

When designing, visual components are essential for the public to have an accurate perception of what we want to show them. Geometric shapes are the first ones that come to mind when we think of shapes. Circles, squares, rectangles, triangles are formed by regular patterns, and are easily recognizable. They give us an idea of order and efficiency. It is essential that the use of these shapes is justified and helps to explain the conceptualization of the project.

● Plácida

Geometric shapes, being a fundamental form, are widely utilized in various ways. Incorporating geometric shapes into designs can involve several elements, such as considering the meaning and symbolism of different shapes. Each shape has its own symbolic significance and can evoke different emotions. To achieve a sense of hierarchy, balance, and harmony, one can experiment with different sizes, positions, and alignment. Additionally, the use of geometric shapes to create patterns and textures can provide visual interest and depth to the design. Typography and letterforms can also be perceived as shapes, and combining them with geometric shapes can result in an aesthetically appealing design.

● Tobias van der Valk

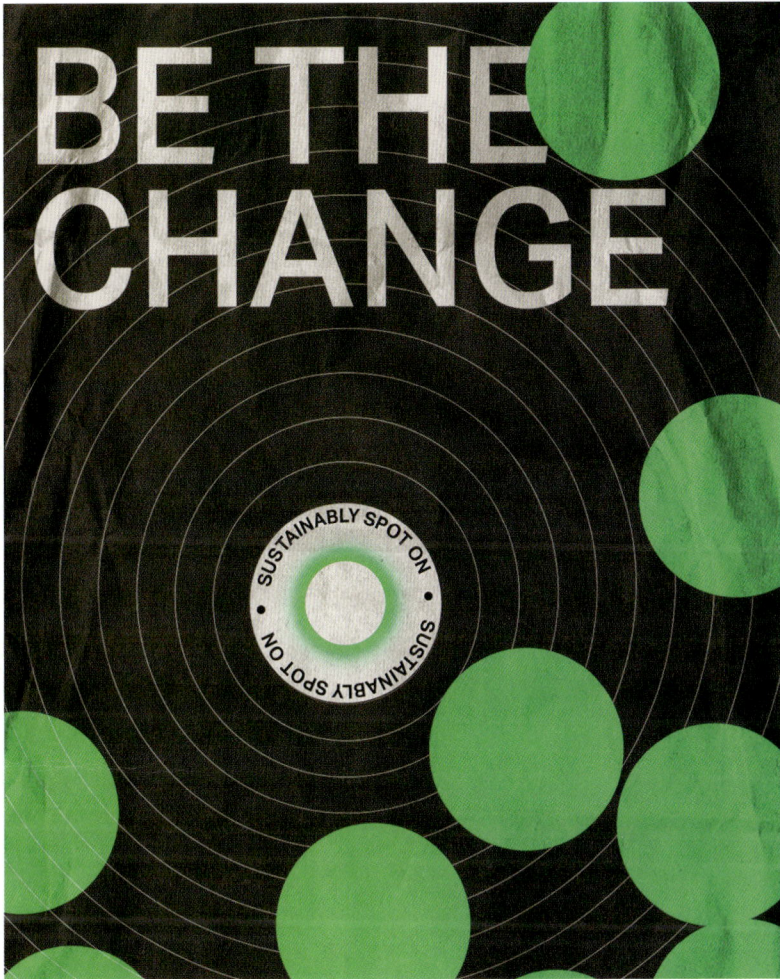

SPORTSPOT

SPORTSPOT is a startup company selling sporting goods that are made out of high quality and sustainable materials. The visual branding for this project consists of a simple motif of a green ball followed by a line representing movement.

Design
Chua Jien Li

sport

SUSTAINABLY SPOT ON

spot

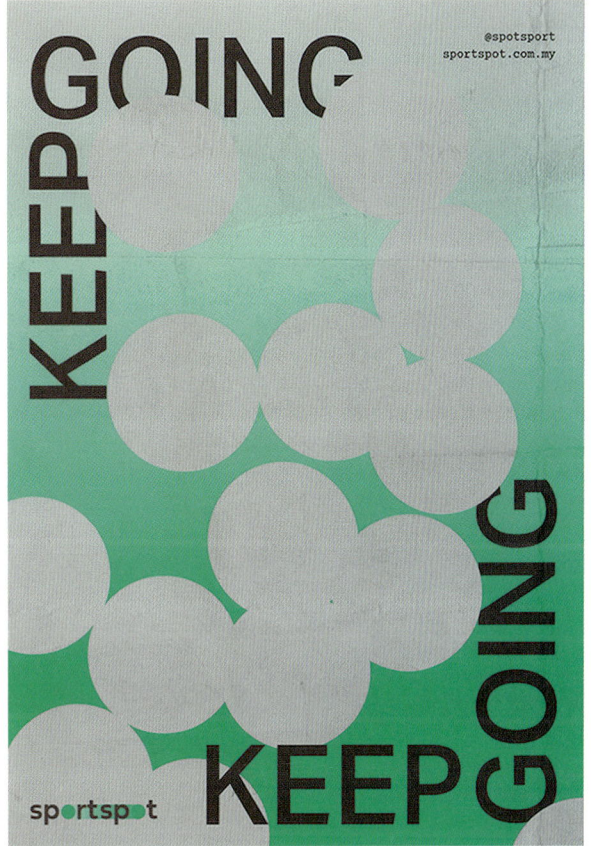

@spotsport
sportspot.com.my

KEEP GOING

KEEP GOING

sportspot

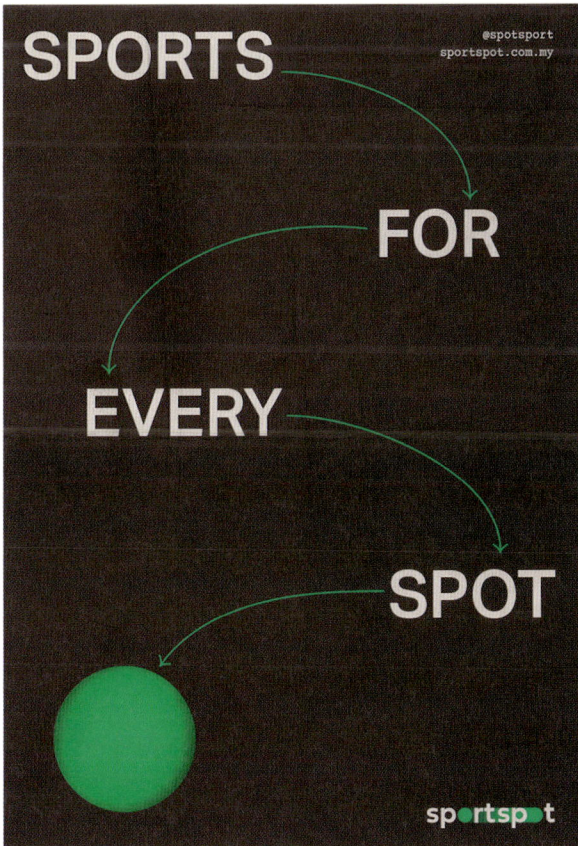

SPORTS

@spotsport
sportspot.com.my

FOR

EVERY

SPOT

sportspot

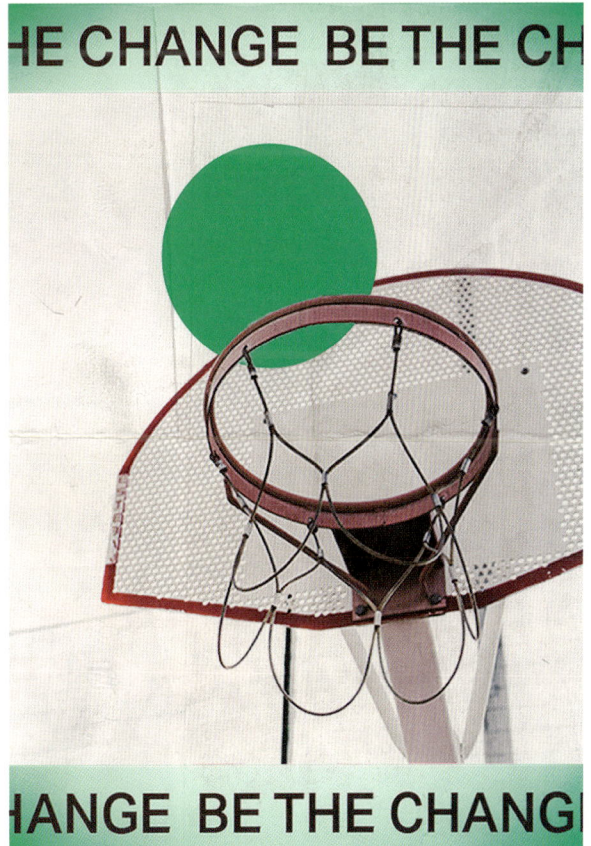

HE CHANGE BE THE CH

HANGE BE THE CHANG

Björkhem

Founded by Emil Björkhem, Björkhem is a newly founded law firm in Stockholm, Sweden. They set off to help founders and entrepreneurs with strategic and legal advisory. The brand identity originates from the core concept of Lady Justice — the goddess of justice within Roman mythology. The identity is bringing out her two main attributes, the sword and the two scale bowls to create an abstract shape that can read as the letter "B", for Björkhem. The attributes symbolize fair and equal administration of the law, without corruption, favor, greed or prejudice.

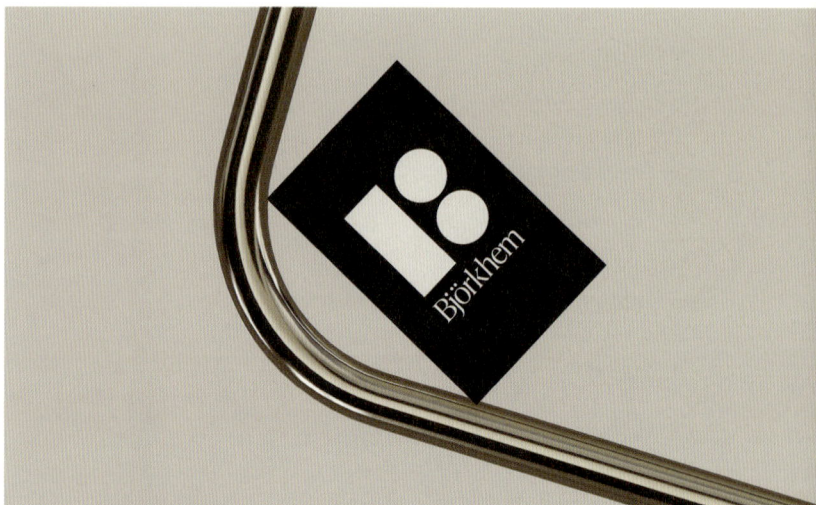

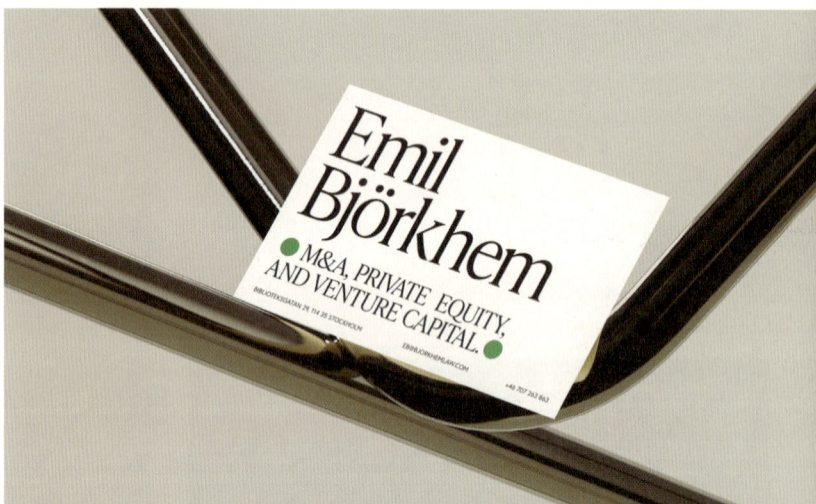

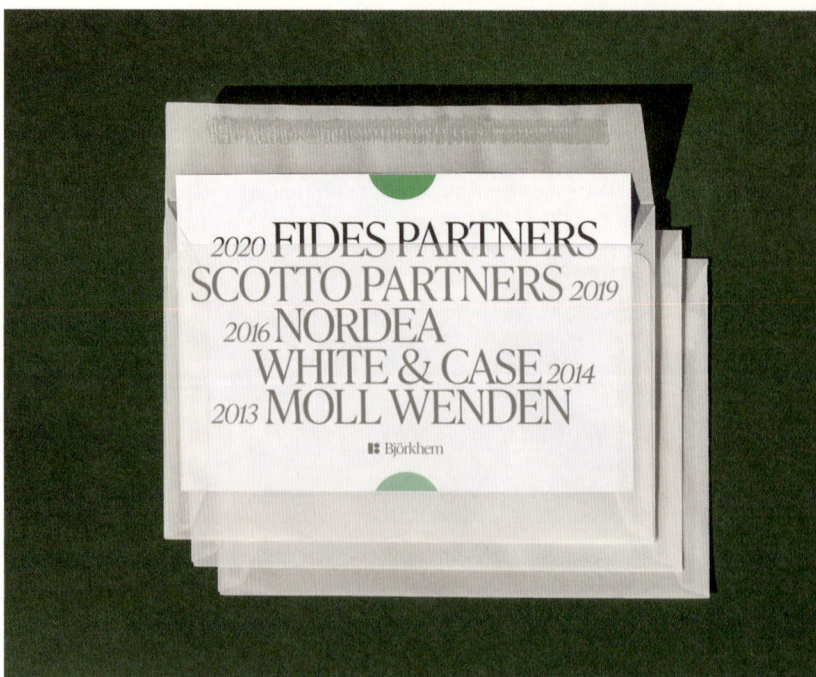

Design Studio
Studio Herrström

Design
Erik Herrström

Creative Assistance
Kerstin Marie Fröhlich

Client
Björkhem

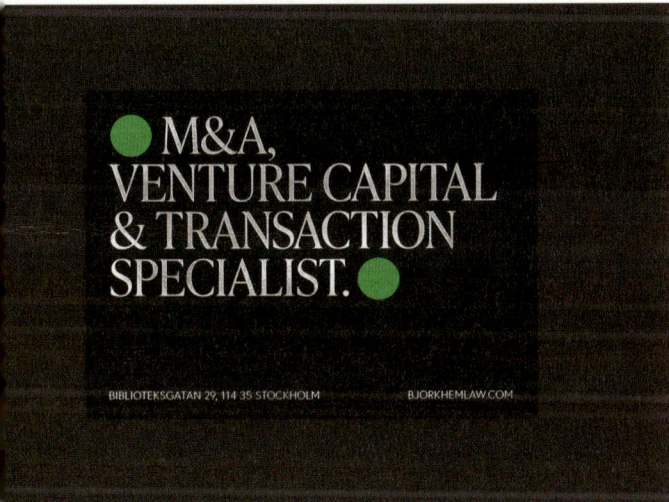

M&A, VENTURE CAPITAL & TRANSACTION SPECIALIST.

BIBLIOTEKSGATAN 29, 114 35 STOCKHOLM   BJORKHEMLAW.COM

Björkhem

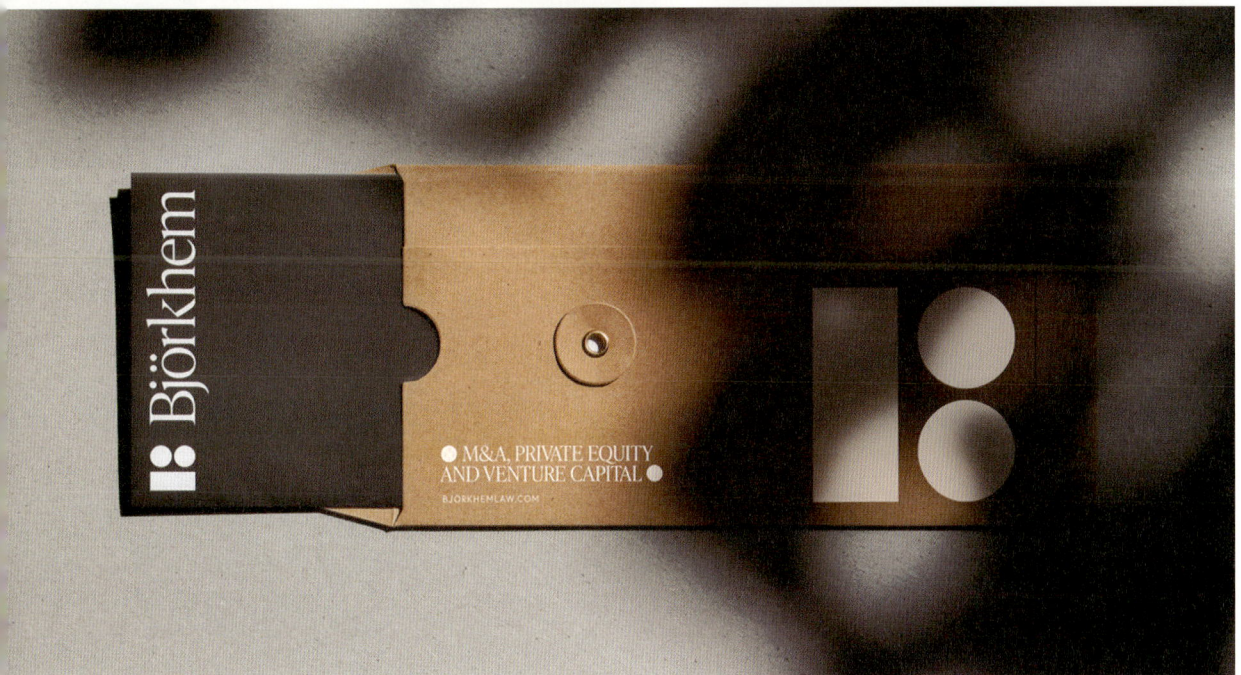

WELLRIGHT

This is a skin care brand rooted in traditional Korean herbs. The brand concept is from the inside to the outside, and then from the outside to the inside. The human body is full of energy. The design constantly emphasizes the inward extension process within the region, creating a dynamic and modern brand language, which is a new presentation of the traditional origin.

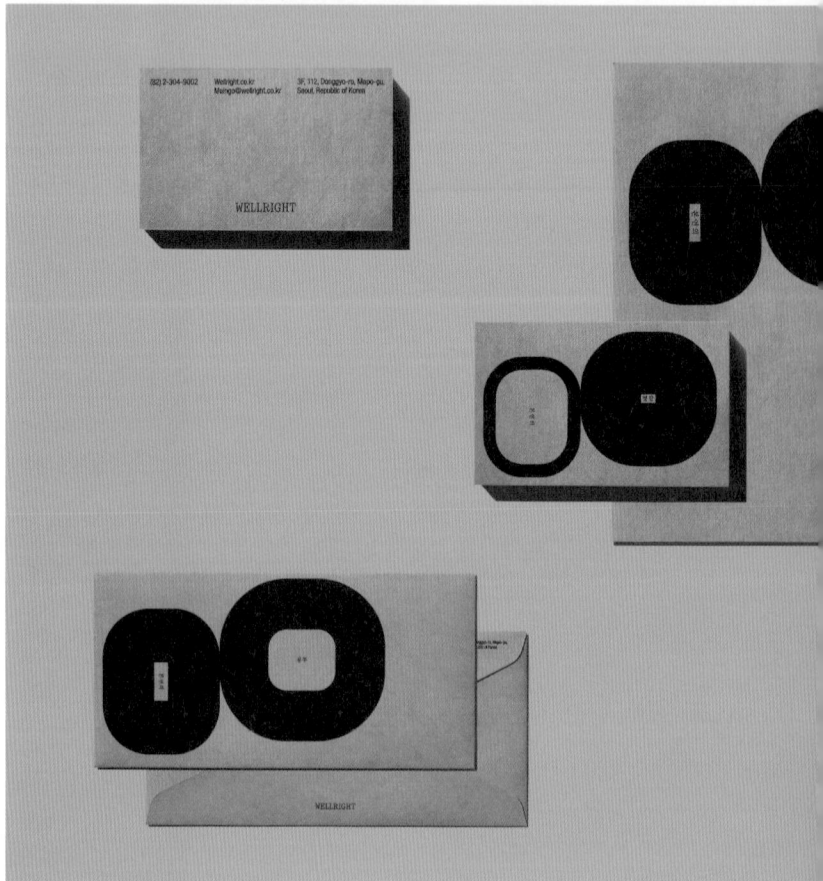

Creative Direction
Han Gao

Art Direction
Han Gao

Design
Han Gao

Client
WELLRIGHT

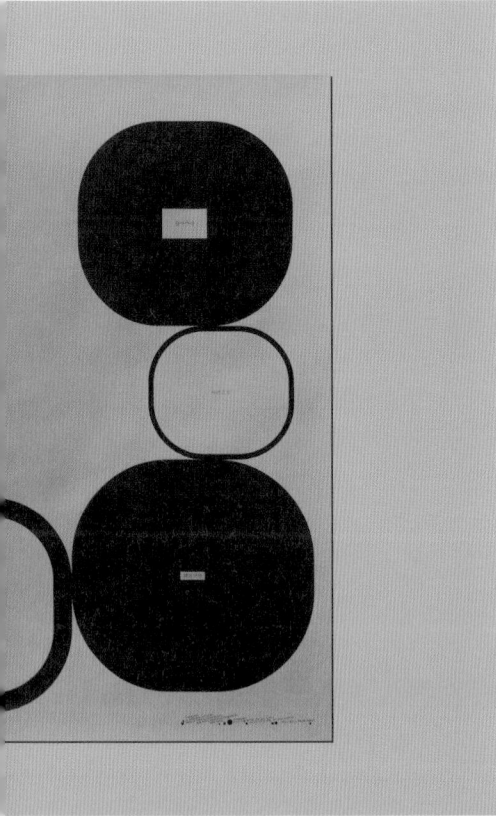

Bureau Buitendienst

This is a placemaking agency. They help governments, urban planners and project developers to think about and act upon the livable environment of the future. That future is not a fixed given but can be shaped in multiple conceivable ways. The identity of Bureau Buitendienst visualizes this idea. Straightforward typography highlights the rational side of their approach, colorful shapes the creative side. It results in a dynamic logo system that can take various forms, yet stays distinct and recognizable.

Design
Tobias van der Valk
(Created at G2K Creative Agency)

Client
Bureau Buitendienst

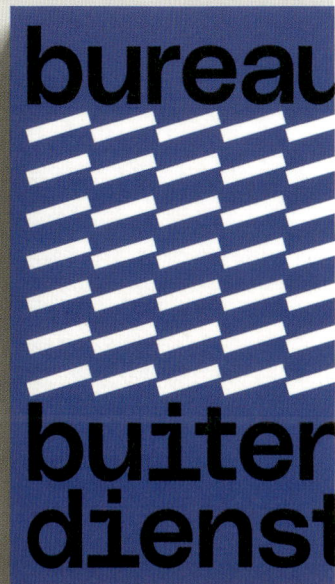

Arts in the Park

Arts in the Park (AIP) is an annual youth education programme through the arts. By providing participants with exciting opportunities, the programme helps them improve their self-confidence and enhance important life skills including creativity, team spirit and leadership.

   The programme is aspiring to create a positive, family-oriented art carnival in Hong Kong to fill the city with positivity and foster creativity and appreciation of local talent.

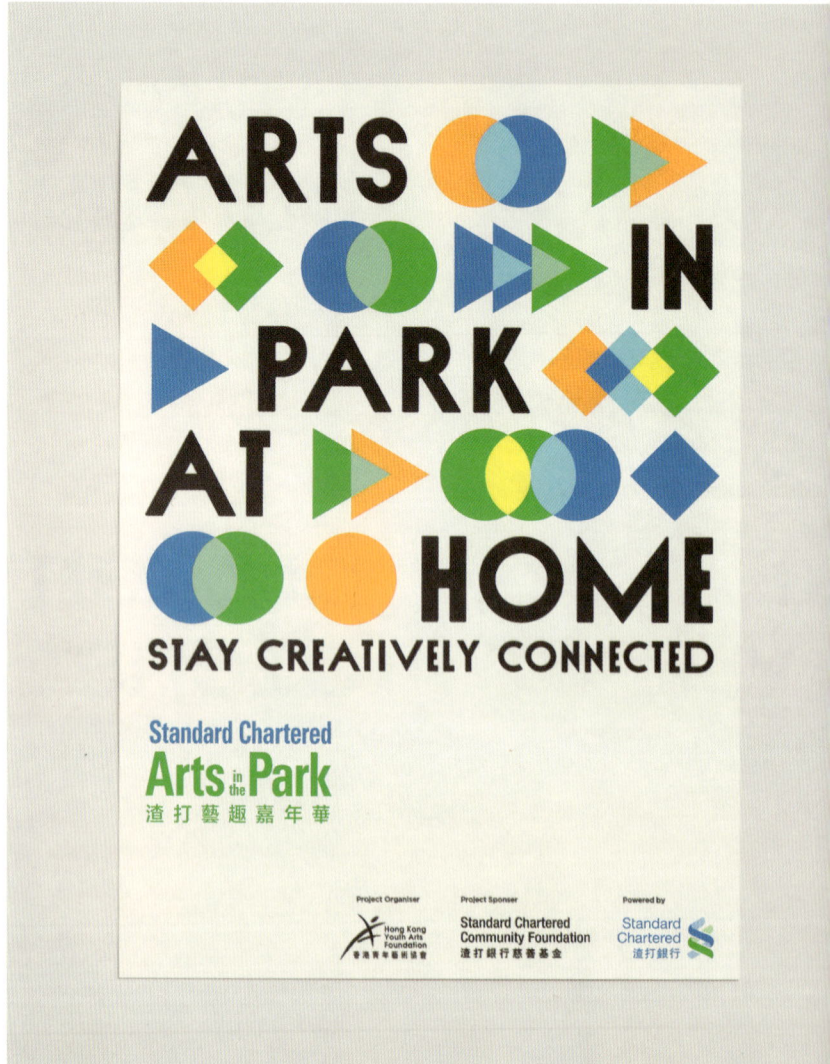

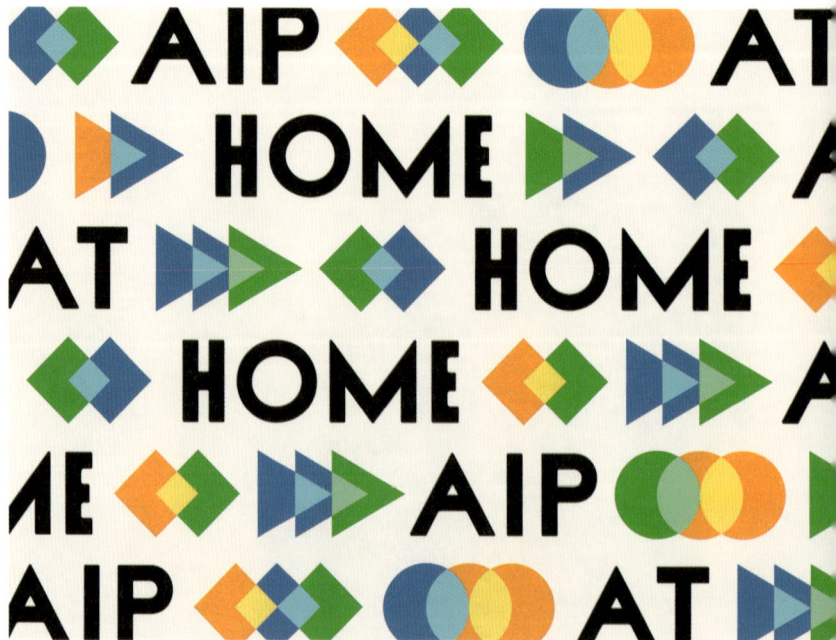

Design
Pengguin

Client
Hong Kong Youth Arts
Foundation

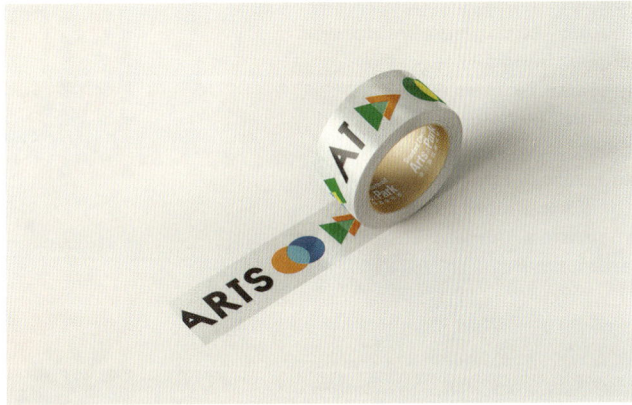

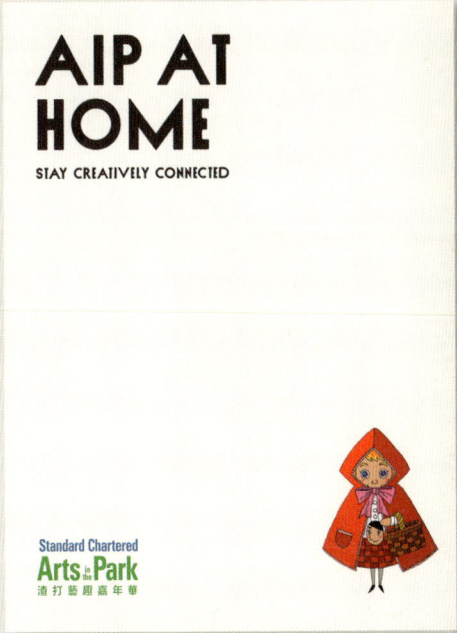

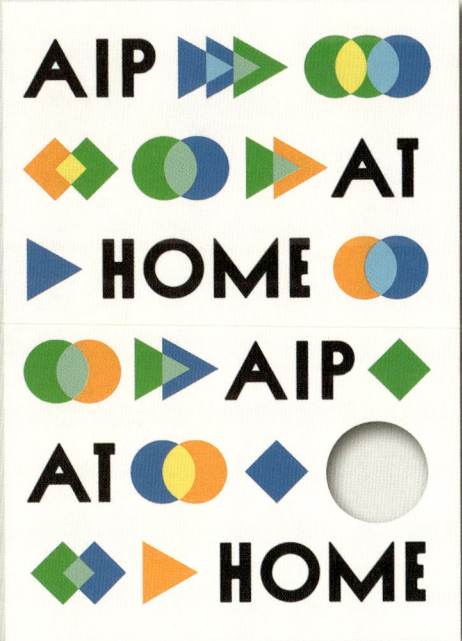

Perfect Print

It is a film development studio based in Shanghai. They help develop film with various artists and offer other services after production. The logo mark itself is a cluster of shapes and colors. It is dynamic and transformable. It speaks for the specific visual legacy in this industry but also is reinterpreted in a modern aesthetic. The logo itself is questioning the definition of logomark in modern design context. Other graphics are trying to use the basic shapes to represent their various processes of development.

Design
Han Gao

Photography
Shilu Wang

Client
Perfect Print

Online   Sale
线上   折扣

Special Sale

up to 50% Off
期间 Period
Oct. 26th - Nov. 25th

Perfect   Workshop
Print   vol. 32

Work shop

Perfect Print
期间 Period
Oct. 26th - Nov. 25th

Perfect   Perfect
Print   Talk vol. 2

Perfect Talk

Perfect Print
时间 Time
June. 20th 6PM - 8PM

Perfect   Open
Print   Studio

Open Studio

All Day Sunday
日期 Date
May 12th 9AM - 5PM

Perfect   ABC
Print   Books

ABC Books

at both D 27
期间 Period
Sep. 10th - Sep. 13th

WILLB

Tangible developed a corporate identity design project for WILLB, an IT company that provides innovative engineering solutions for AR, VR and big data.

New identity system expresses WILLB's corporate philosophy of creating solutions based on strategies and insights on high-tech technologies, and expresses the image of young, driven professionals leading the industry as well.

This project expansively uses square-shaped motifs in different sizes and lengths that represent diverse data of IT and they also represent the value of WILLB to actively lead trends in IT markets. Vivid brand colors are used to build a creative and dynamic corporate image.

Design Studio
Tangible

Creative Direction
Allen Shim

Design
Seohee Min

Client
WILLB

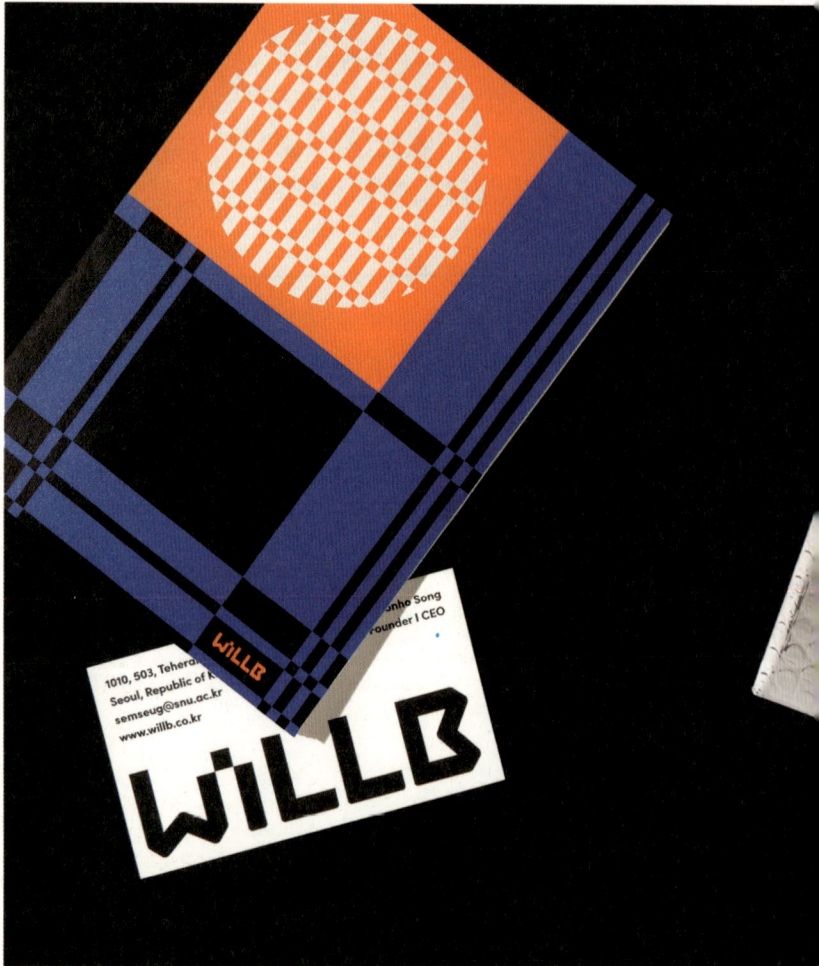

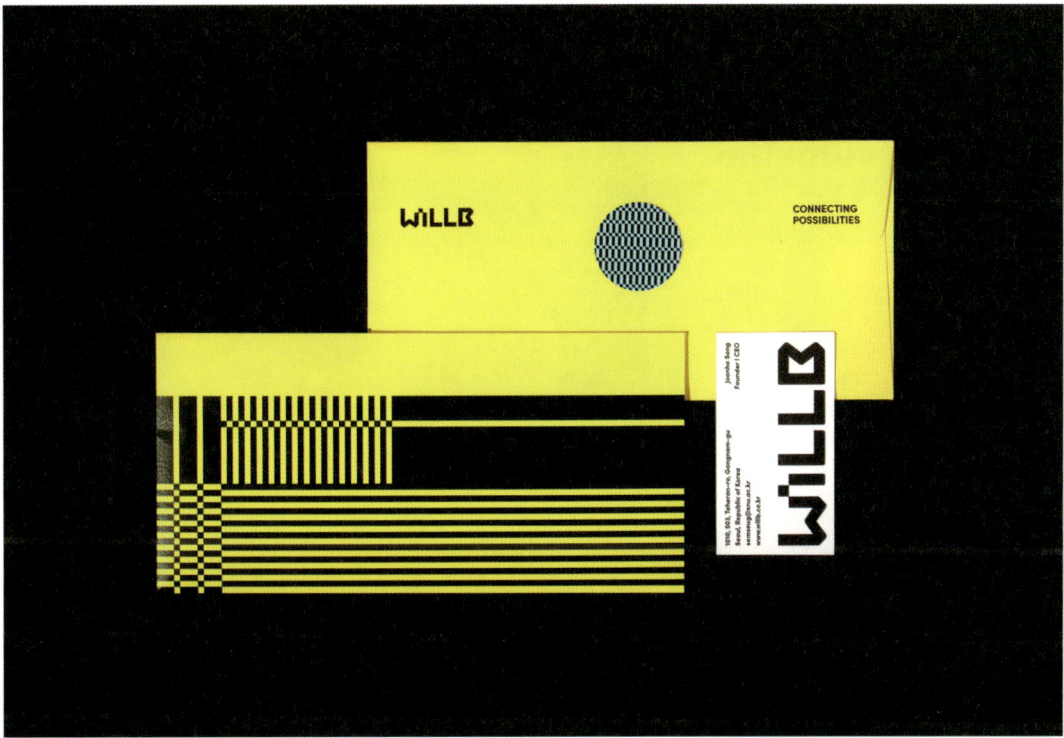

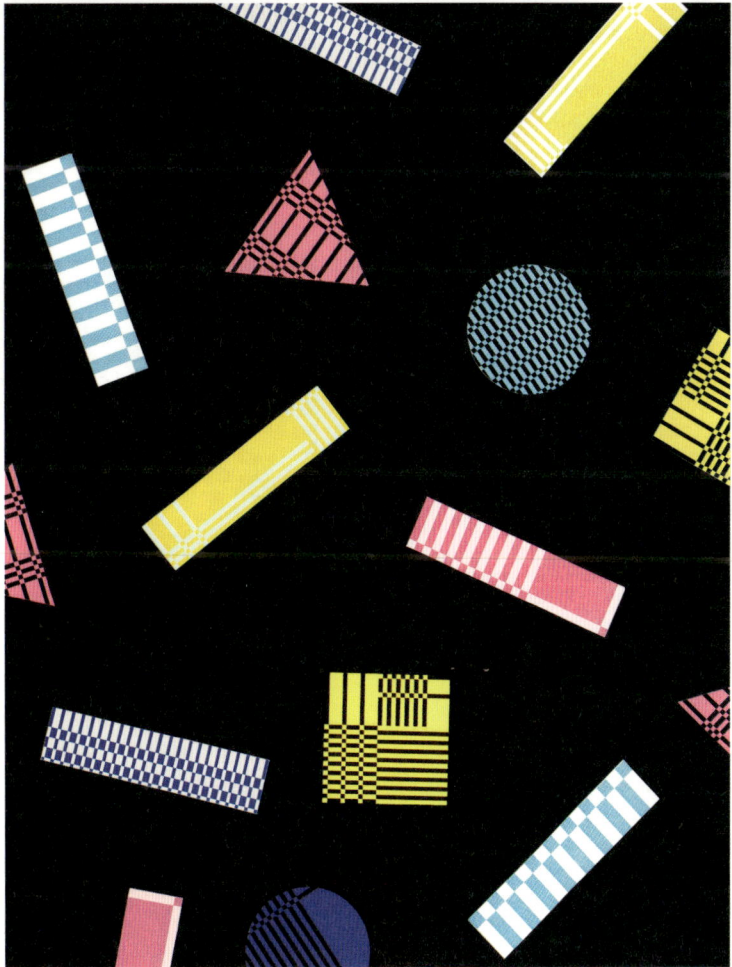

Yatai – La semaine Japon

Baillat Studio handled the branding design for Yatai, the fast-growing Japanese street food festival for its fourth year. For the second pandemic edition of the festival, the goal was to give visitors the "feeling of Japan" without leaving Montreal; the event therefore took an entire week for communication of Japanese culture.

To highlight and promote it, they opted for a minimalist, colorful approach inspired by the widely beloved sakura flowers, which symbolize the end of winter and the coming of spring. Since Yatai was transformed into a Japanese culture week for its fourth edition, the studio also based their design on the imagery of paper Asian calendars mainly (Chinese and Japanese).

Design Studio
Baillat Studio

Creative Direction
Jean-Sébastien Baillat

Photography
Thien Vu Dang,
Yasuko Tadokoro

Brno Design Days

Brno Design Days is a yearly design festival held in Brno, a city located in eastern Czechia. Organized by architects and other design enthusiasts, it habitually takes place in the reconstructed sites which is to be opened soon. This year the venue was transformed from art faculty into a creative hub, launch in its existence with this very design event.

Design Studio
NEON studio

Art Direction
Jakub Konvica

Design
Jakub Konvica,
Martin Egrt

Motion Design
Martin Egrt

Client
Brno Design Days

Brno Design Days — REthink REdesign REstart — 17—20 September 2020 — KUMST Údolní 19 Brno

McCord Museum's 100th Anniversary

The McCord Museum's 100th anniversary is a celebration, but also a chance to look back on its accomplishments. It was an opportunity to demonstrate the scope of this museum institution and its impressive collection, which traces 100 years of history and culture in Montreal. It is a concept that takes its impetus from the way people look at things, through a window to understand the past, the present, and to glimpse the future: like different imprints wink on fleeting existences.

Design Studio
Paprika Design

Creative Direction
Louis Gagnon

Art Direction
Daniel Robitaille

Design
Arthur Grivel, Fanny Roy

Client
McCord Museum

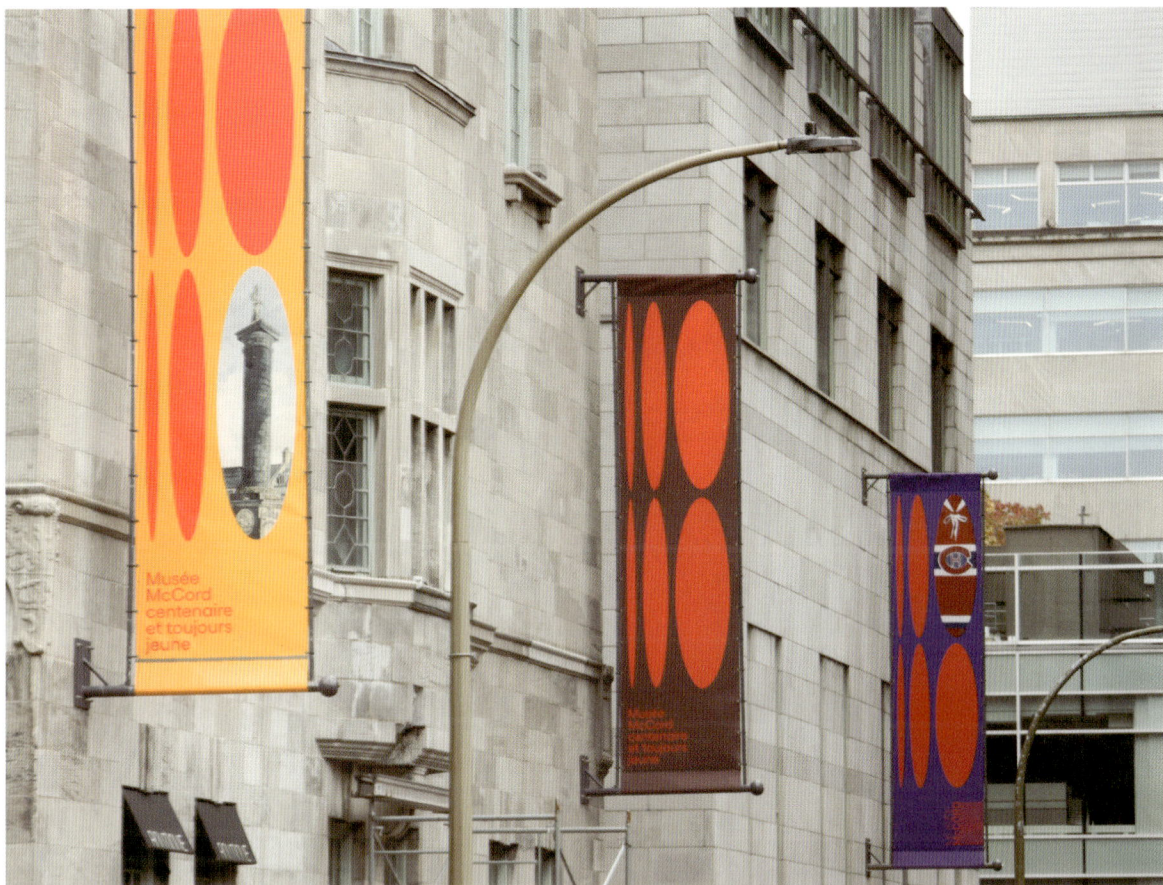

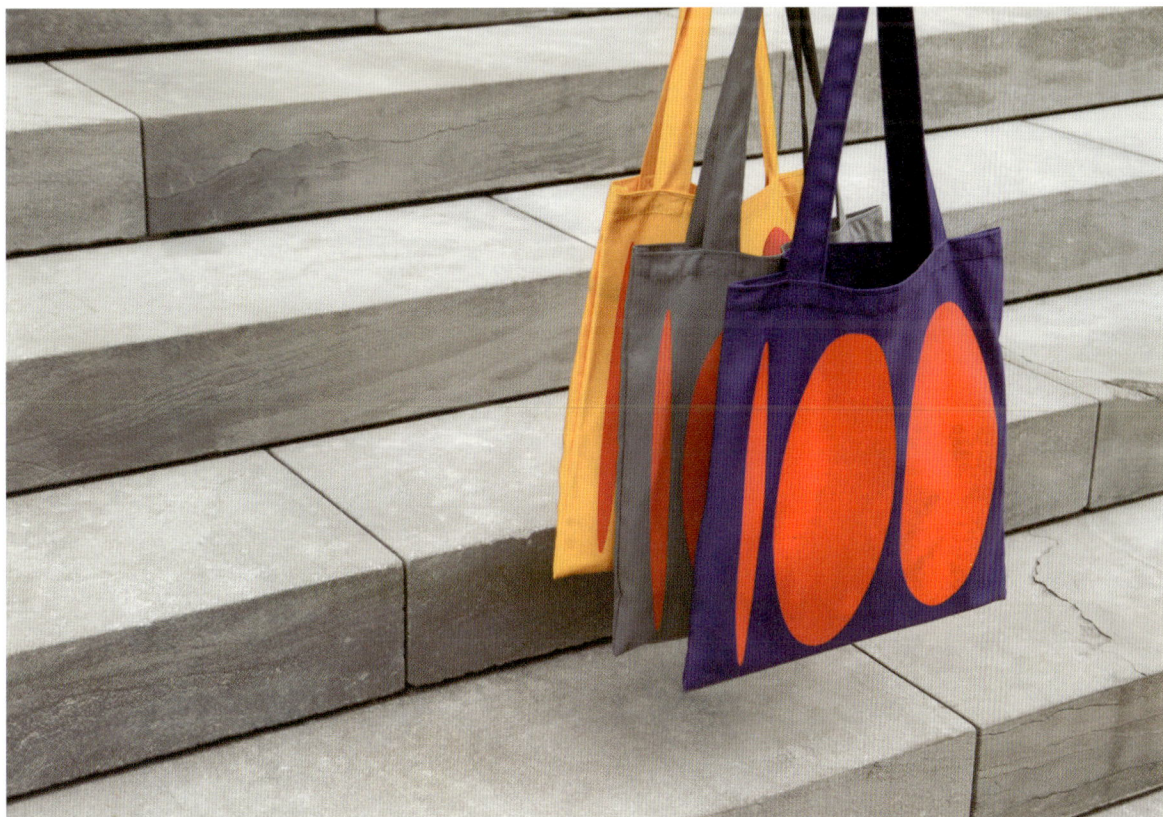

The Studyground

It is an educational company working on creating spaces to learn and enjoy in which children and young people play a leading role in their own learning.

For the naming, designers wanted to bring the idea of the "playground" as the place where students learn indeed rather than in classroom. For the visual identity, they chose a playful color palette, simple but flexible layouts and a dynamic language based on geometric shapes that, as learning is in a continuous motion.

Design Studio
errorerror.studio®

Client
The Studyground

La
letra
jugando
entra.

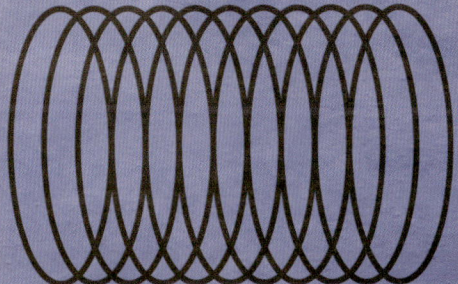

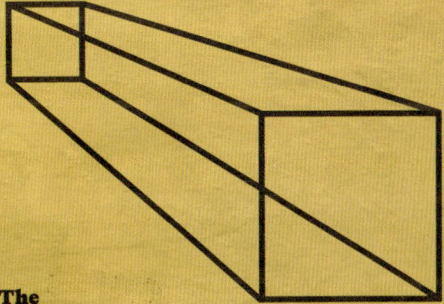

The Study Ground.

Let's costudying!

hi@the-studyground.com   @the_studyground   the-studyground.com

La
letra
jugando
entra.

The Study Ground.

Let's costudying!

hi@the-studyground.com   @the_studyground   the-studyground.com

Let's costudying!
the-studyground.com

Let's costudying!

Let's costudying!

Let's costudying!

Let's costudying!

The Study Ground.   Let's costudying!

The
Study
Ground.

Let's costudying!

La
letra
jugando
entra.

Technical City Engineering Ltd.

It is a local engineering contractor. The construction industry always gives the public an unfriendly image. Through the rebranding, designer hopes to demonstrate to the public a professional image. The uplifted image could help to draw newcomers to the industry to help endure the skills, and most importantly, to showcase how other industry could be benefited from the power of changes brought by design.

This is a brand identity system for a local construction contractor. Taking from the initial "T" of "Technical", which is stacked up to form a concrete structure, symbolizing the rebars used behind everything construction structure. The module system also allows the identity to stack up to different information sections, as the same way construction is built and provides flexible expansion for future usage.

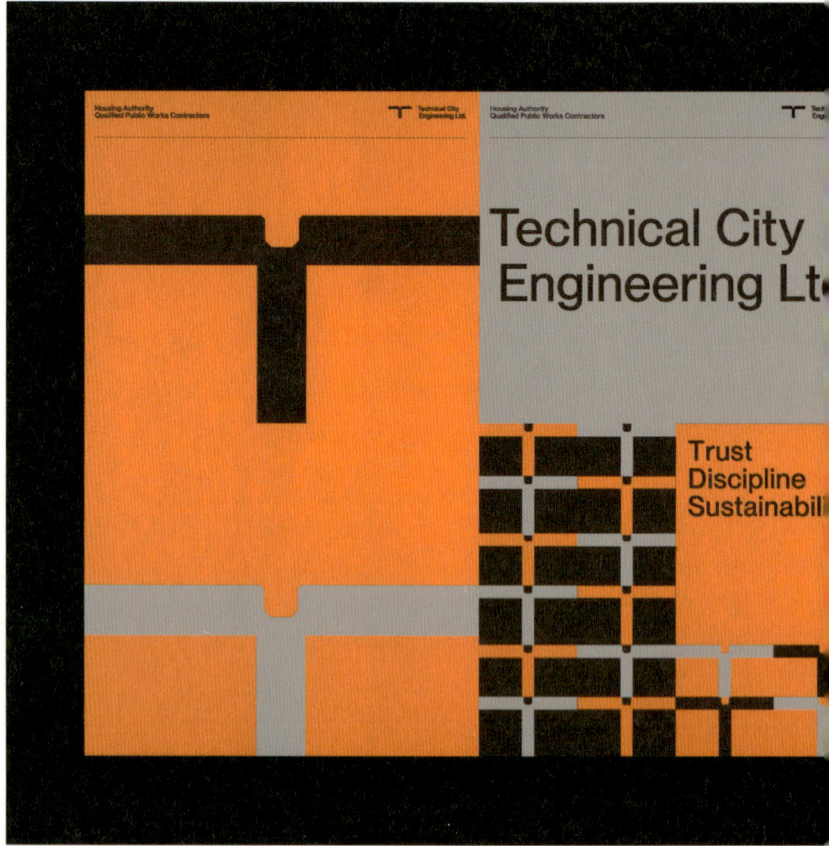

Design Studio
for&st

Design
Ming Cheung

Client
Technical City Engineering Ltd.

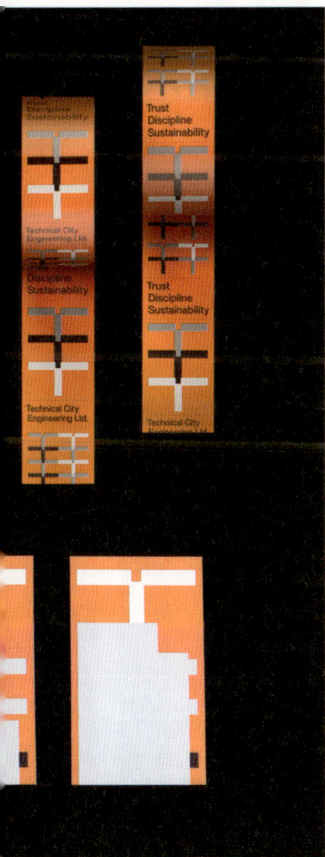

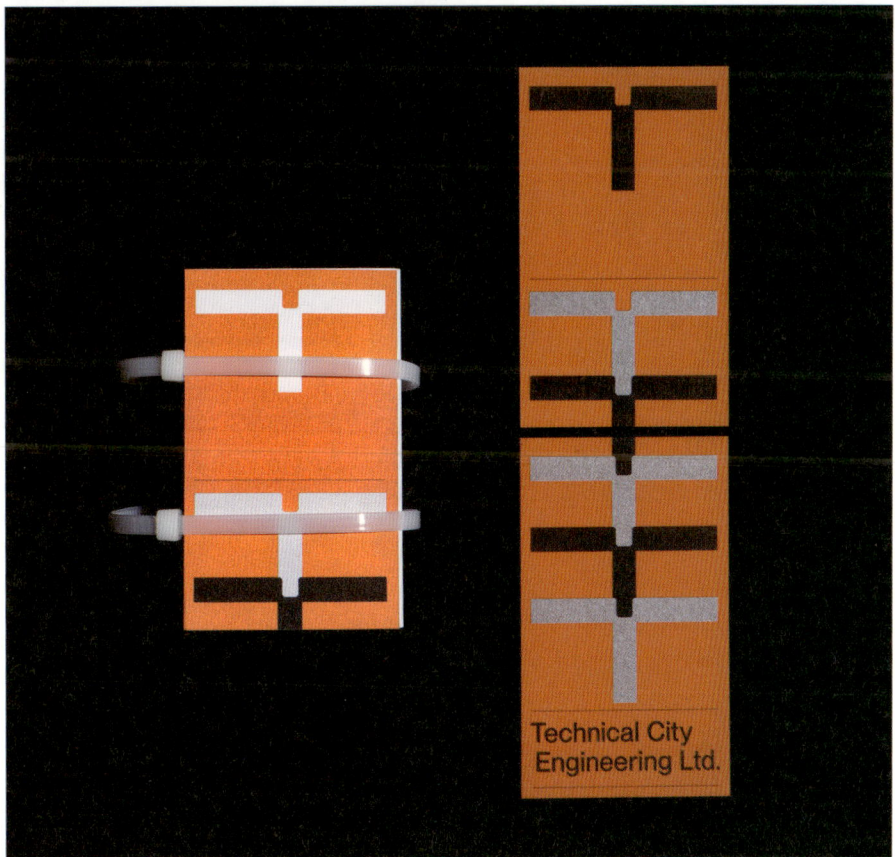

Baehl

Baehl defines itself as a European strategic healthcare boutique, providing services in innovation strategy, market entry, clinical adoption and market launch.

Brand Brothers was commissioned to redefine the company's graphic identity. They opted for a sleek but structured typographyic design, made for the occasion, whose lines subtly evoke a dynamic of growth and forward projection. Based on the curves of the "B", they developed a generative pattern, used in black monochrome or coupled with experimental textures reminiscent of the world of research. This rich and organic texture is complemented by a simple and structured design, based on Labil Grotesk Font.

Design Studio
Brand Brothers

Design
Johan Debit

Innovate↗
↔Collaborate
Accelerate→

European strategic
healthcare boutique

baehl—innovation.com, @baehlinnovation

BAEHL

European
strategic

healthcare
boutique

European strategic
healthcare boutique

baehl—innovation.com, @baehlinnovation

BAEHL

2020
ANNUAL
REPORT

EUROPEAN STRATEGIC
HEALTHCARE
BOUTIQUE

BAEHL—
INNOVATION
.COM

BAEHL.

BAEHL
BUSINESS HUB

BAEHL
PARTNERSHIPS

BAEHL
INTERNATIONAL

10

BAEHL_2020 ANNUAL REPORT

BAEHL_2020 ANNUAL REPORT

11

(SERVICES)
↑↗   (STRATEGY, GROWTH
           & INNOVATION)

Baehl Innovation
leverages the value of
your innovation strategy
from an early-stage by
bringing our knowledge,
creativity, and combined
capabilities to achieve
success in the
increasingly complex life
sciences environment.

**EXPLORE INNOVATION AREAS
IN A SPECIFIC FIELD**

We discover new product & portfolio opportunities by
exploring new markets and territories. We create a panorama
of innovation areas in a specific market/field and bring you
clear, timely and actionable insights associated with a
product / portfolio to define and secure your innovation
pathway, in partnerships with decision makers, clinicians,
influencers and/or potential business players.

**BUILD NEW ASSETS WITH A
CLEAR VALUE PROPOSITION**

We maximize the value of your new assets and
portfolios by generating market landscape insights, clarifying
your strategic options and gauging market drivers and View
case study perceived value proposition of a new product or
asset in the business. We perspectively analyze the reality of
market needs and the main current or emerging applications
that you could address in priority and validate the competitive
position of the new offer or business model. We evaluate new
opportunities that the competition will find hard to emulate
through a combination of extensive publication research, as
well as targeted interviews with key market leaders,
clinicians, payers and stakeholders in your industry.

**STIMULATE EXTERNAL
INNOVATION IN LIFE SCIENCES**

If you want to launch or support open innovation
initiatives, we can help you open up your innovation process
and explore innovative targets in France and abroad. We
provide support in a variety of activities, including setting up
bioincubators, assessing and launching scouting initiatives or
just bringing or selling new technologies or innovative
solutions to an existing portfolio or business. We explore the
best collaboration opportunities in your market through the
search for specific skill sets, technologies and/or startups
with high potential and accompany you in ranking selected
targets and establishing successful partnerships.

egotree Nootropics

The very first nootropic dietary supplement company in Taipei, egotree began in 2020. The combination of the ego and tree in brand identity, started from the exercise of spherical energy body. By capturing the process of brain, transferring the floating, the bumping, the gathering and dispersing of energy into a symbol, and further extending the concept of the package. Constructing the unique graphics of capsule, one (zone) and two (still), in addition to conveying the abstract experience of the product.

In order to divide the stereotype that marketing of dietary supplement usually emphasis the ingredient and the effect, by using the abstract visual with the warm tones color system to build up the image of the brand, connecting egotree's brand definition "start from people" and the idea of bring the revolutionary experience to the consumer.

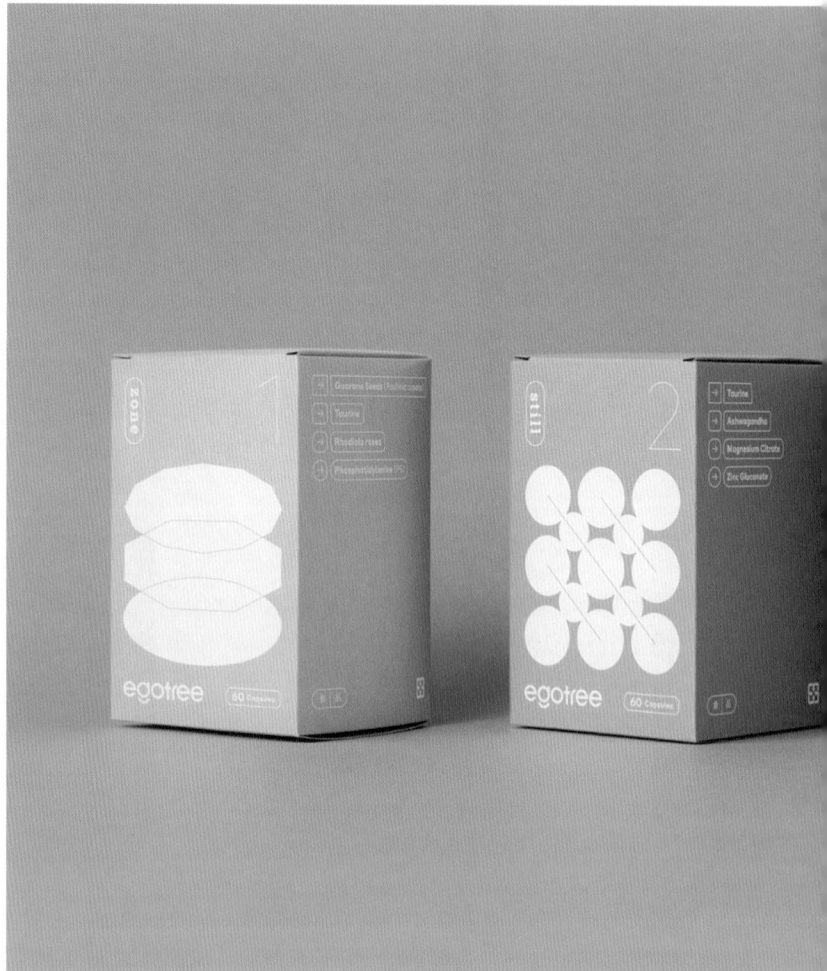

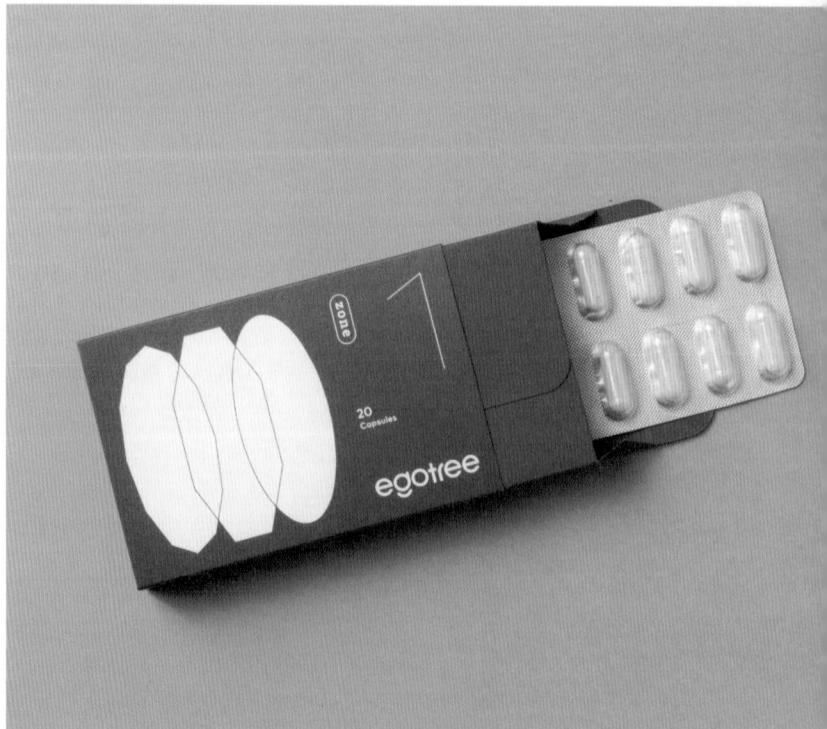

Design Studio
nomo®creative

Creative Direction
Lin Chi Tai

Art Direction
Lin Yu Chien

Design
Lin Yu Chien, Lin Chi Tai,
Kan Wei Yun, Allison Hsiao

Client
Egotree

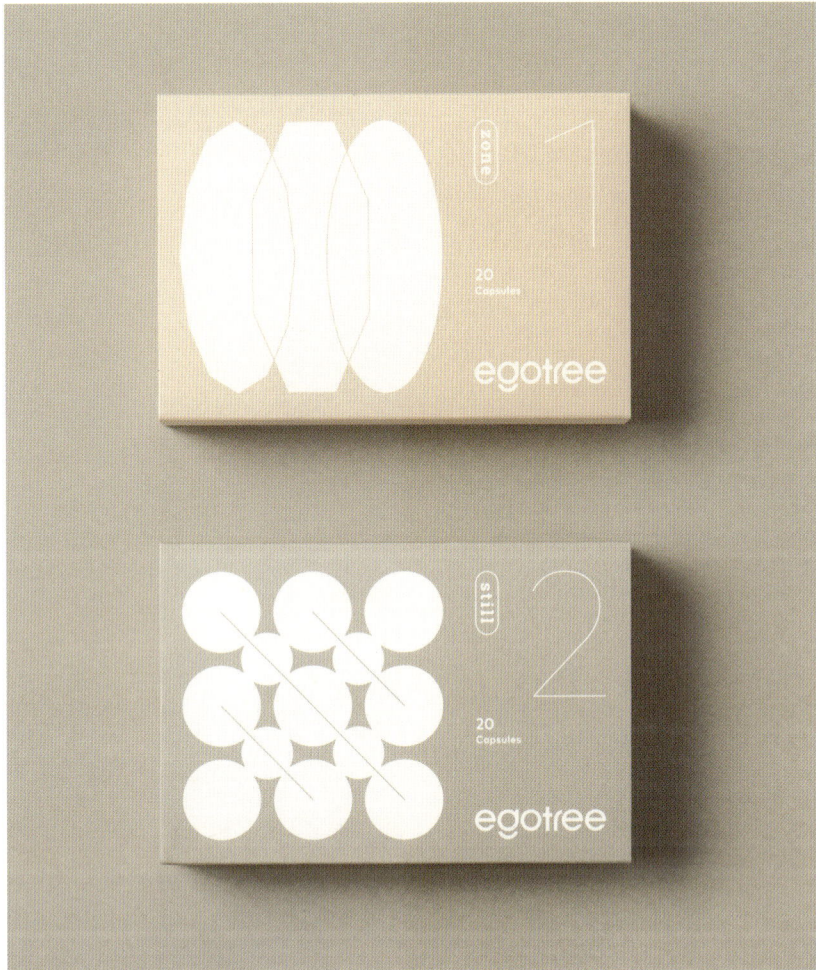

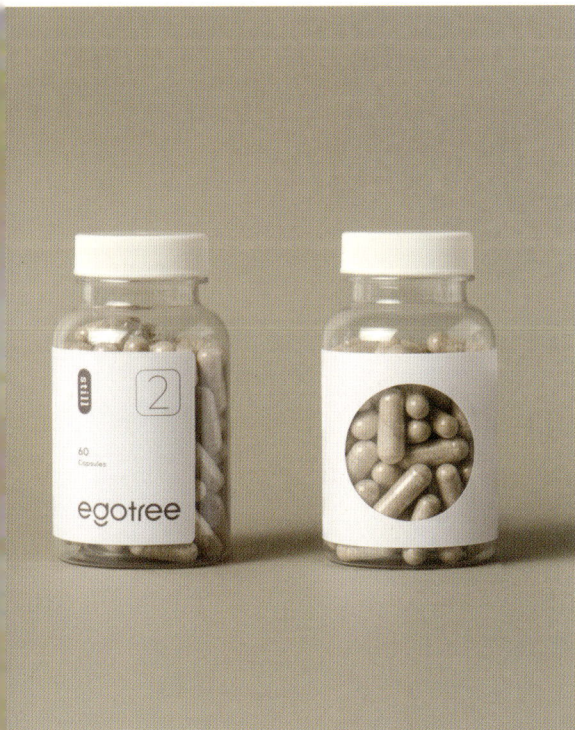

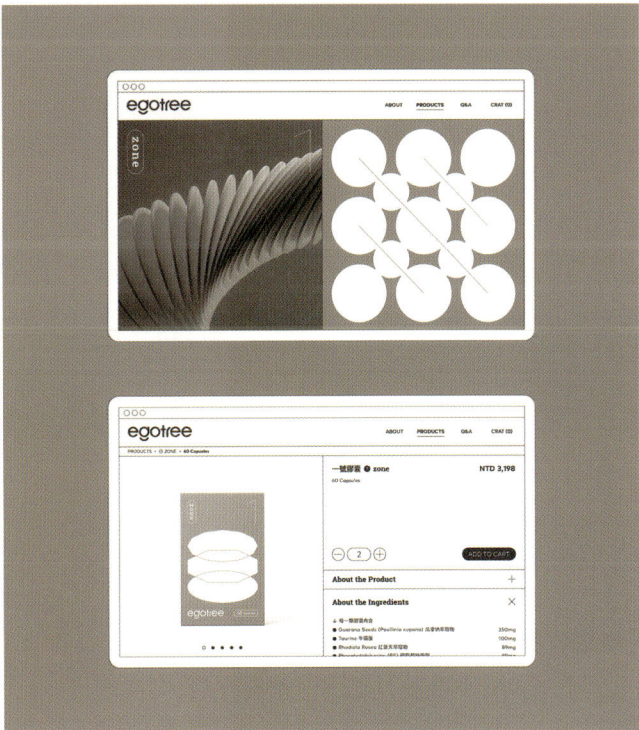

Derprosa

Derprosa is the brand of laminating films for paper and cardboard for the packaging and print communication sector. The aim of the project is to convey its corporate identity to a visual system more akin to the world of graphic design. It is proposed a modular solution based on geometric synthesis, which is proposed as a universal and timeless language. For this, it undergoes two axes of product classification, such as their finishes and ranges.

Design Studio
Plácida

Photography
Colectivo Verbena

Client
Derprosa

Derprosa™ Select Films Collection

Derprosa™ Gloss DL Pro-Shield™
Extra gloss film, specifically designed to prevent any scratch on the surface

Laminated with Derprosa™ Gloss Bacterstop

Leading manufactu
innovative films for
cardboard laminat

Derprosa™ Gloss DL Pro-Shield™
Extra gloss film, specifically designed to prevent any scratch on the surface

Derprosa™ Matte Premier reLIFE™ 50
Super matte finish
with 50% PCR
chemically r

BAMBUYU

BAMBUYU is a toilet paper brand that speaks to a global environmental challenge, deforestation. Therefore, a striking design is the most suitable solution to once again emphasize the feature of the product and draw the consumer's attention to it.

The design used rich colors and contrasting combinations. The pattern was made predominantly with sharp shapes that emphasize the bold character of the brand. Bright design gave the brand courage, emotionality and at the same time modernity, and the very specificity of the product — awareness and involvement in global problems and problems of consumers.

Design Studio
PG Brand Reforming

Creative Direction
Vitaly Yatskevich

Client
BAMBUYU, UAE

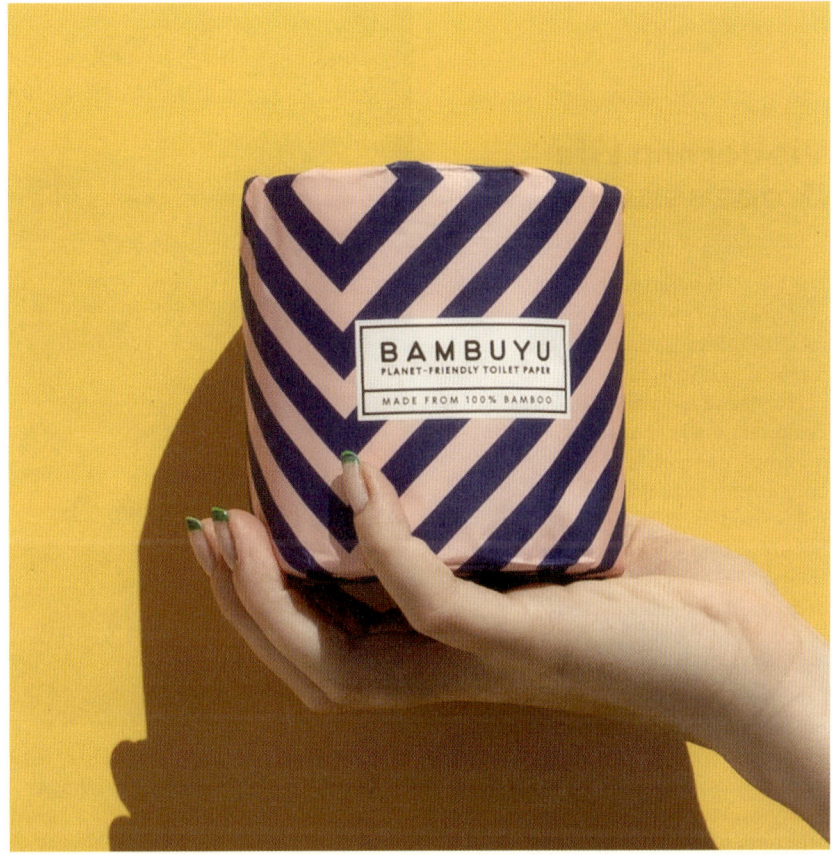

Viodermin Life Drops serums

The Life Drops products are composed of three serums providing intense treatment of facial skin and eyes.

For these specialized serums, designers created a small family of minimal, geometric illustrations in connection to their benefits. Gold foil is used in all of the designs, accentuating the transformations taking place through the product's dedicated application. The white, black and gold palette emphasizes the directness and efficiency of the brand and particularly this range of products. The very subtle, geometric pattern of the white relief paper, gives the packaging a premium look and feel and sets the products apart from other ranges.

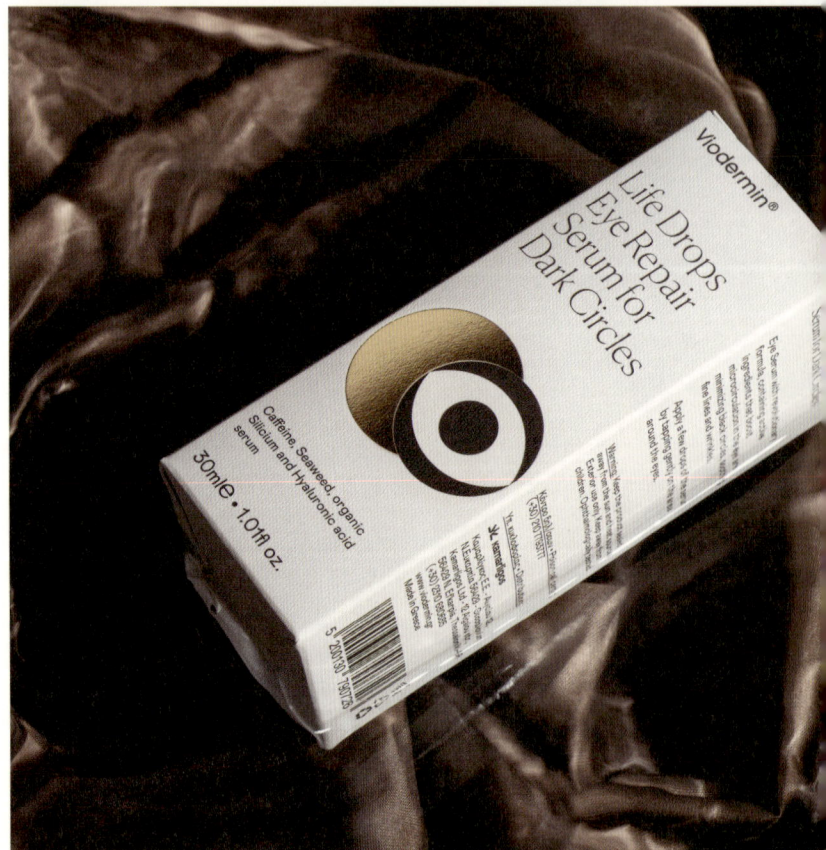

Design Studio
Boo Republic

Design
Boo Republic

Client
Kamarligos LTD / Viodermin

Love Beauty Foods

Love Beauty Foods (LBF) is a purpose-driven brand located in Newcastle, Australia. The brand narrative takes inspiration from cairn sculptures traditionally used to mark paths in nature. MAKEBARDO uses this symbol to represent the essence of LBF — a company that guides people towards more conscious and balanced consumption. To bring this concept to life, they designed a monogram with geometric shapes that, when used vertically, creates a balanced cairn that embodies the brand's concept. The logo maintains readability even when rotated, making it adaptable to any brand asset and converting it into the protagonist over the identity.

The packaging is easily recognizable thanks to the large-scale logo displayed on the front. The cohesive look created by the repetitive layout and clear color system across all products ensures that the brand will not go unnoticed. The logo changes the color to define each product's flavor/scent, and the rest of the content is tinted with the same color to reduce ink usage.

Design Studio
MAKEBARDO

Design
Bren Imboden & Luis Viale

Photography
Lifestyle by Ruby Blake,
Studio by Lucy Alcorn,
Web Development by New Territory

Client
Love Beauty Foods

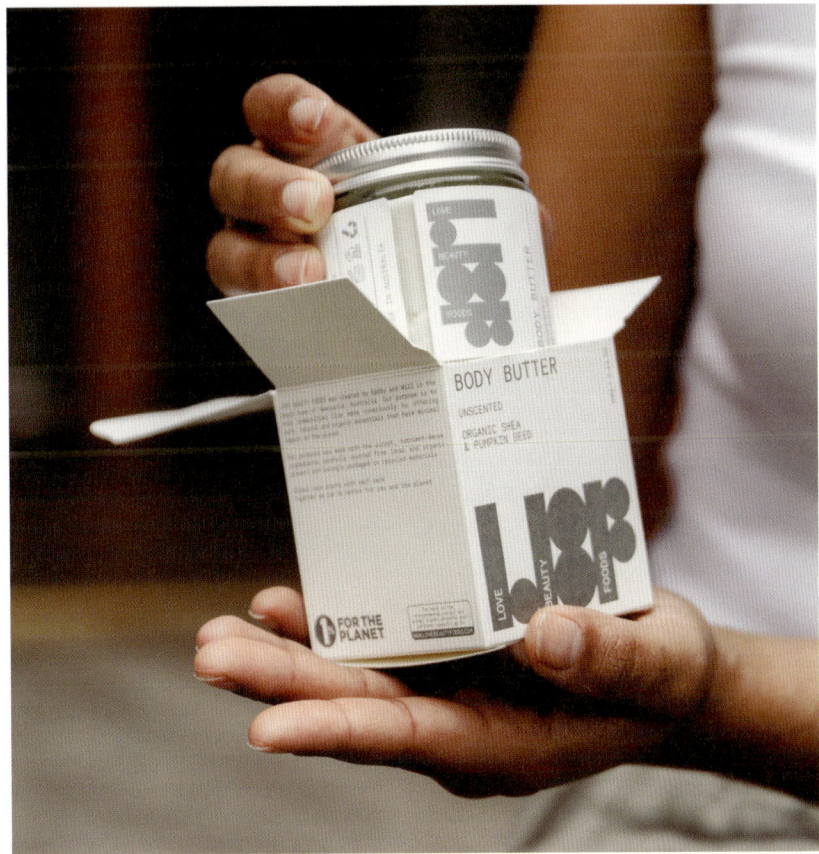

zerolens

zerolens is a brand of cosmetic contact lenses that focuses on natural and comfortable wearing. cheeer STUDIO has designed the visual identity and packaging system for it. The overall vision revolves around the moist and relaxed characteristics, as if reflecting bubbles of different gloss, which is light and changeable, conforming to the brand's concept: beauty is natural. The surface of the packaging box uses UV and laser hot stamping technology, which presents a variety of glossy states in more dimensions.

Design Studio
cheeer STUDIO

Art Direction
Mia Liu, Yan Yaoming

Photography
Kiwi Foto

Client
zerolens

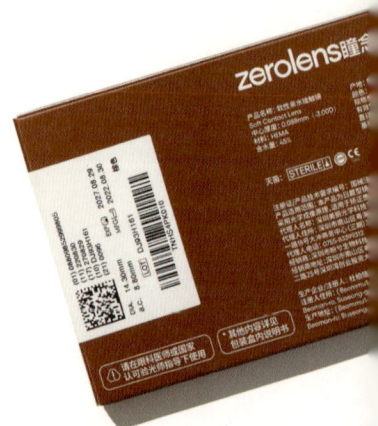

Team Korea

maum studio planned, designed, and produced goods to promote and commemorate the Korean Sport & Olymmpic Committee.

The shapes and colors of the stadium, which are characteristic of each of seven events of the Korea Sport & Olympic Committee, became the motif of the graphic design, and they are used on light postcards, stickers, pouches, towels, and bowls. They hope that light products with graphics will be more friendly to people.

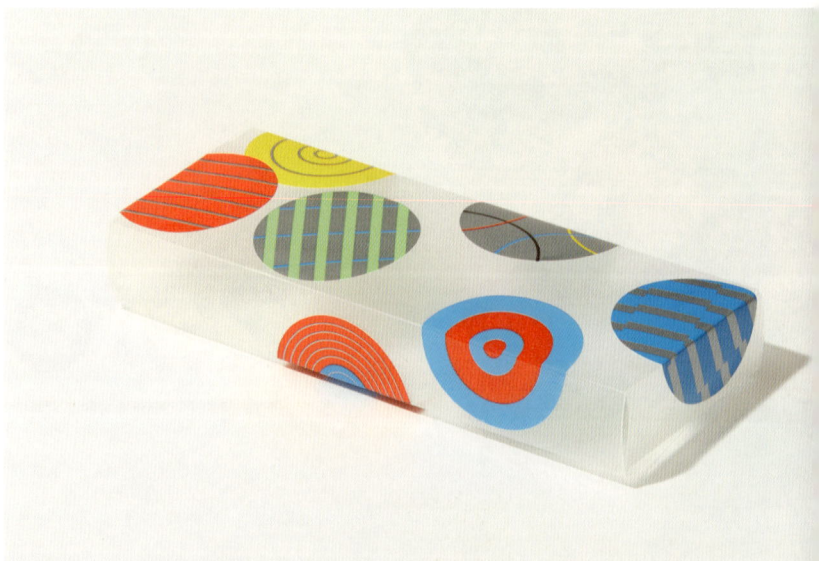

Design Studio
maum studio

Creative Direction
Dalwoo Lee

Art Direction
Yoonji Lee

Design
Jeawon Chung

Ceramics Cooperation
Playing Dish

Client
TEAM KOREA

The Hyundai Seoul ALT.1 – I am Ground

maum studio designed the graphic and space of the exhibition "I am Ground" to commemorate the first anniversary of the opening of The Hyundai Seoul ALT.1 Gallery. Five artists from different media, genres, and generations gathered here to design key visuals, motion, transfer spaces, lounges, and captions, which meant that it would be good to introduce their works and art galleries like a game of self-introduction.

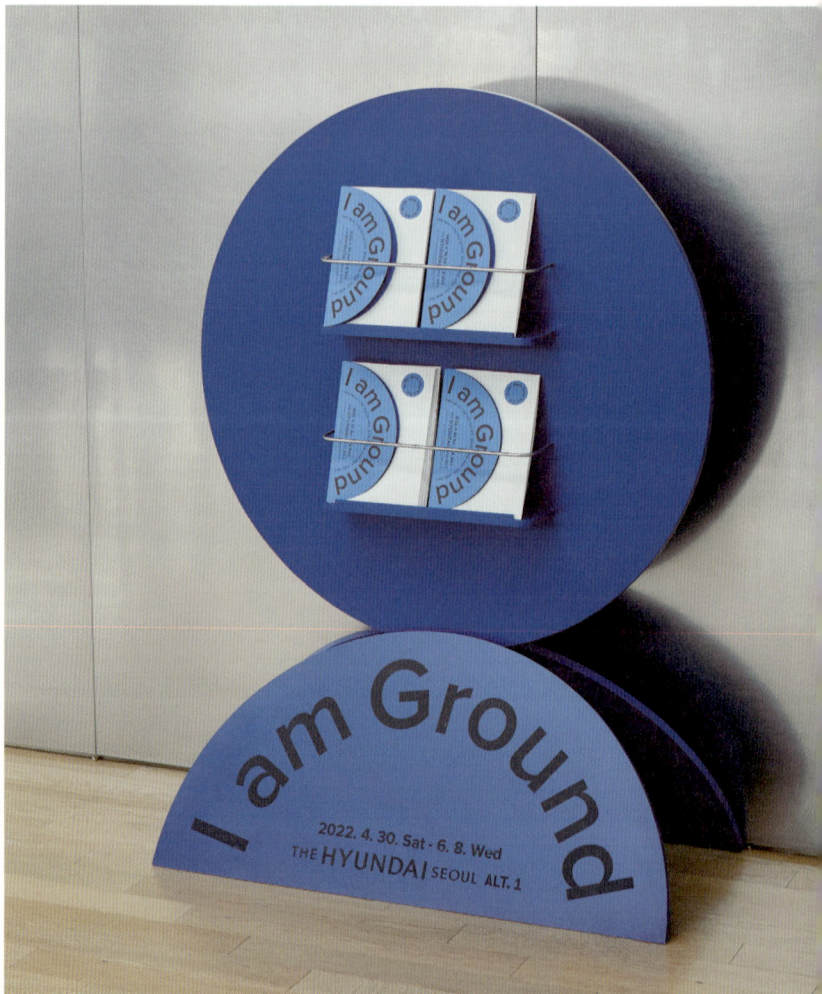

Design Studio
maum studio

Creative Direction
Dalwoo Lee

Art Direction
Yoonji Lee

Design
Yoonji Lee,
Jaewon Chung

Motion
Hyunjin Lee

Space Design
Eunhye Oh,
Youngbak Jeong

Client
THE HYUNDAI

Linkurious

Linkurious was founded in 2013 in Paris and has developed the most advanced investigative detection solution to date, working with many governments, NGOs and corporations to uncover the most sophisticated criminal networks.

Linkurious has engaged Brand Brothers to redesign its entire graphic identity in spring 2021. Until then, the identity had too many weaknesses in relation to the scope of the topics covered and the power of the technology developed by the company. Designers have therefore developed a visual grammar that is both more raw and richer, based on several elements. First, the logo is a lettering designed for Linkurious, geometric and orderly, but with many graphic features (curves, inktraps). The "O" holds the brand's symbol, two overlapping discs that convey the notions of investigation and highlighting, and will serve as a canvas for the entire visual language.

Design Studio
Brand Brothers

Design
Johan Debit

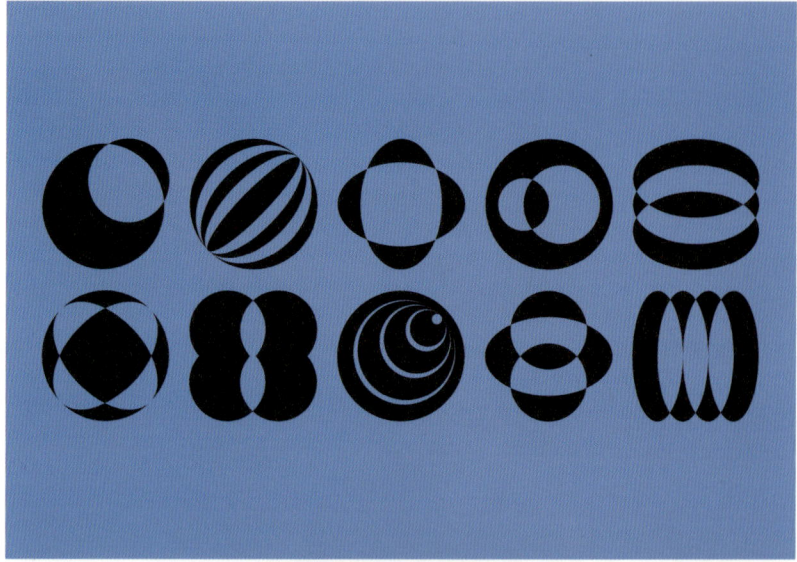

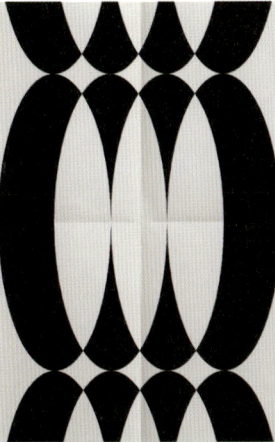

Criminals are not thinking in silos. Neither should you.

When financial crime lies in the shadows, we turn the lights on.

linkurious .com

Financial crime
Anti—fraud
Anti—money laundering
Law enforcement

Follow
@ linkurious

LINKURIOUS

Visualize everything connected to a suspicious client in 30 seconds.

When financial crime lies in the shadows, we turn the lights on.

linkurious .com

Financial crime
Anti—fraud
Anti—money laundering
Law enforcement

Follow
@ linkurious

LINKURIOUS

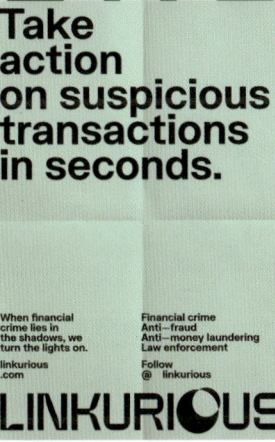

Take action on suspicious transactions in seconds.

When financial crime lies in the shadows, we turn the lights on.

linkurious .com

Financial crime
Anti—fraud
Anti—money laundering
Law enforcement

Follow
@ linkurious

LINKURIOUS

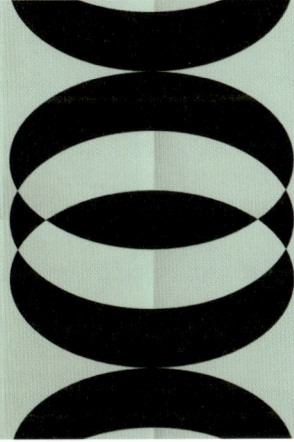

Stop criminals in their tracks no matter how they hide.

When financial crime lies in the shadows, we turn the lights on.

linkurious .com

Financial crime
Anti—fraud
Anti—money laundering
Law enforcement

Follow
@ linkurious

LINKURIOUS

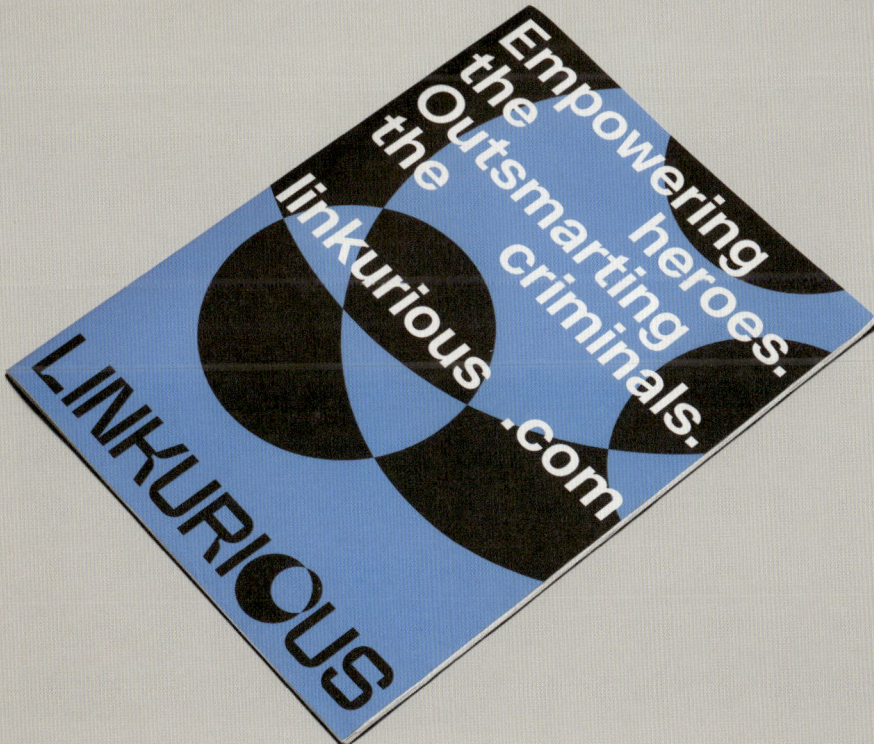

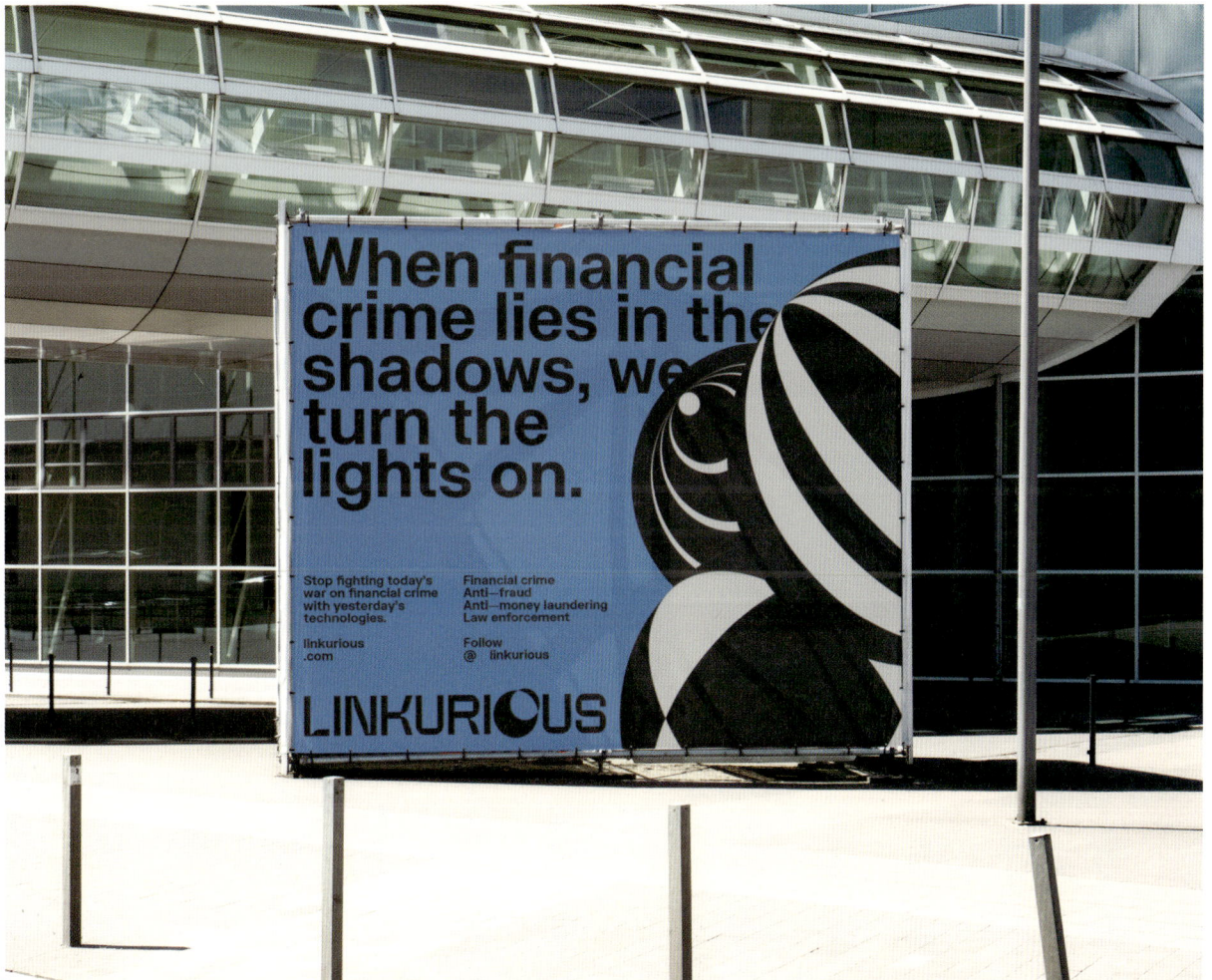

PPGMAT

The work undertaken involved the visual identity of PPGMAT — the Mathematics Education Postgraduate Program at Federal Technological University of Paraná. This design aimed to solidify the visual identity of the program's professors, students, and staff, imparting a sense of seriousness and professionalism to the department.

The central idea was to highlight the department's own personality: welcoming, human, and reflecting in the performance and craft of the mathematics education program. Leste created a logo with hand-drawn letters that strongly draws inspiration from humanist typography, while simultaneously carrying a strong geometric relationship in its form. For the illustrations, they used basic geometric shapes and playful variations: addition, division, multiplication, progression of forms, among others. The shapes interact with each other — within the application possibilities. Each element can engage with others and create new forms of visualization.

Design Studio
Leste

Art Direction
Felipe Augusto

Logo Design
Gustavo Andre

Production
Marina Bigardi

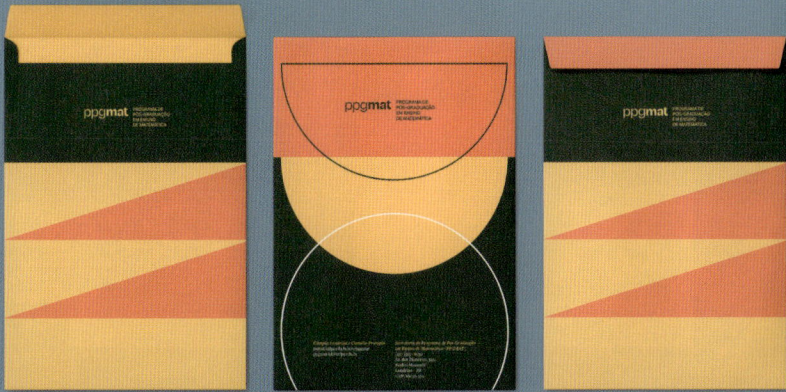

Mizna Film Festival

The campaign and identity for the Mizna Film Festival revolve around a tapestry of screens, seamlessly blending the realms of analogue and digital. The graphic system not only pays homage to the intricate artistry of Palestinian cross stitch embroidery but also serves as a symbolic representation of the interplay between traditional and contemporary storytelling. The tapestry of screens becomes a visual narrative, reflecting the festival's commitment to showcasing diverse voices and narratives while bridging the gap between heritage and innovation.

Design Studio
Morcos Key

Creative Direction
Wael Morcos

Design
**Chuck Gonzales,
Rouba Yammine**

Client
Mizna Arab Film Festival

YOU RESEMBLE ME
A FILMMAKER DISCUSSION
Pre-recorded, Virtual

mizna a
16TH ARAB FILM FEST

MAY GOD BE WITH YOU
POST-SCREENING DISCUSSION WITH CLÉO COHEN
Oct. 1 at 3 p.m., In-person at Trylon Cinema

mizna a
16TH ARAB FILM FEST

FILMMAKING BETWEEN FICTION & REALITY
A WORKSHOP WITH KHALIL JOREIGE
Oct. 1 at 3 p.m., In-person at Trylon Cinema

mizna a
16TH ARAB FILM FEST

FADIA'S TREE
A CONVERSATION
Pre-recorded, Virtual

mizna a
16TH ARAB FILM FEST

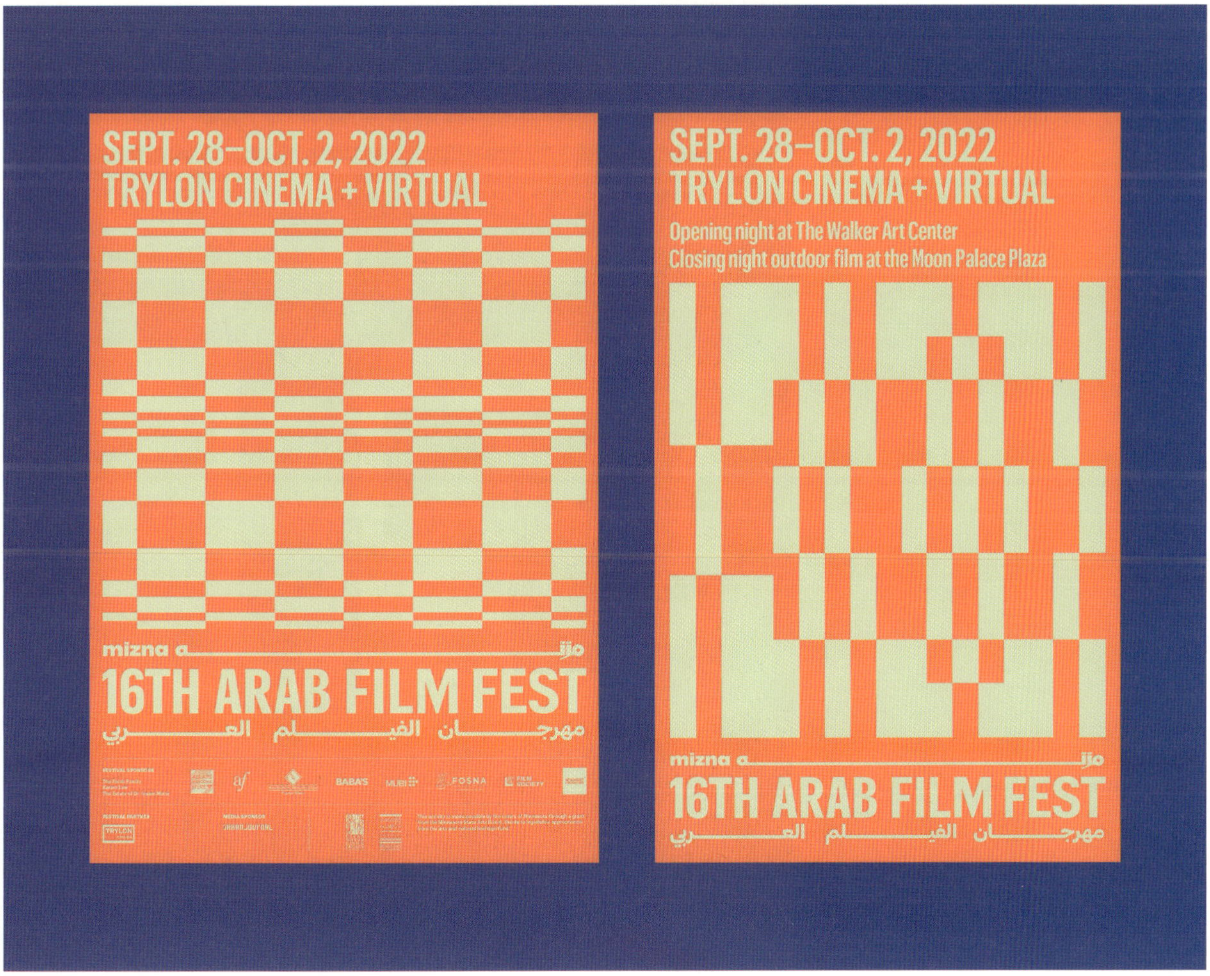

SEPT. 28–OCT. 2, 2022
TRYLON CINEMA + VIRTUAL

mizna a
16TH ARAB FILM FEST

SEPT. 28–OCT. 2, 2022
TRYLON CINEMA + VIRTUAL
Opening night at The Walker Art Center
Closing night outdoor film at the Moon Palace Plaza

mizna a
16TH ARAB FILM FEST

FCM – Festival Caxiense de Museus

The visual identity of the Festival Caxiense de Museus emerges to resignify the way of telling the story of the past, transforming the present into a cultural and educational moment.

With an aesthetic that overflows plurality, the brand is composed by the acronym "FCM" represented in geometric form. The project based on culture and on the multifaceted points of view portrayed in historical works and objects. Here, all comes together with the same purpose: to retell the history.

Design Studio
Anselmi Branding Corp.

Design
João Pedro Anselmi Jr

Client
Festival Caxiense de Museus

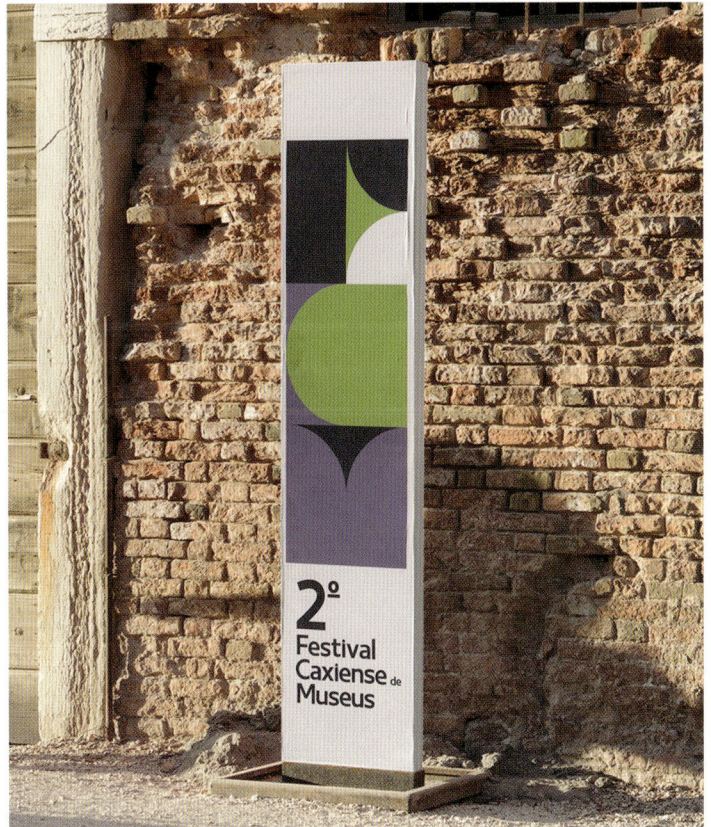

Infiniti Graphics

This is an advertising company based in Dammam City, Saudi Arabia, providing services like designing, printing, and 3D signboards. Designer built the logo concept based on the relationship between the clients and their customers.

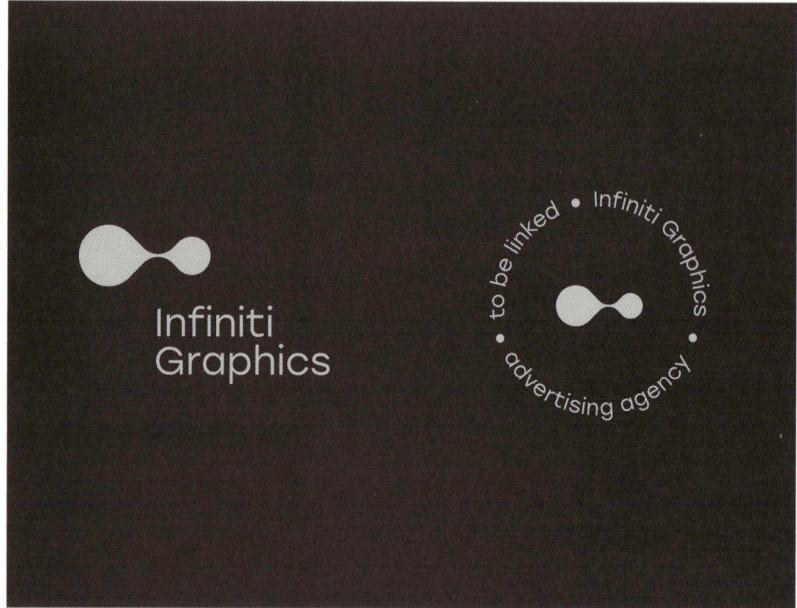

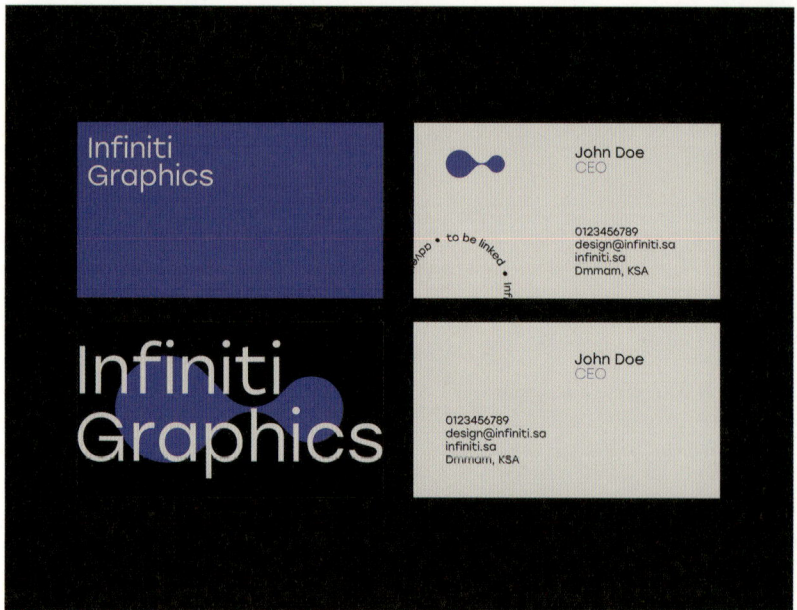

Design
Omar H. Abdulqadir

Client
Infiniti Graphics

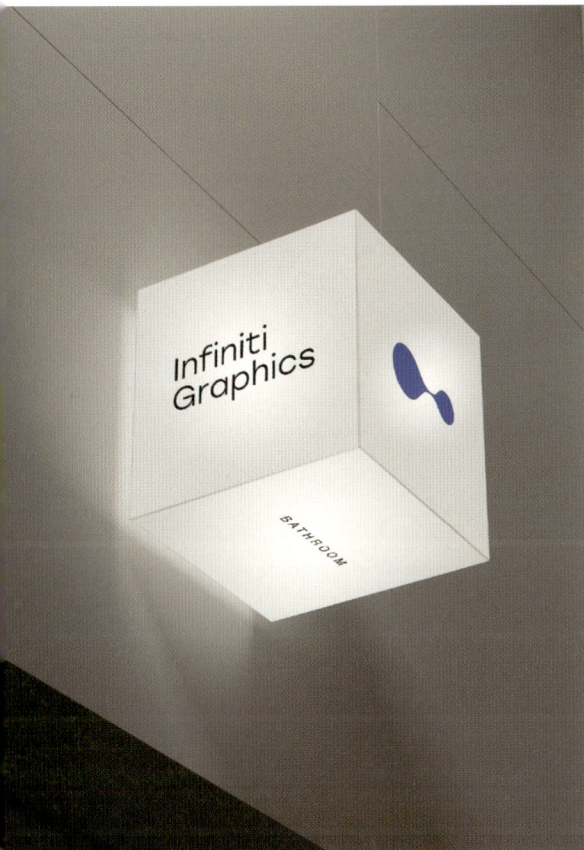

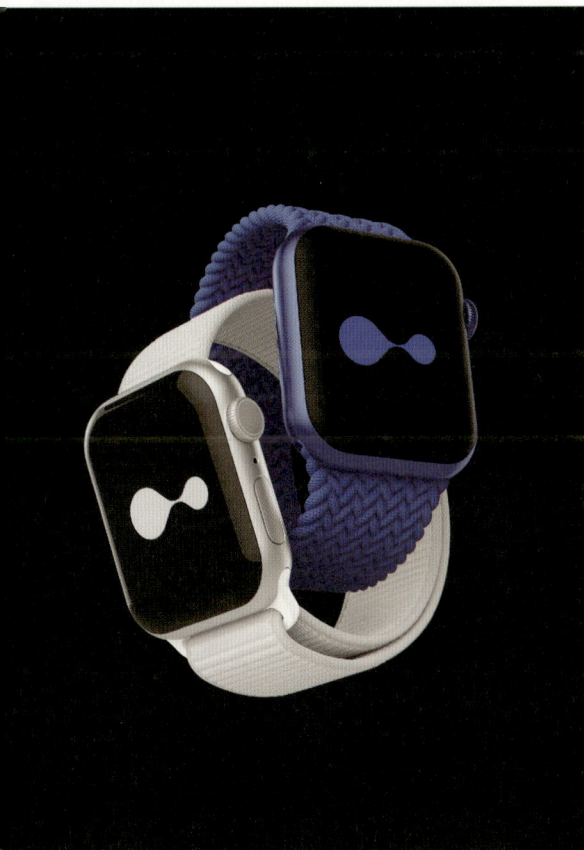

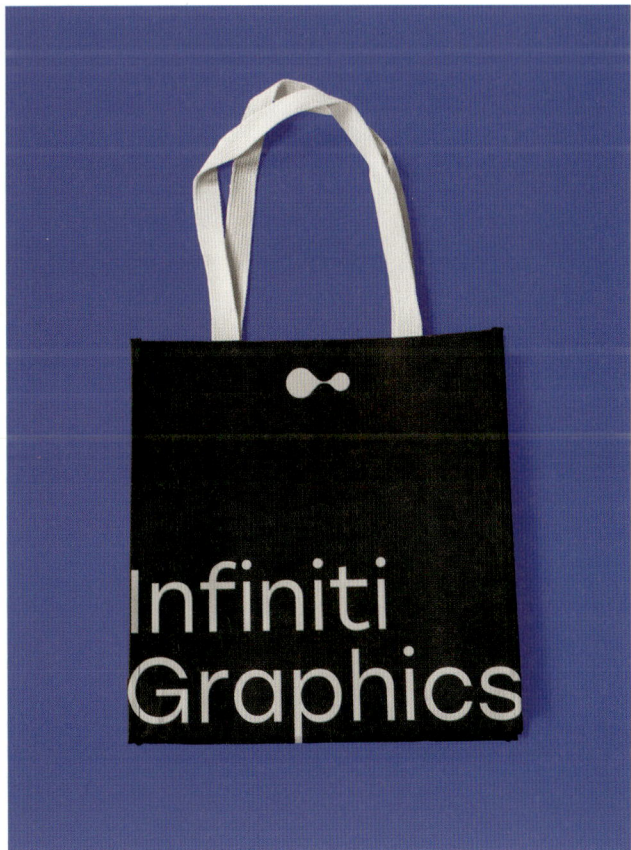

MORECHKA

MORECHKA is a brand of sculptural designs for the interior. "Morechka" is exactly how the great-grandmother called the creator of the brand. So it is no coincidence that the blue color appears in branding (In Russian, the word "more" means "sea").

The essence of the brand: the search for pure proportions in personality and sculpture, the knowledge of emptiness through manifestation. People can see an ellipse in the logo, which actually doesn't exist. It is a void. However, the manifestation of the background rectangle helps people to see it.

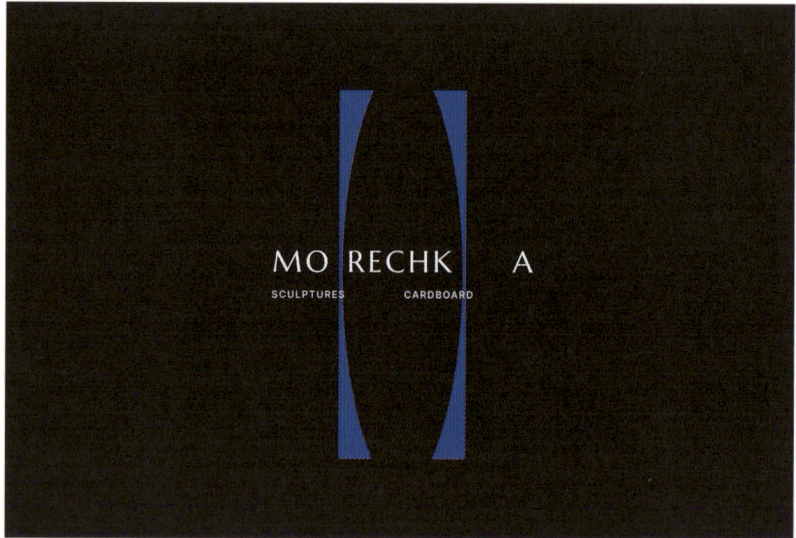

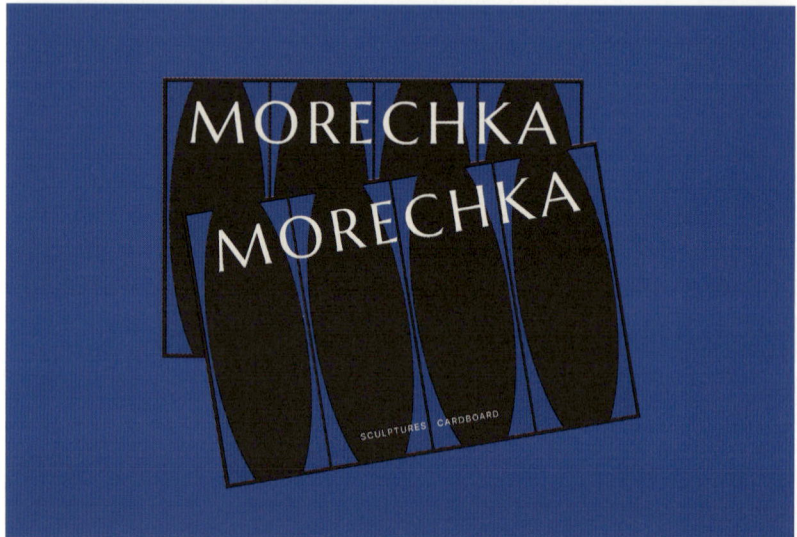

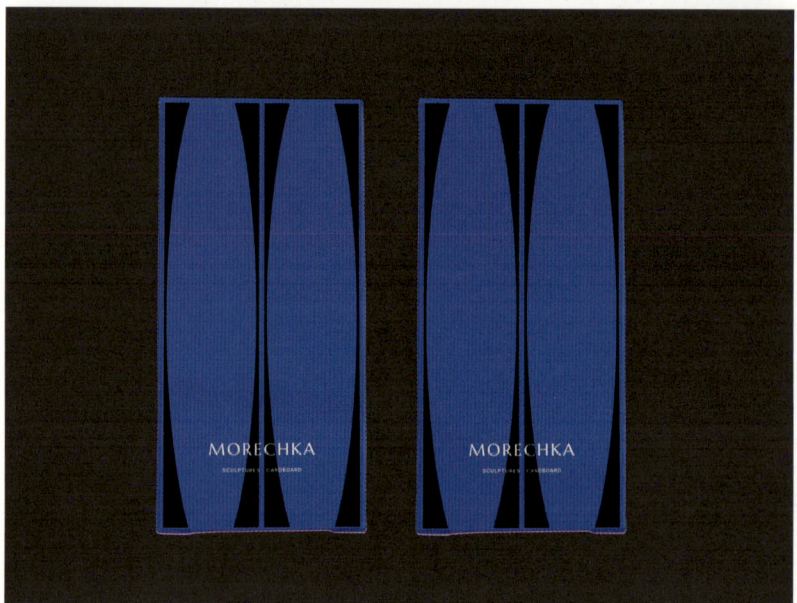

Design
Evgeniia Prokopeva

Client
Marina Varnashova

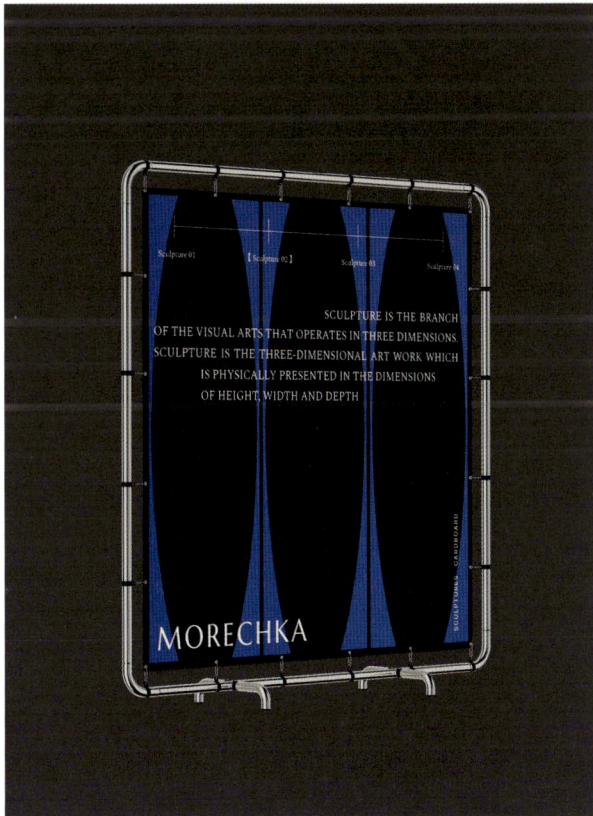

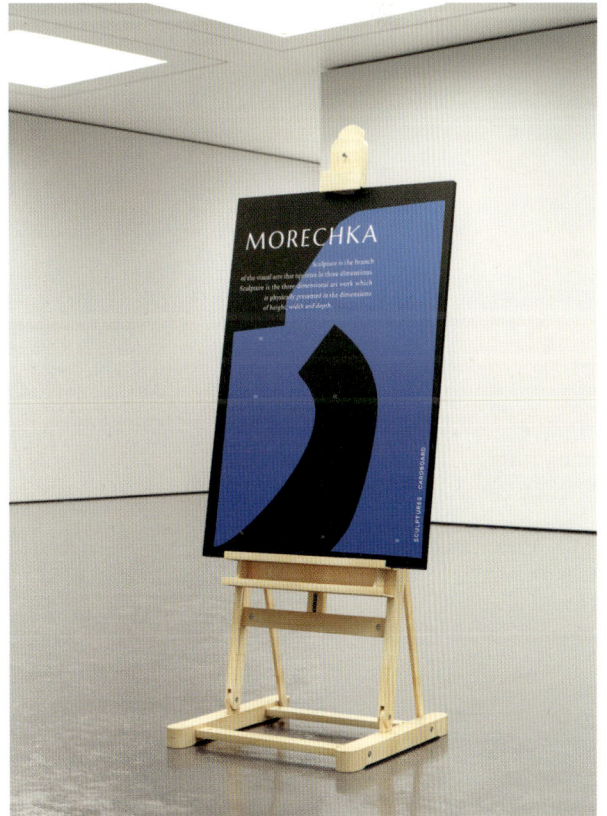

f(u) = formule CAFÉ

f(u) = formule CAFÉ is the full name of f(u) CAFÉ. The concept of an equation is the unique design language of f(u) = formule CAFÉ. As a result, its graphic area proportions are all due to the changing shapes between the four letters of "CAFÉ". BY-ENJOY DESIGN tries to emphasize the unbounded sense of the brand image through such creativity, expanding the possibility of filling and extending the application content and making it derive the expression image of multiple existence under random conditions.

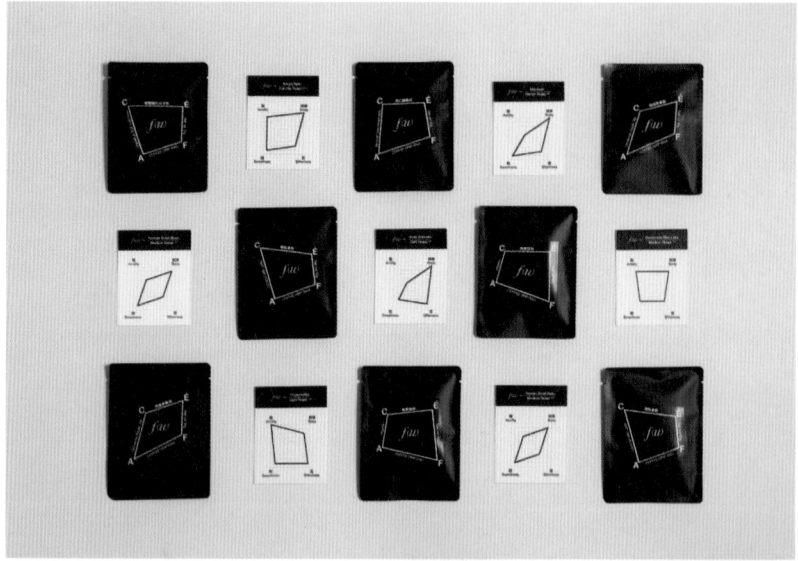

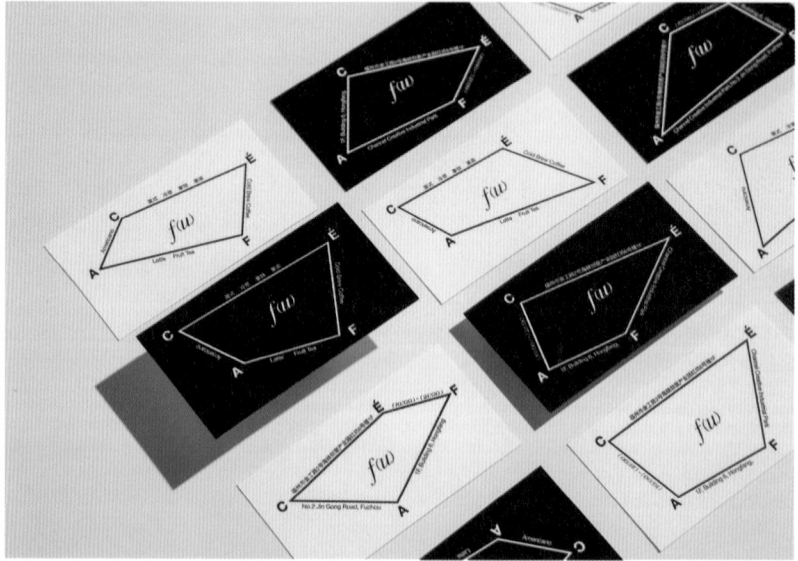

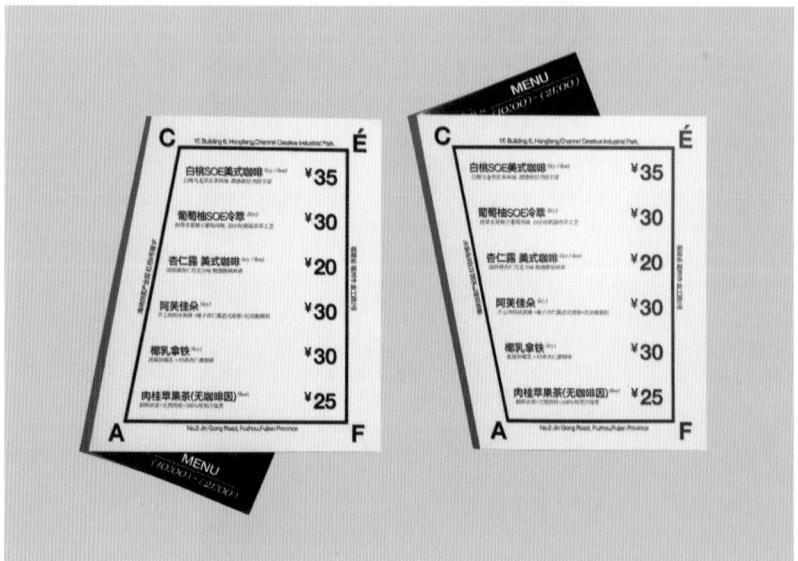

Design Studio
BY-ENJOY DESIGN

Art Direction
Yang Huale

Design
Yang Huale, Zheng Ziyang

Motion
Zhou Minqi

Photography
Zou Xunkai

Client
f(u) CAFÉ

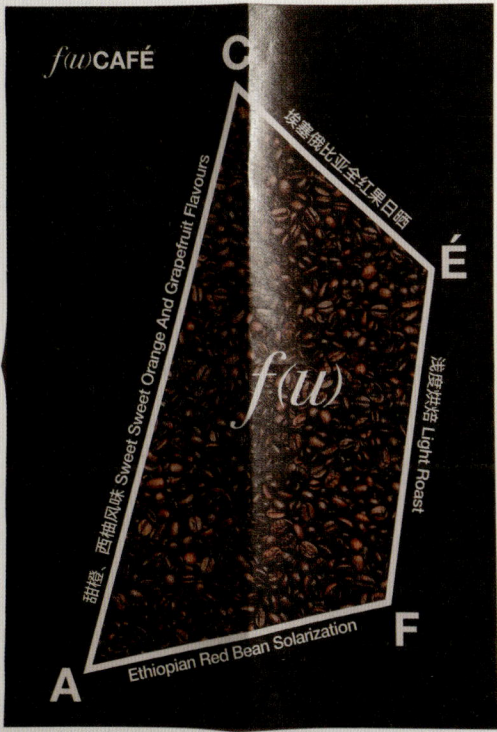

f(u)CAFÉ

埃塞俄比亚全红果日晒

埃塞俄比亚全红果日晒 Sweet Sweet Orange And Grapefruit Flavours

浅度烘焙 Light Roast

f(u)

Ethiopian Red Bean Solarization

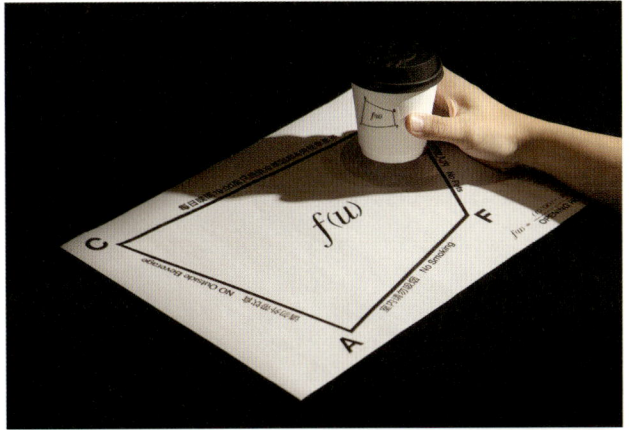

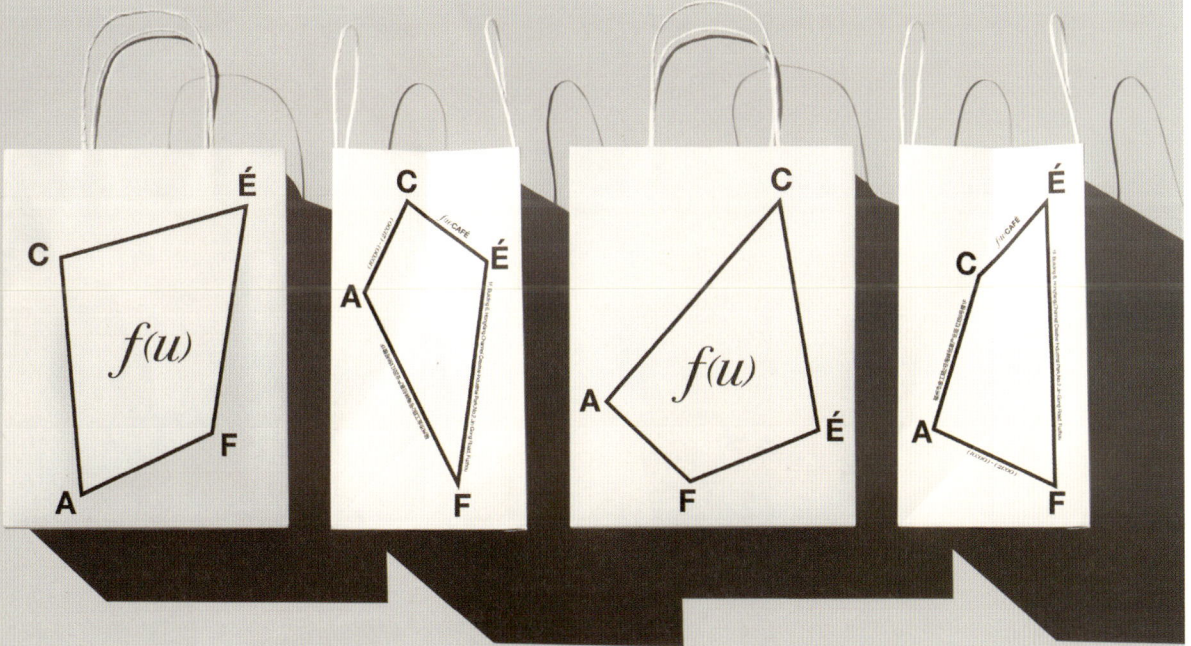

HKRITA – Fabric Poster System

The Hong Kong Research Institute of Textiles and Apparel (HKRITA), is the leading center of excellence in research, development and technology transfer in fashion and textile industry.

The center focused research and development efforts, pursuance of continual technological development and facilitation of technology transfers of research and development results, thus designers have developed a brand pillars extension system to help them demonstrate their cutting-edge results. The extension system is made with a flexible module system, to be effectively showcasing the different aspects of HKRITA, and regarding to the professionalism of HKRITA in the textile industry. The poster system is printed with fabric instead of paper, to echo the brand's industry-changing visions.

Design Studio
for&st

Design
Ming Cheung

Client
The Hong Kong Research Institute of Textiles and Apparel

Abstract

Shapes

Abstract shapes are simplified versions of common elements or forms. In addition to geometric shapes, they are mostly based on organic shapes although lacking definition. Abstract shapes are usually arbitrary since they can take many different forms.

01. Under what circumstances would you choose abstract graphics as elements for your work?

The studio is characterized by a composite methodology between in-depth research and creative intuition. Experimentation is a fundamental step that guides all our work. Through historical, linguistic, iconographic and semiological exploration, it is the pursuit of meaning and the unique piece that drives us to build honest and accurate visual identities, without artifice. Abstract forms allow for a freedom of interpretation that often exceeds our original intentions. I consider it a kind of narrative and visual poetry.

● **AB Projets Studio**

I work more often with abstract graphic elements than illustrative shapes, often in the borderland between simple and illustrative. Abstract elements can create an interest to see more and are well suited when there is a lot of text in a material. I would also chose to twist abstract elements whose shapes we take for granted — like the dots in a bullet list. Small details like that can do a lot. But with this said, it is always the idea and content that must guide the solution.

● **Lina Forsgren**

In expressing the sense of atmosphere and visual concept, we will try to use abstract graphics to present, which is general and direct in itself, it removes some details to make things more pure and essential.

● **B&W Graphic Lab**

First and foremost, abstract graphics can elicit emotions and captivate viewers. A brand can succeed creating intrigue and a strong connection with the public while establishing a unique visual identity. Abstract elements in graphic design can also symbolize ideas, values, virtues, by allowing deeper layers of meaning. Another big advantage is that the brand can stand out within a crowded market by using a strong contrast, an iconic pattern, a bold form, an unexpected or fresh symbol.

Furthermore, abstract graphics follow the minimal aesthetics. This means that you keep it as simple, clean and balanced as it gets to convey the message directly. Abstract visual elements can also easily adapt or adjust in different shapes, sizes or formats. This flexibility offers a great design freedom especially when designing a series of products.

Shapes and symbols are often used by us as a systematic approach to brand identity and packaging design. Rather than just creating a logo or designing single bits and bops for a brand identity, we always want to tell a story. We aim to create an opening to a world that people can dive into. By crafting a system out of simple, abstracted elements we are able to build a holistic concept.

● **KR8 bureau**

● **Loukas Chondros**

When I want to express some complex psychology such as emotions or feelings, or some concepts that are difficult to give a definite conclusion such as thinking, I choose to use abstract graphics as an element to create. Just like an article with open proposition or a film without a conclusion, I hope to use abstract graphics as a medium to trigger the viewer's association and link their emotions when interacting with them.

● Peng Cheng

I always start with an idea that rules the brand concept. Sometimes, these ideas naturally evolve into geometric forms. I don't use geometric shapes randomly; instead, I strive to ensure that they serve a purpose and derive meaning from a specific source. While geometric shapes can be found everywhere, for them to truly resonate and become synonymous with a particular brand, they must always originate from a conceptual idea that guides their existence.

● Sofia Noceti

Abstract graphics can be chosen as elements for work in various circumstances, depending on the specific objectives and desired aesthetic. Sometimes adding visual interest or energy. Abstract graphics can inject vibrancy, dynamism, and visual excitement into a composition. They can be used to create eye-catching focal points, enhance visual hierarchy, or add a sense of movement and energy to the overall design.

● Studio Woork

When we going to visualizing an idea which is conceptual or non-visualized, we will consider abstract graphics as visual elements to communicate with the audience.

● Pengguin

The tone of voice and target audience are important considerations. In this case, the use of a shape-mixed logo and abstract graphics, inspired by paper-cut icons, help to create an authoritative logo and a clear wayfinding system that blends seamlessly into the natural and open campus space. These graphics have a balanced and artistic tone that appeals to both parents and students, without being too childish or too mature.

● Toby Ng Design

I will use shapes when the information I need to convey is more emotional and imaginative but not specific; when I need to convey the concept of diversity and inclusiveness in brand logos or visual design. Designs using abstract graphics are easier to stand out in competitive products. When designs with shapes are easier to print, add more processing or artistic; when I want to convey a more experimental, youthful and innovative feeling.

● Triangler

It all depends on the project and its requirements. We often propose an abstract graphic when we think it is interesting for the audience/consumer to be able to give it their own personal meaning in order to involve them in a subtle way.

● Wikka

02. How do you come up with a concept in design and turn them into shapes?

We are committed to crafting identities based on artisanal design with the belief that stories are told through original logos: we design our own typograms and wordmarks to find unexpected angles and enrich identities with a systemic approach. We develop shapes based on the same construction rules as typefaces, which allows us to practise a free and precise design.

● **AB Projets Studio**

For the beginning of the creation, we will have deep divergent thinking, try to be as far away from the case itself as possible, so that the distant observation can see a bigger outline, and the thinking process will form a network to encompass the rich content. The visual logic is sorted out by graphically depicting the big outline, the details of the graphic structure and rules.

● **B&W Graphic Lab**

Through our strategies we usually create some sort of brand narrative or brand character, which is the base for every approach. Our work BEYA for instance was inspired by "Gestalt Therapy". I'm sure you're familiar with the Rorschach Test. The shapes for BEYA work are in a similar way. Just the other way around. BEYA works with a library of 15 shapes that you can combine to create your personal message with. Shapes and symbols can work in many ways. Consciously, subconsciously, directly or metaphorically. All our work that include shapes and symbols have different narratives and functions.

● **KR8 bureau**

I read about the background to the project, figure out what we want to say with the material and what the recipient should think and feel. I often work with moodboards that I boil down to a core visual expression and then do a lot of sketching, and somewhere in the sketching process the shapes emerge.

● **Lina Forsgren**

When it comes to ideation in design process, inspiration is derived from different sources. It all starts with the strategic approach, such as, client — competitors — market research. However the main focus of research is the product itself, getting to know more and more the narrative behind that.

Especially when designing food and beverages, the core point is the story from seed to shelf. The most important values of the brand are mainly narrated throughout this journey, such as sustainability, cultivation ethos, etc. These are the elements that inspire the concept development and convey the brand's message. Together with that, the goal is to create shapes that are visually engaging, meaningful, and resonate with the target audience.

● **Loukas Chondros**

Well communicating with clients / audiences can always help us to generate the concept. When there is a concept behind the shapes, they can always deliver a message through the overall design layout.

● **Pengguin**

I would first go for a limit of subtraction, just like making a logo by reducing a figurative concept to a basic geometric figure. For example, in my "Dong Creation" illustration series, I extracted the most iconic coiffure of the Dong women, they use a comb to coiffure their hair in the shape of an infinite symbol like "∞", I found that this graphic element is a unique feature of the Dong women, so I incorporated this simple graphic into my creation and used this special graphic into my creation and used this particular graphic element in the gesture of the Dong women weaving.

● **Peng Cheng**

I don't have a single approach or a fixed working process. With each brand I collaborate with, I engage in research and analysis, posing numerous questions to both the client and myself. Through this exploration and investigation, answers emerge and act as catalysts for ideas.

Occasionally, when ideas or concepts don't arise directly from these answers, I allow intuition to guide the flow of ideas until I discover something that resonates with the project's theme. My creative process doesn't follow a linear path, making it challenging to articulate in words. I would describe it as a fusion of research, intuition, and extensive experimentation. Ultimately, the essence of my work lies in form and color, as I strive to uncover the perfect combination of hues and shapes that align with an identity.

● **Sofia Noceti**

By understand the context, coming up with a concept in design and translating it into shapes involves a creative process that combines ideation, visualization, and iteration.

● **Studio Woork**

We begin by identifying the core elements that define United Christian Music Kindergarten (UCM). From these, we select the essence that best represents UCM and transform it into a multitude of motifs that reflect the core values and beliefs that shape the kindergarten.

● **Toby Ng Design**

Different design types will have different methods. In layout or poster design, I will first think about the main message to be conveyed by the overall picture, arrange it with geometric figures, and then evaluate whether it needs to be replaced by other methods. In logo design or illustrations, the brand's information is the focus of the design, and then the shape of the real object is referenced and displayed through lines, circles, and squares, thereby triggering the viewer's association and giving it emotion and narrative feeling.

● **Triangler**

We try not to stay with the same methodology, because each project is unique. But broadly speaking, the concept is always based on the brand strategy and its value proposal. Once defined, we use graphic references to determine the style and that is where we define what kind of shapes we will create, depending on the message we want to transmit.

● **Wikka**

03. How to convey the message behind the shapes accurately?

Research is the driving force behind our studio, and strategy is one of our complementary pillars: we accompany companies in their visual and narrative positioning through visual identity. We often submit iconographic choices, interdependent with the visual identity.

It is also a question of coherence between the message and the design. The message always serves the design and vice versa so we make sure that our deliverables are consistent with the positioning of the company.

● AB Projets Studio

Graphic representation is not a single, but a systematic concept output.

When sorting out the concept, you need to find clues and expression logic, and build a graphic visual to form a systematic framework so that all the details of expression will be unified and accurate.

● B&W Graphic Lab

That's a good question. Our take is always: It works like art. You are invited to find your own meaning in it, but you don't have to, necessarily. I think working with metaphors is not comparable with how pictographs need to function. And it's fun! A sense of mystery and exploration leaves opportunity to play.

● KR8 bureau

I think it's about in which context they are in and how they support and cooperate with the message. The shapes should be relevant to the content and in some way highlight it.

● Lina Forsgren

To effectively communicate the brand's message, a strategic approach is totally required. Firstly, as a designer you get to understand the brand identity in terms of philosophy, values, scope, target audience etc. Then the ideation includes the generation of symbols, visual elements that represent the above meanings. Depending on the main message, the shapes and forms will be developed respectively. The position, composition and hierarchy of the visual information also plays a vital role, depending on the brand's key points.

Another significant factor when designing is the typography and the use or non-use of color. A thoughtful selection of both should be aligned with the brand's identity. Finally, throughout the process, client's feedback is really useful to ensure that the message is communicated effectively.

● Loukas Chondros

Every shape has their own characters, for example, square is a regular quadrilateral, it represents balance, stable, volume and prefect, etc. Through their unique features, the audience may catch up the message you want to deliver naturally.

● Pengguin

To convey the message with communicate more effectively by understanding the psychology or concept of shapes. They help you convey the exact vibe and message that we have in mind and our design. It varies based on the specific context and we need to visualize the shapes and help people identify the shapes easily.

● Studio Woork

I think graphics are a language in themselves, for example, a stable square and a tilted parallelogram must be perceived differently, and I will connect the "language" of the graphic itself with the emotion I want to convey to help set the mood or convey the message. In addition, I think symbols can be very useful, and they can be defined as "perceptions that are perceived as carrying meaning", just like the universal script of the world, which is also a good way.

● Peng Cheng

We derive meaning from the core values of UCM to create effective and accurate communication that resonates with our audience.

● Toby Ng Design

Different shapes convey different meanings, but the focus still must be to confirm the culture, background and language awareness of the target audience to ensure that the graphics can convey the correct meaning among them. Ask different people to evaluate whether they correctly understand what the graphics represent. Accept the feedback and make any necessary changes to ensure accuracy of graphic meaning.

● Triangler

Shapes have their own language and the way we present them communicates our message. Shapes can take on various forms, whether rigid, organic, or geometric. They can repeat, interact with one another, break free from the plane, change in size, or expand. Countless actions can be applied to shapes to convey ideas, tell stories, and transform them from mere forms into concepts full of meaning. Let's not overlook the power of color as well!

● Sofia Noceti

In brand design, shapes are always accompanied by other graphic elements such as typography, colors, layouts, photographs, etc. A good approach to the composition of all these elements helps the message to be transmitted correctly.

● Wikka

04. How to keep the graphics coordinated with other visual elements in the work?

Research allows us to collect visual information and codes that we try to reinject into the composition of our projects. There is both a question of organizing the elements between them to create a new language and an artistic intuition. Experimenting with new things is one of our most ambitious challenges. We take risks to make magic happen.

● AB Projets Studio

This totally depends on the systematic approach. You need to have a strong concept first. Limit yourself to as little "ingredients" as you need, but give every bit a sense function. If you can't explain why you added this element, or what it represents, you can mostly always let it go. For us even typefaces carry a message. It's like creating a beautiful ikebana piece. The art to know when to stop, and what is needed for it make the right impact.

● KR8 bureau

Seize the visual priority, pull away the contrast of graphic expression, locate the position of graphic expression in this case, and need to have design white space to match the application of the rest elements at the beginning of creation.

● B&W Graphic Lab

It can differ so much from project to project. In some cases it could be finding something that i.e. a shape and a letter have in common, and in other cases it's better if they stand in contrast to each other. If a typeface that is used is thin, the balance can get better if the shapes are chunkier. The contrast can then make it easier to sort and take in the information – and create a strong visual expression.

● Lina Forsgren

By establishing a design system, aligning with the brand's identity, maintaining a consistent visual language, harmonizing typography and colors, considering proportions and scale, and embracing an iterative design process, ensure that all elements work together cohesively, the overall aesthetic is uniform and so the sense of unity can reinforce the brand's identity.

● Loukas Chondros

It really depends on the overall feeling or message we want to present. Having a strong visual impact is the most important thing to consider.

● **Pengguin**

The first thing that comes to my mind is similarity, creating a main graphic, other elements in the feeling can be consistent with the feeling of the main graphic, for example, the main graphic of the picture conveys the feeling of roundness, then the corresponding text, typography, color scheme can refer to the perception associated with it. Or a strong contrast in the picture to create a sharp impact of equal strength, so that is also a kind of coordination. I feel that coordinating all the elements in the picture is the goal of each creation, each time is a different game, there is no fixed answer.

● **Peng Cheng**

By understanding the visual language that sends messages to the target audience and maintaining consistency in visual elements such as color palette, typography, layout, photography, and more in visual communication.

● **Studio Woork**

We ensure that all graphic elements are in alignment with one another. The paper-cut inspired icons were specifically designed to coordinate with the other visual components in the project.

● **Toby Ng Design**

Harmony is not achieved in isolation; it is nurtured throughout the entire process. I firmly believe that every element holds significance, and I don't prioritize one over another. Graphic elements, typography, and color must coexist in harmony or intentionally contrast, as dictated by the concept. Personally, I have a predilection for meticulously justifying every decision. Whether elements coexist or not depends on what we want to communicate, but it always originates from strong ideas.

● **Sofia Noceti**

My understanding of coordination is whether it plays its role competently; the size and placement of shapes vary from design to design. Color choices should be coordinated to ensure that colors blend into each other without causing visual clutter. Just like all design elements, whether it is images, fonts, or geometric figures, there are considerations of basic formal principles such as color, lines, style, contrast, etc.

● **Triangler**

This is defined when we propose the graphic style through visual references. Through moodboards we propose which type of graphics go with which type of typography, colors, photography, etc.

We normally propose a very clean style so that all the elements can coexist in harmony.

● **Wikka**

Engetsu Consulting

Engetsu Consulting is a London based company offering Cyber security and penetration testing services. Engetsu (crescent moon) is a highly defensive formation which was adopted by samurai soldiers when they are outnumbered.

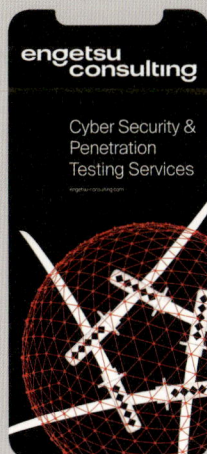

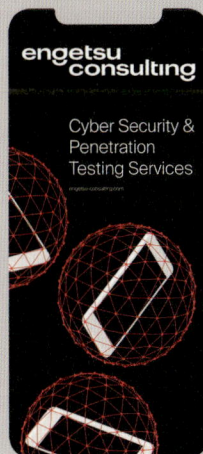

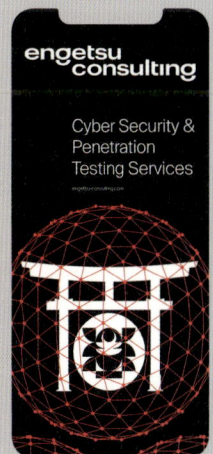

Art Direction
Bogdan Katsuba

Design
Ophiuchus Design

Client
Engetsu Consulting

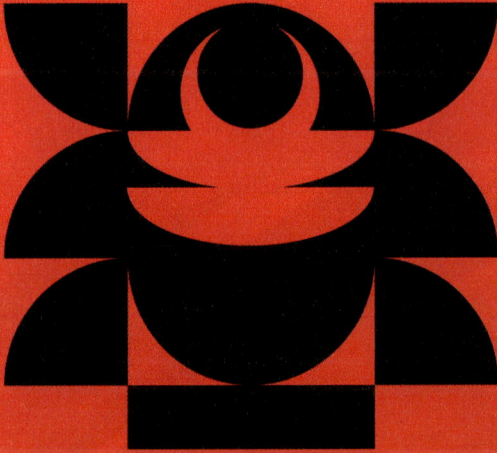

Samsen Kit

Samsen is a consultant company designed around the idea to adapt work to life rather than life to work, for example, by choosing how and when they want to work and which clients they feel passionate about working with. The Samsen Kit is a theme box and tool to help the members to identify opportunities for professional and personal development, and through self-leadership and coaching achieve an increased quality of life. The opportunities can range from issues with relationships, personal health, stress management and career challenges, to smaller things like time management and daily habits.

Art Direction
Lina Forsgren

Design
Lina Forsgren

Copy
Tomas Måsviken,
Samsen

Client
Samsen

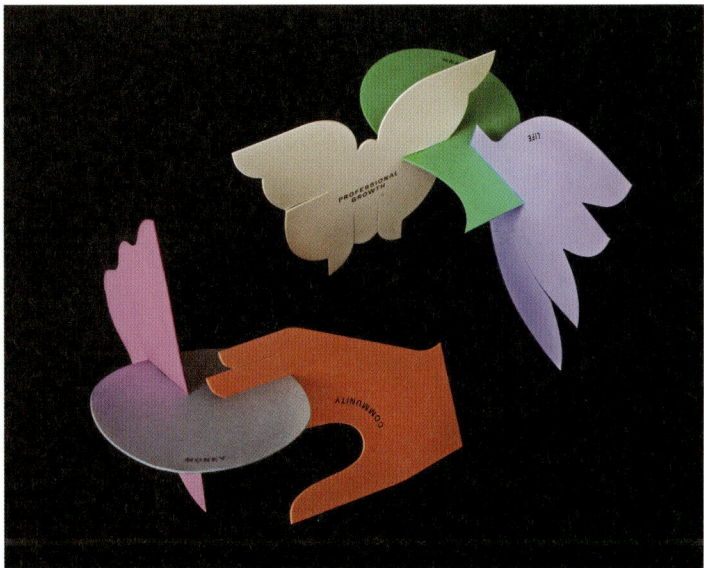

③ Pick *the most inpactful objective*

Now, pick the one objective that would have the largest impact on where you are in life right now. We will help you scope the objective to make it actionable in your first coaching session.

I want to reduce stress

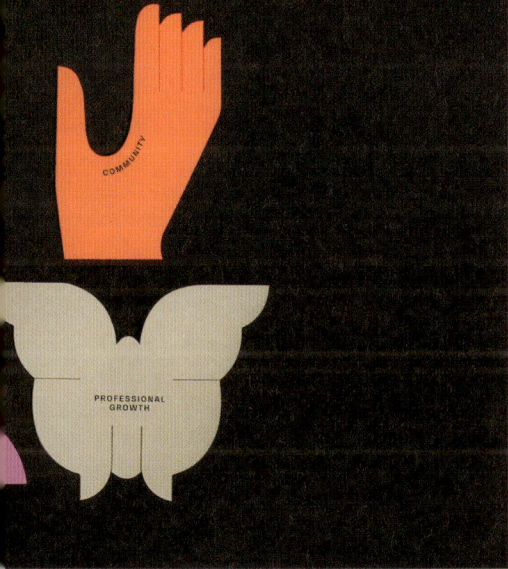

COMMUNITY

PROFESSIONAL GROWTH

CLIENT WORK

"I like my client project, but this specific person I work with drives me nuts"

PROFESSIONAL GROWTH

"I want to become more organized"

LIFE

"I'm moving house in two months and need some time off"

Pez Negro

Pez Negro is a bookstore and publisher based in La Plata, Buenos Aires, Argentina. The space brings together a selection of poetry books, fanzines, essays, photography, illustrated books and novels. The identity design was inspired by two axes: on the one hand, in the geometry and figures of tangram (the ancient Chinese game) and on the other, in the urban layout of the city of La Plata organized by diagonals.

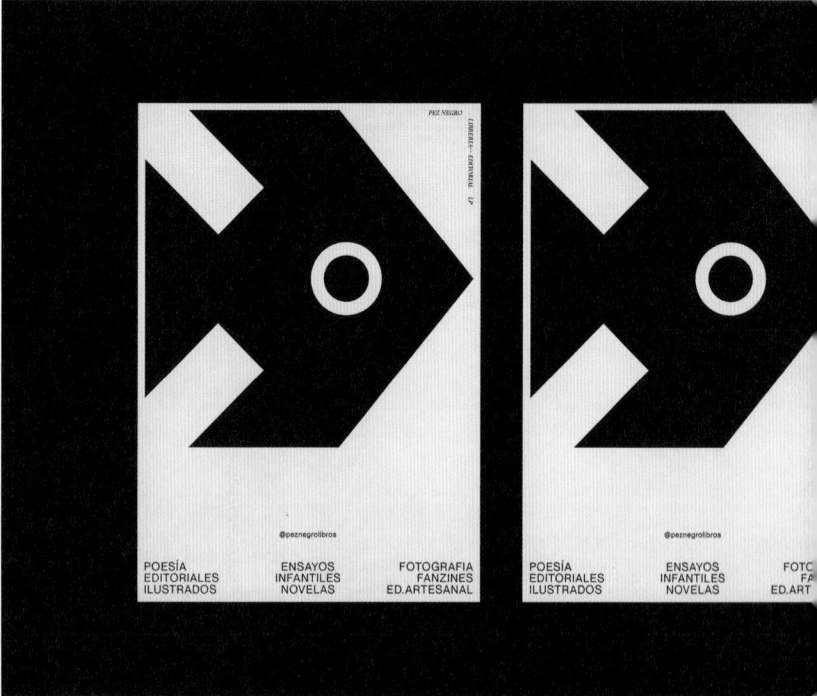

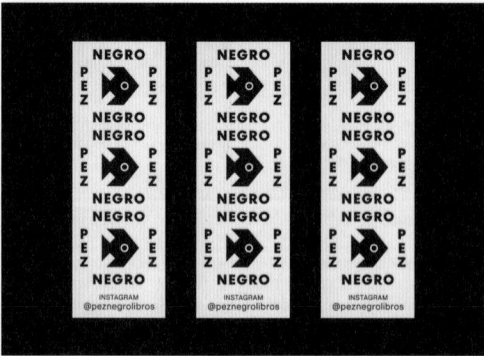

Design
Un Barco

Photography
Un Barco

Client
Florencia Mendoza

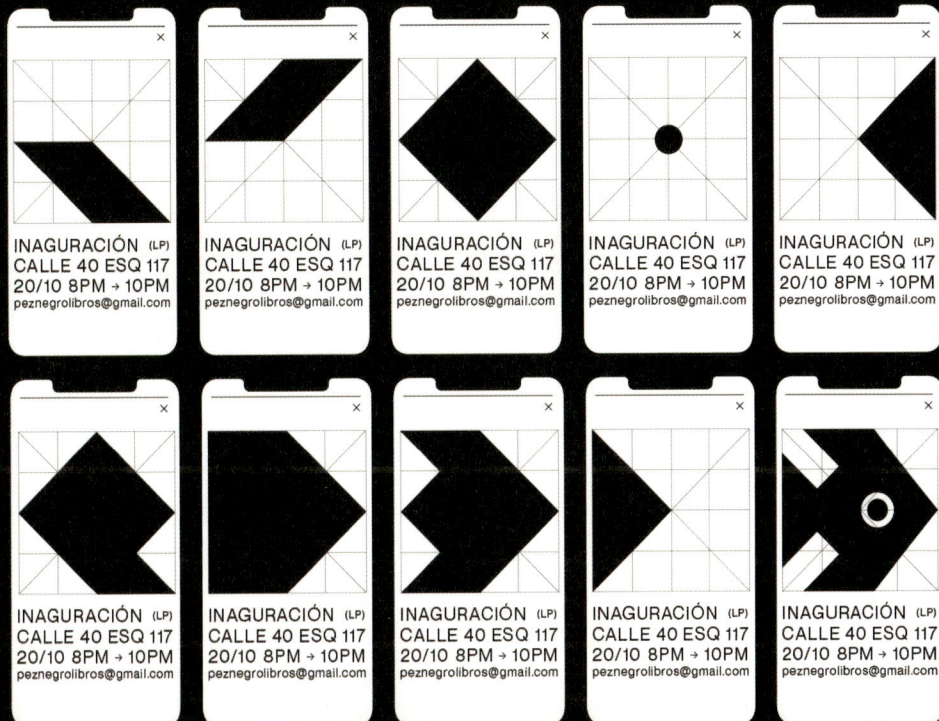

INAGURACIÓN (LP)
CALLE 40 ESQ 117
20/10 8PM → 10PM
peznegrolibros@gmail.com

INAGURACIÓN (LP)
CALLE 40 ESQ 117
20/10 8PM → 10PM
peznegrolibros@gmail.com

INAGURACIÓN (LP)
CALLE 40 ESQ 117
20/10 8PM → 10PM
peznegrolibros@gmail.com

INAGURACIÓN (LP)
CALLE 40 ESQ 117
20/10 8PM → 10PM
peznegrolibros@gmail.com

INAGURACIÓN (LP)
CALLE 40 ESQ 117
20/10 8PM → 10PM
peznegrolibros@gmail.com

INAGURACIÓN (LP)
CALLE 40 ESQ 117
20/10 8PM → 10PM
peznegrolibros@gmail.com

INAGURACIÓN (LP)
CALLE 40 ESQ 117
20/10 8PM → 10PM
peznegrolibros@gmail.com

INAGURACIÓN (LP)
CALLE 40 ESQ 117
20/10 8PM → 10PM
peznegrolibros@gmail.com

INAGURACIÓN (LP)
CALLE 40 ESQ 117
20/10 8PM → 10PM
peznegrolibros@gmail.com

INAGURACIÓN (LP)
CALLE 40 ESQ 117
20/10 8PM → 10PM
peznegrolibros@gmail.com

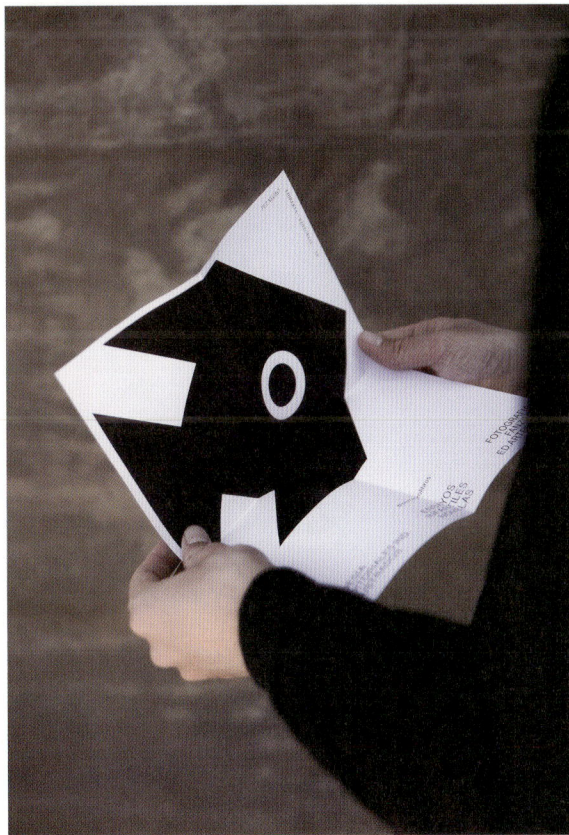

Nut Butters

It is a new series of Nut Butter packaging for Fig Shop. It is to reveal the pureness of 100% nut butter solely made from almond, pistachio, cashews, hazelnut and sesame. The strong contrast and iconic patterns identify the brand and its different flavors.

Design
Loukas Chondros

Client
Fig Shop

Braw Liquor Club

Braw Liquor Club blends locally sourced, small batch cocktails. My Creative produced a full brand identity and label system that reflected the misologists craft when layering flavors and spirits together to create a delicious cocktail. These flavor profiles were then used to depict Scottish landscapes. Layers of color form a mountain range or seascape, which links the product and source directly to the brand. A simple but iconic sun shape was adopted into the brand and then hole punched out of each label and drinks card. They frame the liquor as a jewel in the label and throughout the brand.

Art Direction
My Creative

Design
Ewan Leckie

3D Rendering
Jamie Cardo

Client
Braw Liquor Club

Amuleto Portal

This line is made up of a selection of 12 plants that act on different body systems. Each color identifies a different system. Red color identifies the circulatory system, blue color identifies the nervous system and orange color identifies digestive system. From the design of the packaging, designers took the aesthetics of a common medicine and linked it with the world of plants, making a lot of focus on the medicinal.

Design
Un Barco

Photography
Un Barco

Client
Amuleto Portal

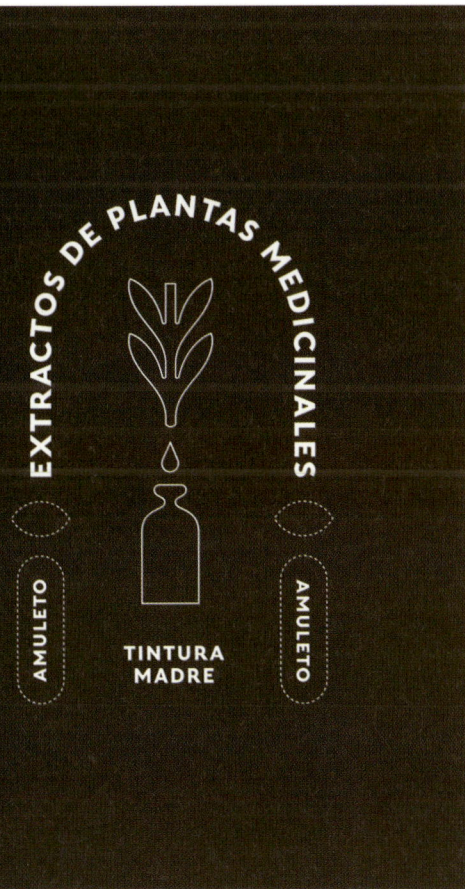

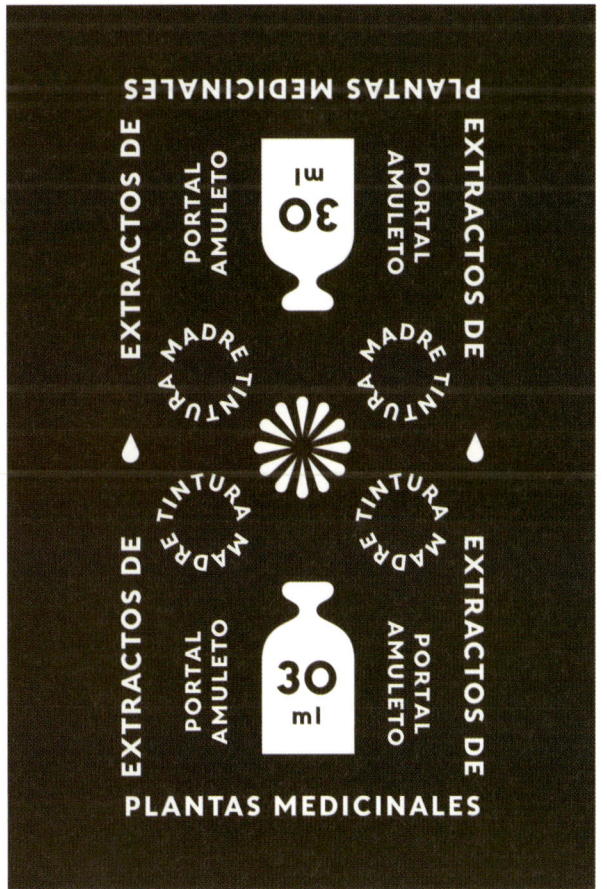

Floresta

Floresta is a kit of ceramic pieces inspired by sunflowers and cherry blossoms. The kit contains one pipe, one drying box and one storage box. Un Barco created the Floresta's visual system.

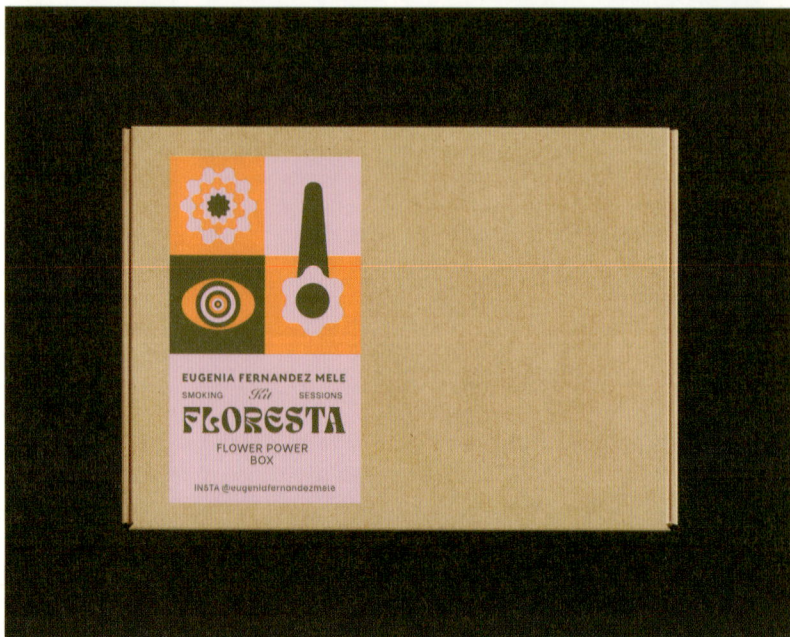

Design
Un Barco

Photography
Lucia Baldi

Client
Eugenia Fernandez Mele

FLORESTA

SMOKING SESSIONS   PIPA

Esta pieza fue horneada a 1100° y revestida con esmaltes no tóxicos.

@eugeniafernandezmele

PIPA *PIPE*

Inspirada en los girasoles y las flores del cerezo

Esta pieza fue horneada a 1100° y revestida con esmaltes no tóxicos.

Medidas
Ancho 8cm. Alto 3cm.

FLOWER POWER BOX   SMOKING *Kit* SESSIONS

SECADO *DRYING BOX*

Inspirada en los girasoles y las flores del cerezo

Esta pieza fue horneada a 1100° y revestida con esmaltes no tóxicos.

Medidas
Diámetro 6,5cm. Alto 6cm.

FLOWER POWER BOX   SMOKING *Kit* SESSIONS

GUARDADO *SAVED BOX*

Inspirada en los girasoles y las flores del cerezo

Esta pieza fue horneada a 1100° y revestida con esmaltes no tóxicos.

Medidas
Diámetro 10cm. Alto 6cm.

FLOWER POWER BOX   SMOKING *Kit* SESSIONS

FLORESTA
FLORESTA
FLORESTA
FLORESTA

SMOKING *Kit* SESSIONS
SAFETY 40 MATCHES

Mastea

The rich taste of tea leaves mixed with a delicate sense of layering. Every bite is filled with a sweet and natural flavor. The visual overall combines simple composition with rhythmic lines to express the visual fragrance of tea.

Bold bright colors are used, comparing and pairing with graphic lines filled with sense of design. It presents a visual image that is deeply loved by young people.

Design Studio
B&W Graphic Lab

Creative Direction
Ben

Art Direction
Wynne

Design
Ben, Wynne

Client
Mastea

för ägg

This is the rebranding design for för ägg, a company that sells chiffon cakes and other western-style confections, while running a poultry farm. The design concept is the integrated production process from the poultry farm to the cake factory and the change and development from eggs to chiffon cakes. When designing the logotype, the designer took the raw egg as a double circle, put the cracked egg in the grid, and showed the process of making chiffon cake. The typography allows for individualistic change within the constraints of the divided double circle.

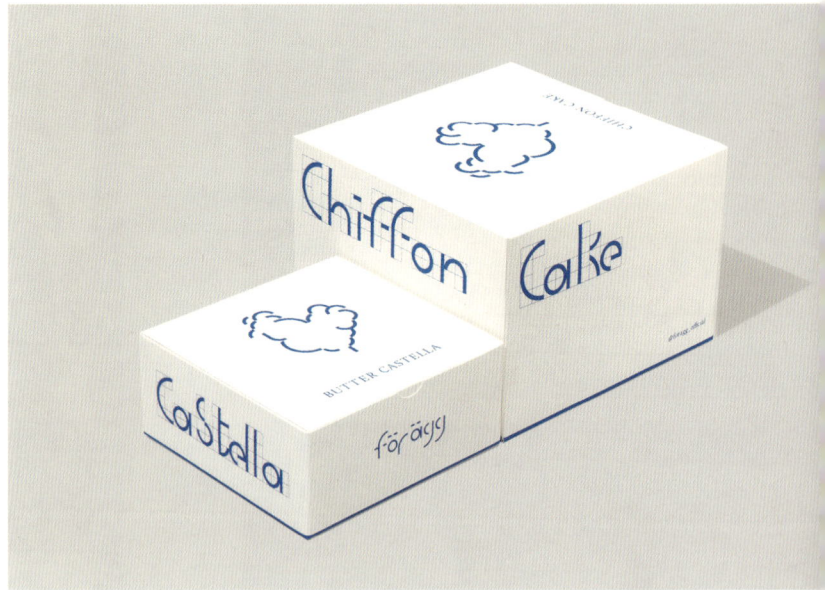

Design Studio
Sitoh inc.

Art Direction
Sitoh inc.

Design
Motoi Shito

Client
för ägg

volcanicafé

volcanicafé is a coffee brand created specifically for YANGMING MOUNTAIN LAB.

The logo design of the brand is marked by the Chinese character structure of "fire"(火) and the image of fire eruption, combining the baking degree with the geomorphic characteristics, and incorporating the blue, red, and rock ash into the identification spectrum.

The visual identity system is mainly based on the volcanic outline and the "fire" character knot, using bright lines to outline the logo and extend the flavor icon, matching three different flavors with geological colors. The fog (blue), lava (orange), and volcanic gravel (ash) have a large area of substrate as identification points, making the shape unconventional and used as a modeling sticker for bean bags and cup stickers. The public can get the knowledge of Yangming Mountain while tasting the coffee.

Design Studio
InFormat Design Curating

Art Direction
Pang Wang

Design
Tzou Yun Da

Client
YANG MING MOUNTAIN LAB

La Hidalgo

La Hidalgo is a local bakery shop located in Chapala, Jalisco Mexico, offering home bakery with a contemporary twist. The design of the identity is based on the stylization of the dough with simple and geometric figures creating silhouettes that suggest the shape of the traditional bread. In this way, the possibilities of creating an infinite number of patterns are opened up in the visual system that are used as an iconic graphic resource of the project, as well as in the packaging and other applications, achieving the unity of the entire brand.

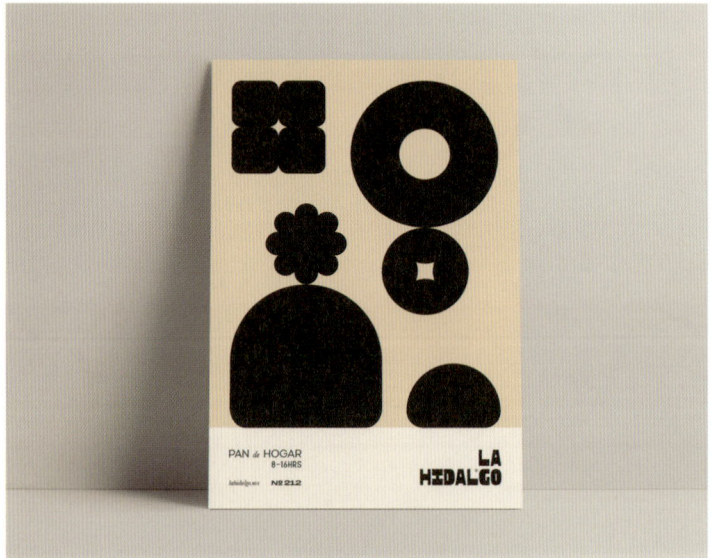

Design Studio
Culto Creative

Design
Daniel Duran Hernández

Client
La Hidalgo

Travelling Through Sham Tseng

Sham Tseng is a village in Hong Kong, China that has a history of hundreds of years and full of integration of cultural intersection.

The visual identity represents the concept of "integration". By combining different graphic elements, the experiment created a brand new visual system. The visual extends from graphic design to exhibition space and the community.

Design
Pengguin

Client
The Conservancy
Association Centre
for Heritage

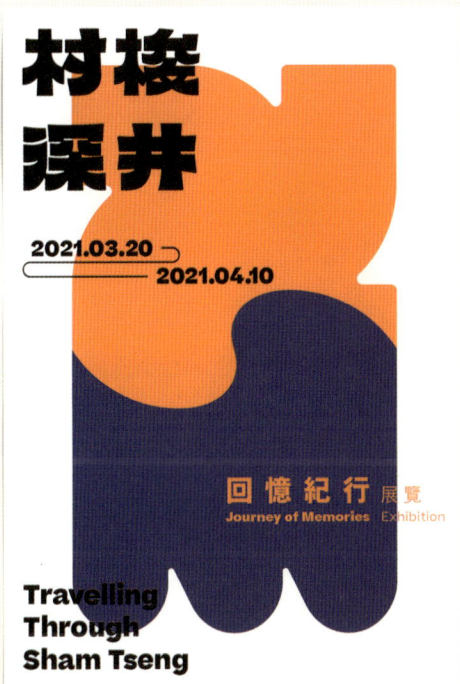
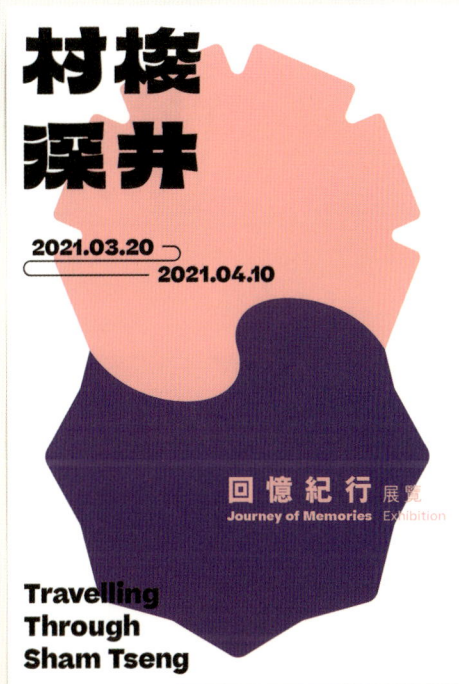
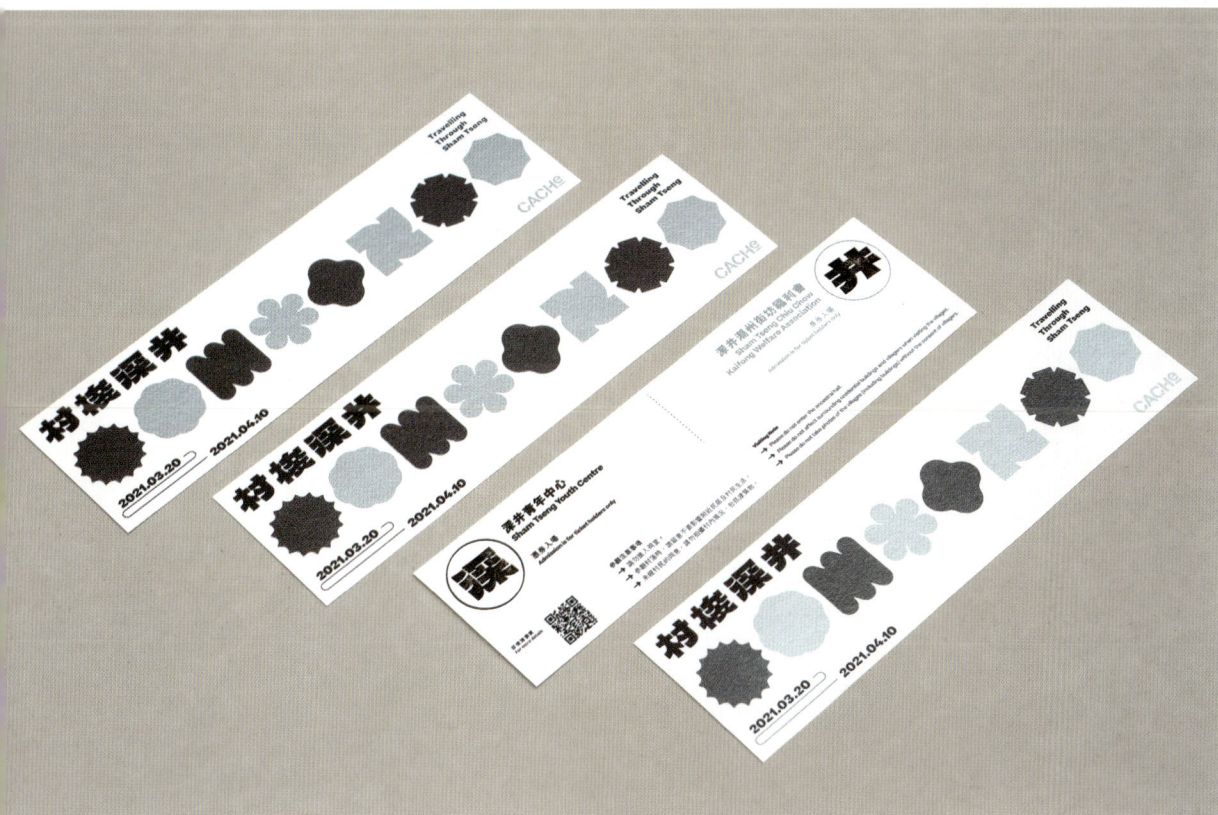

Grow Deal

Grow Deal is the first vertical farm in Toulouse, located in the heart of the city's Marché d'Intérêt National. It is the first indoor vertical farm in France to grow directly on site, and also runs a second farm in the basement and on the roof of a Toulouse supermarket.

Brand Brothers worked with Grow Deal's founder to completely redesign its visual identity. They went for a strong graphic and typographic system, out of the usual codes of the food and vegetal sectors. The typogram, designed in the studio, uses a strict geometric structure and curves that form outgrowths, reminding the budding of plants. On this basis, a system of shapes enriches the visual grammar and forms the backbone of the graphic applications, which are deployed in environments as varied as monochrome labels, textiles or social networks.

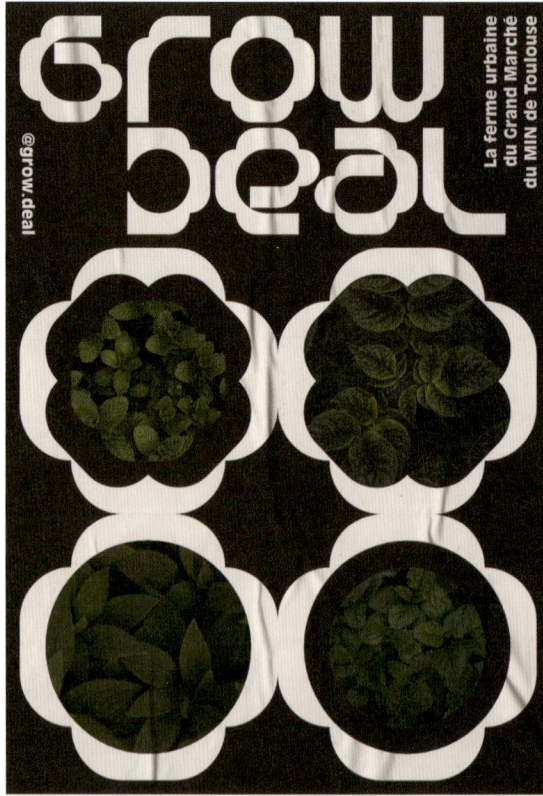

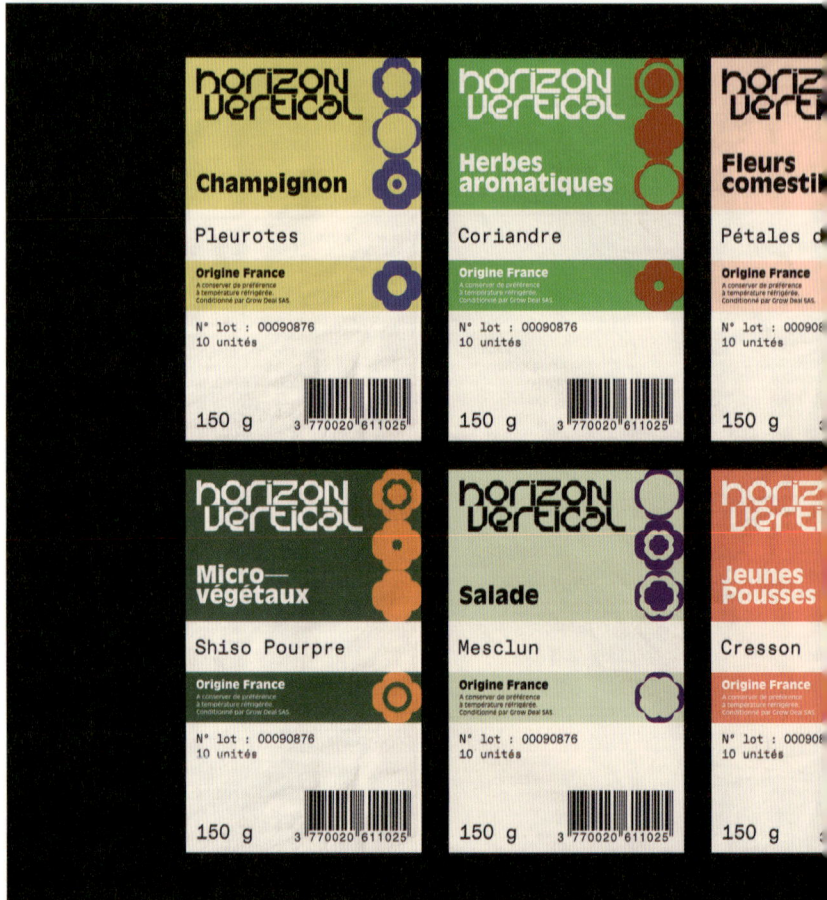

Design Studio
Brand Brothers

Design
Johan Debit

DOOD COFFEE

DOOD is a young plant-based, plastic-free and biodegradable coffee brand whose visual image is inspired by the time hourglass and "time, sunshine, heat".

The brand's use of strong color contrasts is a nod to the Instagram-friendly nature of the tones, while also hoping to combine the brand with fashion and youth. The side of the package uses a unique color block to distinguish the taste and series. This design makes the brand have a strong identification.

DOOD's visual presentation is around the process description. color gradient is connected to the conversion of energy and the change of flavor. The graphics show the transformation process of detail. The negative graphics are the form of an abstract hourglass, representing the passage of time and the details of filtering.

Design Studio
B&W Graphic Lab

Creative Direction
Ben

Art Direction
Wynne

Design
Ben, Wynne

Client
DOOD COFFEE

Infinite Love Marathon Concerts

This "Infinite Love Marathon Concerts" is a local concert held under the epidemic. Music uplifts the soul and infuses vitality into the society. It brings together local entertainers to give marathon musical performances.

This design is gorgeous in color and romantic in font. The fragrance and shapes of flowers light up everyone's hope. Each flower is blooming with enthusiasm, ready to greet everyone in the best posture. The purpose is to clarify the theme of "love", and attract people to experience the enthusiasm of the concert.

Creative Direction
Au Chon Hin

Art Direction
Au Chon Hin

Design
Untitled Macao,
Untitled Design Ltd.

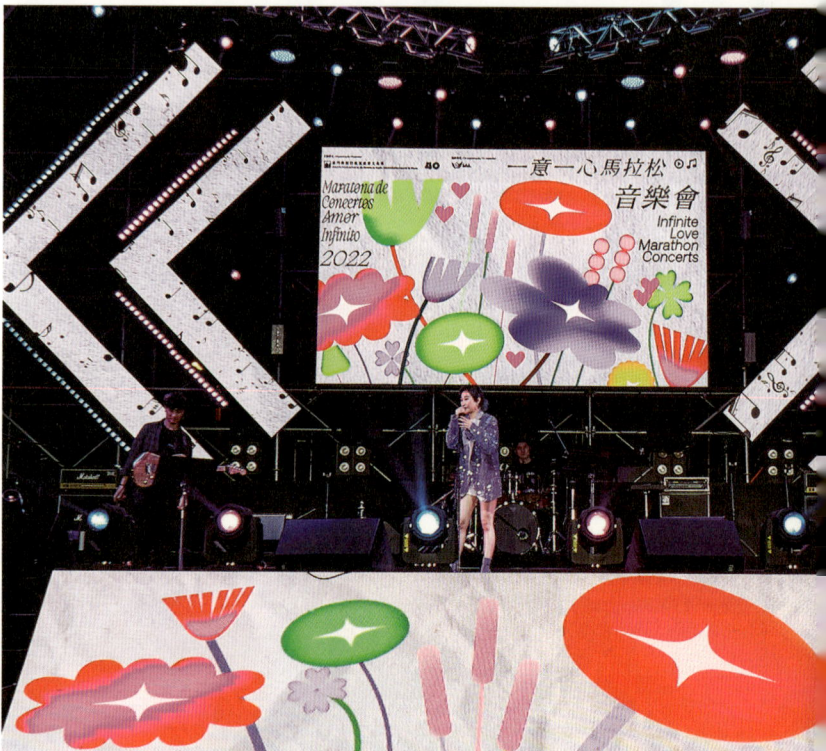

Bongja Festival

maum studio designed the main graphic of the Bonghwa Natural Plant Festival (Bongja Festival) in the summer of 2022.

The festival atmosphere with fresh and pleasant colors is expressed so that people can feel the pink plants unique to the arboretum. 2022's summer plants in season, the main motifs of the graphic are the Lythrum salicaria, Aster koraiensis, speedwell, Belamcanda chinensis flower.

Design Studio
muam studio

Art Direction
Yoonji Lee

Design
Hyunjin Lee, Yoonji Lee

Lythrum salicaria L.

Aster koraiensis Nakai

Iris domestica (L.) Goldblatt & Mabb.

Pseudolysimachion longifolium (L.) Opiz

Fleurs 2.0 – Pop Art Flowers

This is a series of imaginary playful flowers, which are geometric and infinitely modular.

Design
Laura Normand

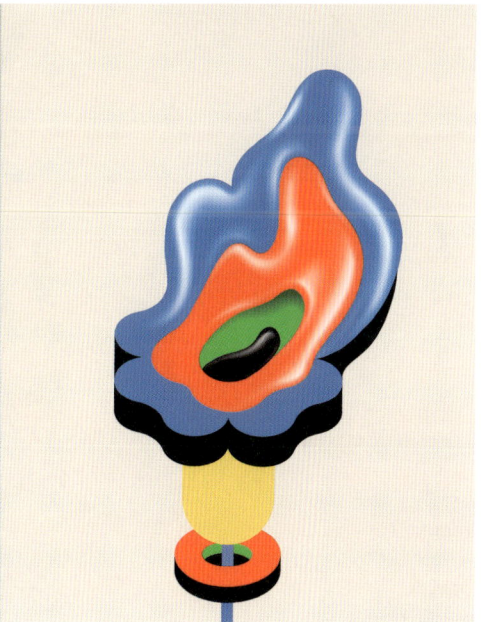

Dongba
New Year Gift Box

Dongba is the language used by the Naxi people of eastern Tibet and northern Yunnan in China and is the only pictographic character still alive in the world. Designer has recreated it based on its aesthetics and hopes that people can feel the charm of the "new" traditional Chinese culture in this work.

Design Agency
Tencent | FXD | :Daily Studio

Art Direction
yecoir

Design
paulinepeng

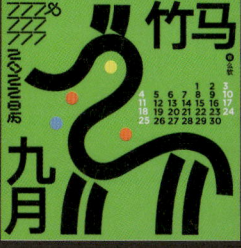

BEAN'S

Brewing in constant tumbling, the aroma slowly and thickly rises, and the rhythm constitutes a visual. The image of the Chinese character "豆"(bean) is formed. Designers restore the scene of coffee beans when they are roasted, and disassemble them to form "beans" to express the unique flavor of this batch of coffee beans and the taste core from Yunnan, China.

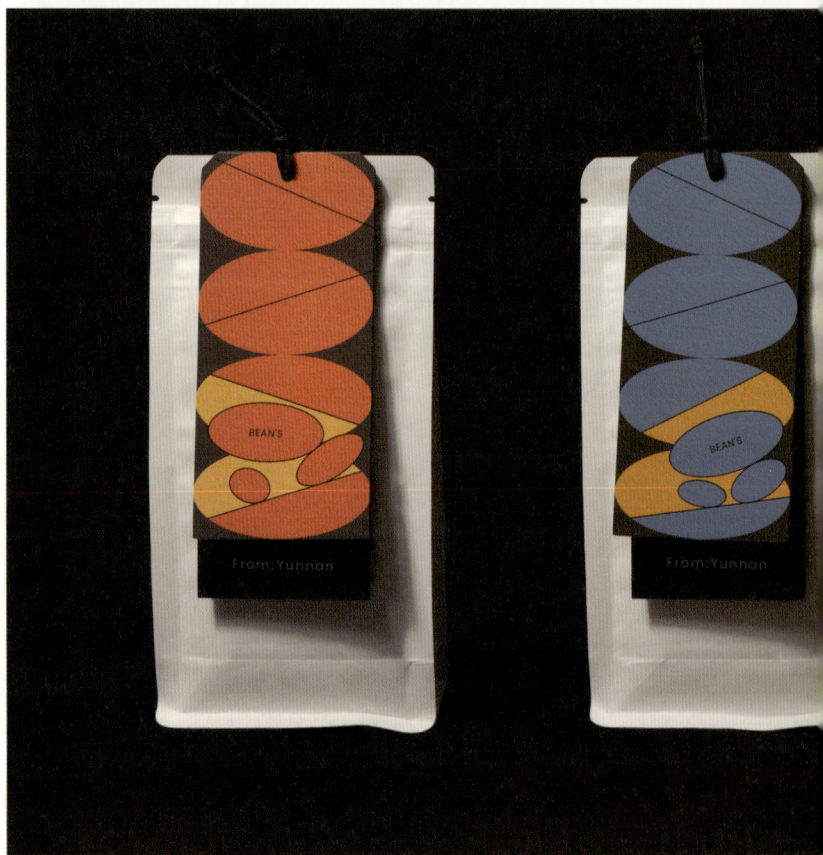

Design Studio
B&W Graphic Lab

Creative Direction
Ben

Art Direction
Wynne

Design
Ben, Wynne

Client
Bean's

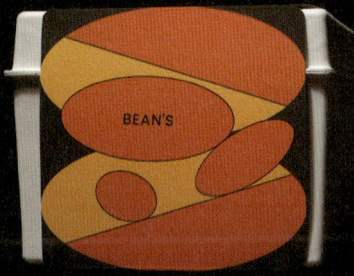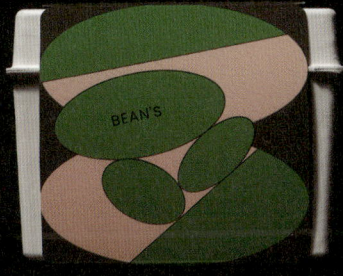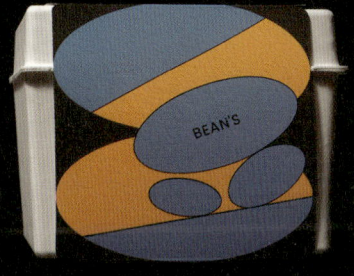

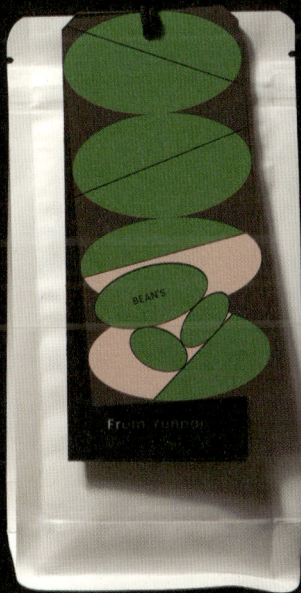

Buds

It is a visual identity including posters, invitation cards and supergraphics for art exhibition "Buds", by Minna Sakaria in Mölle, Sweden 2021.

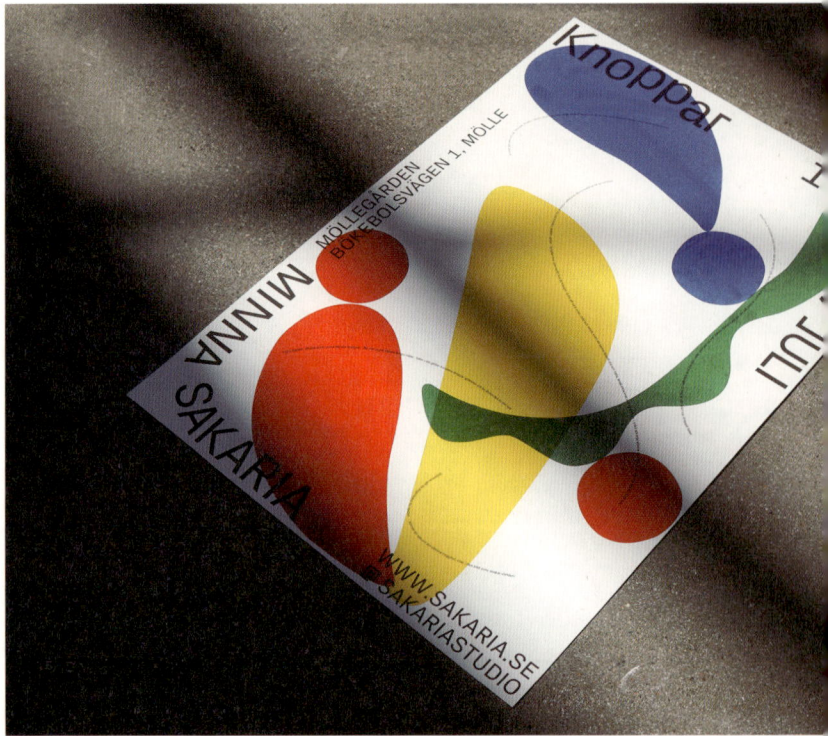

Design
Sakaria Studio

Client
Buds

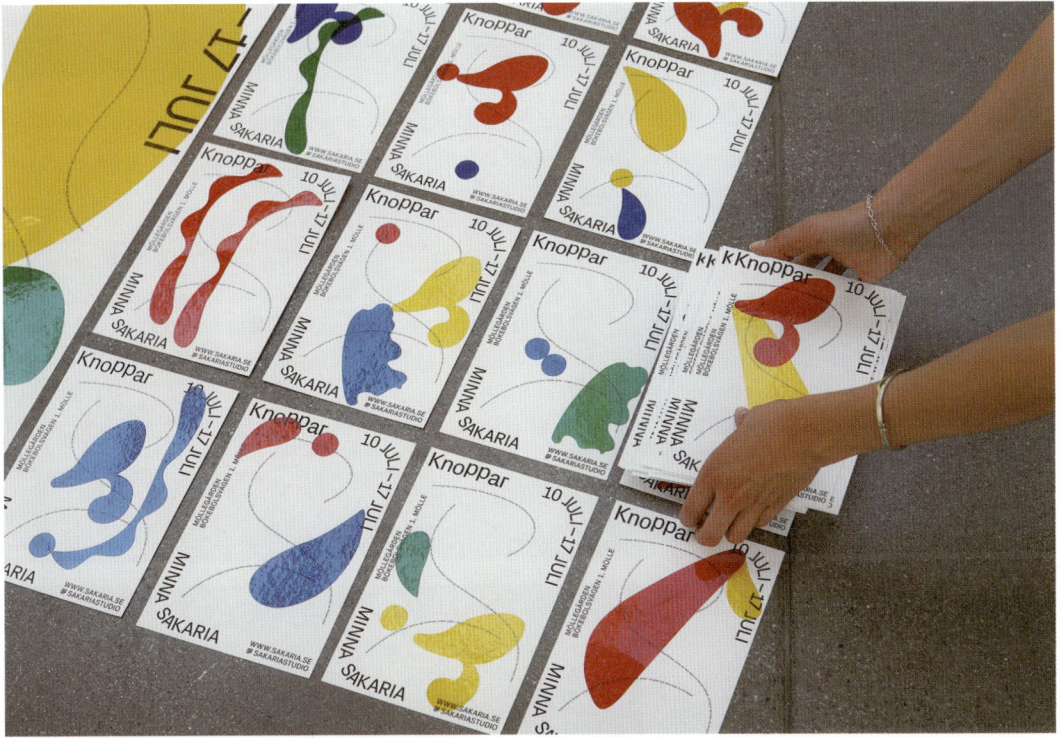

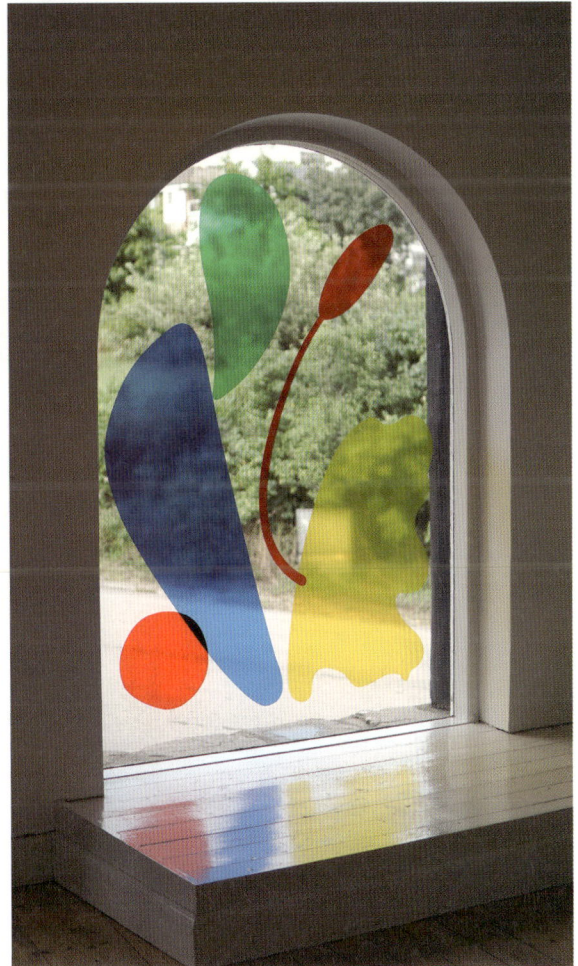

Drip Come True

A selection of two Taiwanese coffee beans is carried out based on the concept of "Bwa Bwei" (a traditional Chinese divination method), combining the living scene of folk beliefs with coffee. Each bean is the prayer of small coffee farmers and bean roasters. The bamboo mug carrying wishes and freshly roasted coffee are both sonorous in sound. Every cup of coffee is a powerful thought, from a raw bean to a cup of coffee, to brew a cup of divine bamboo shoots (cups).

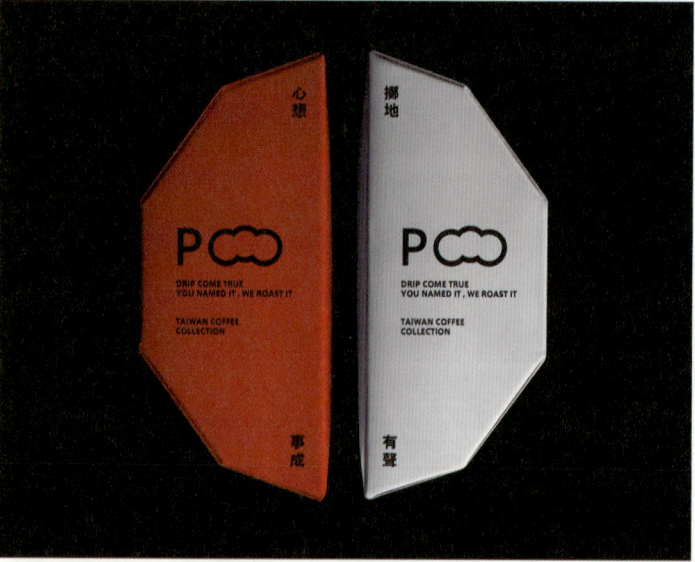

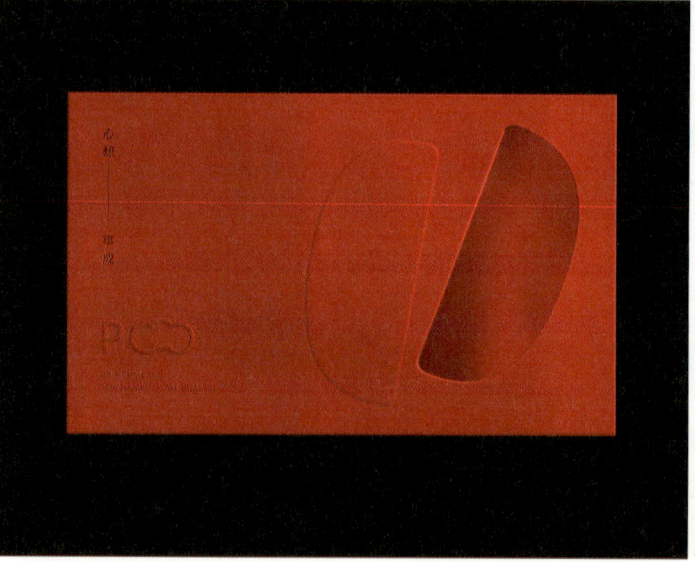

Design
Lung-Hao Chiang

Client
PO CAFE

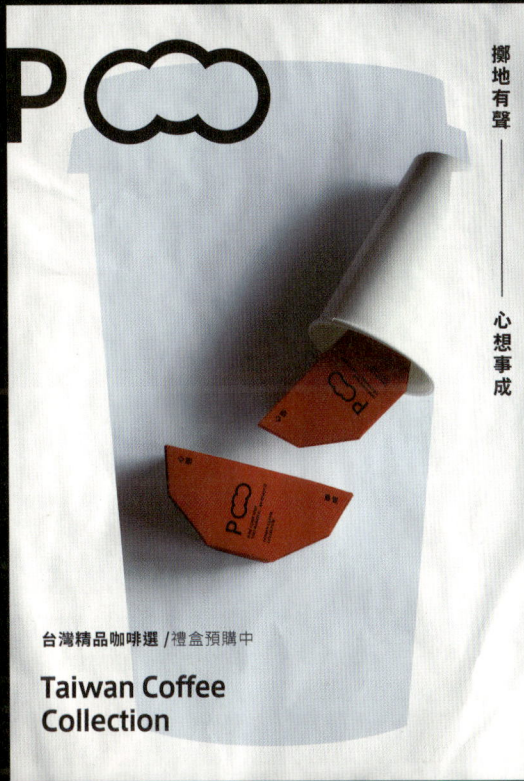

BEYA

It is a brand identity for a consulting firm.

Design Studio
KR8 bureau

Creative Direction
Florian Kowatz

Art Direction
Denise Schindele

Illustration
Denise Schindele

Client
BEYA

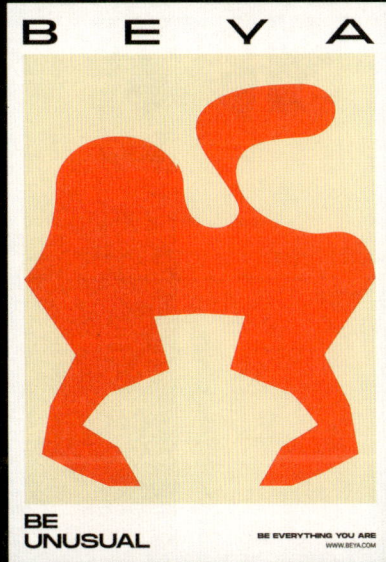

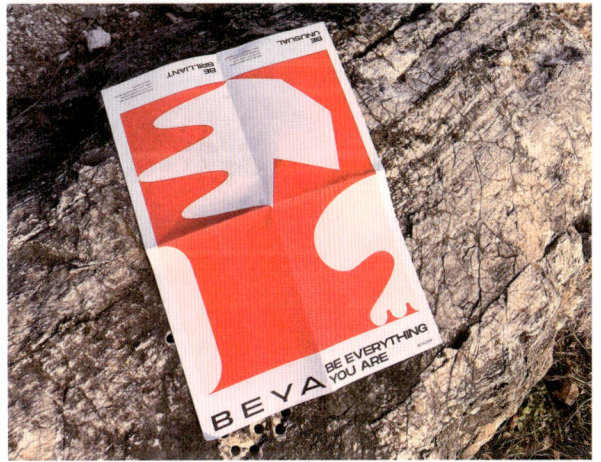

Witte Doos

Pure geometric shapes are displayed as the basis of the construction. Also the basic 3D shapes are geometric. With these shapes designer can later build infinite compositions. The icon tells about light on objects. In a render, light is one of the most important elements. It is the one that gives reality to it, with a well directed light, the space is real.

The color palette is inspired by noble interior materials: wood, concrete, tiles, fabrics and elements in warm colors.

Taking the basic shapes of the logo, designer takes them apart and uses it to build new compositions. Small structures are like totems. Infinite combinations invite people to visualize new constructions and ideas.

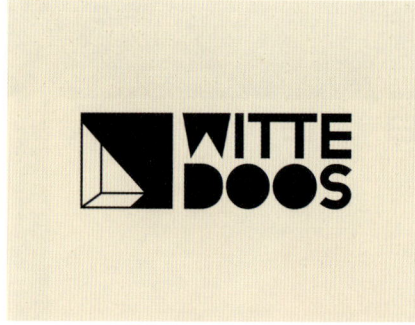

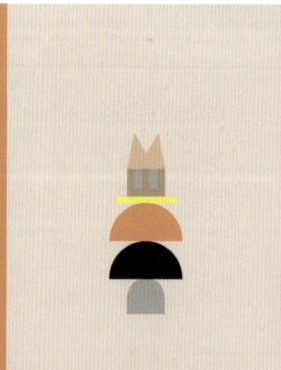

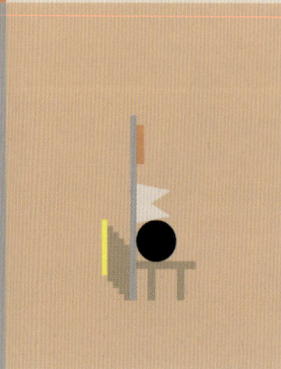

Design Studio
Sofia Noceti Studio

Design
Sofia Noceti

Client
Witte Doos

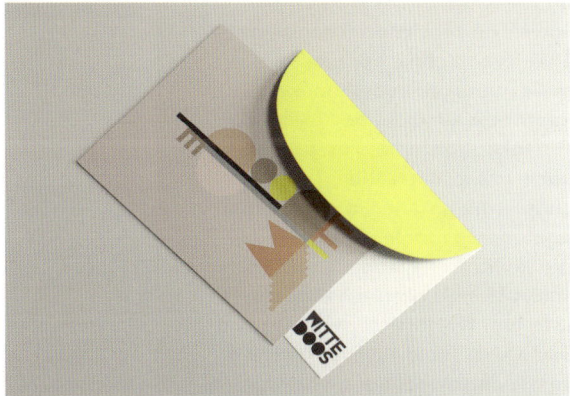

Pass Pro

Pass Pro is the podcast that takes people behind the scenes of the music industry.

For this identity, the studio designed a special typeface with a rhythm that focuses primarily on the width of the lowercase vowels and the capital consonants. Their typographic approach gives full expression for an imposing geometric symbol. The "p" in Pass Pro takes up the idea of a sound wave or a conversation. These shapes are declined in a modular and unpredictable system like an audiogram. The studio has chosen the sans serif typeface Aspekta in different weights for headings and body text. The guidelines have led to the deployment of an Instagram grid: from the publication through a principle of reels and stories.

Design
AB Projets Studio

Typeface
Aspekta by Ivo Dolenc

Client
Pass Pro

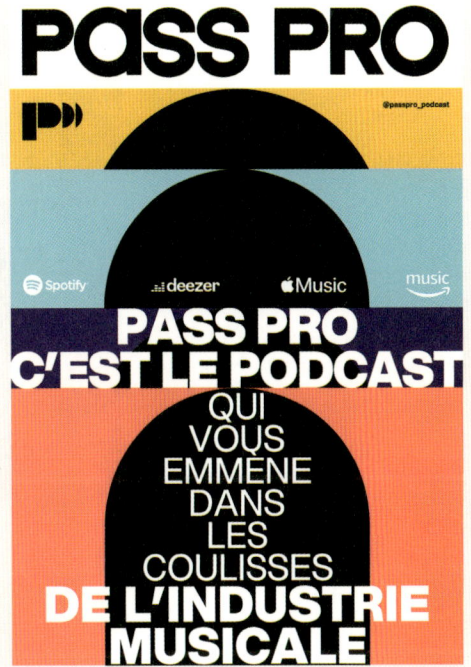

Brunning

Brunning is a concept that combines running and gourmet pleasures. It targets regular or Sunday joggers in search of conviviality and good mood. The formula is easy: once a week, the idea is to get together with friends to run a circuit in Paris and meet at each other's homes for brunch.

The logo aims to reinterpret both the impulse of a stride and the deliciousness of a hearty brunch. Anaïs Bonder decided to create a geometrical typographic design with the letter "R" as monogram and to create a pattern of a group of runners in order to humanize the identity. She also developed Brunning's circuits based on the typographic design to give a light spirit to the visual universe: "At Brunning, we do things seriously, without taking ourselves too seriously".

Design Studio
AB Projets Studio

Typeface
**Fractul by Adam Ladd
(Linotype)**

Client
Brunning Associative

B&W Alphabet

Every time people meditate, they are in the bondage of cognition. There is a fixed frame structure in the communication of words, which is not only conducive to people's efficient communication but also constrains the thinking. To break the shackles of communication and obtain more space and imagination, to bind and reshape letter elements is a desire for breakthrough.

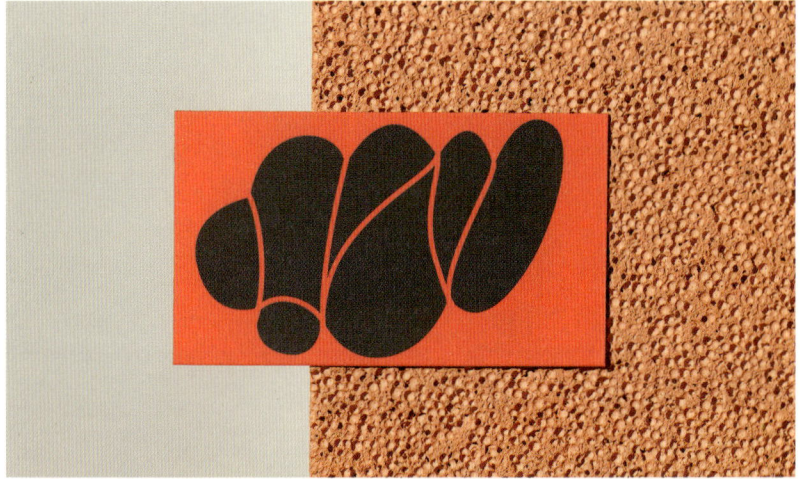

Design Studio
B&W Graphic Lab

Creative Direction
Ben

Art Direction
Wynne

Design
Ben, Wynne

Bourgie Hall 10th Anniversary

As part of its 10th anniversary, Bourgie Hall is looking forward to a celebratory campaign that focuses on the multiplicity of its programming and the musical genres that inhabit it venue.

Opened in September 2011, the hall offers a high level of programming welcoming both Canadian and international musicians. Housed in a church, now part of the Canadian and Quebec Arts Pavilion, Bourgie Hall offers music lovers musical experiences that reflect the encyclopedic diversity of the Montreal Museum of Fine Arts in an intimate setting, bathed in the soft light of early 20th century Tiffany windows.

Through a convincing collage exercise, the number "10" is created by the entanglement of the various instruments featured. These instrumental constructions are combined with a soft color palette of yellow, pink and green, as well as a visual direction inspired by analog photography, to create a campaign as noble as it is contemporary.

Design Studio
Paprika Design

Creative Direction
Louis Gagnon

Art Direction
Daniel Robitaille

Design
Marianne St-Pierre,
Vedran Vaskovic,
Virginie Jamison

Client
Arte Musica

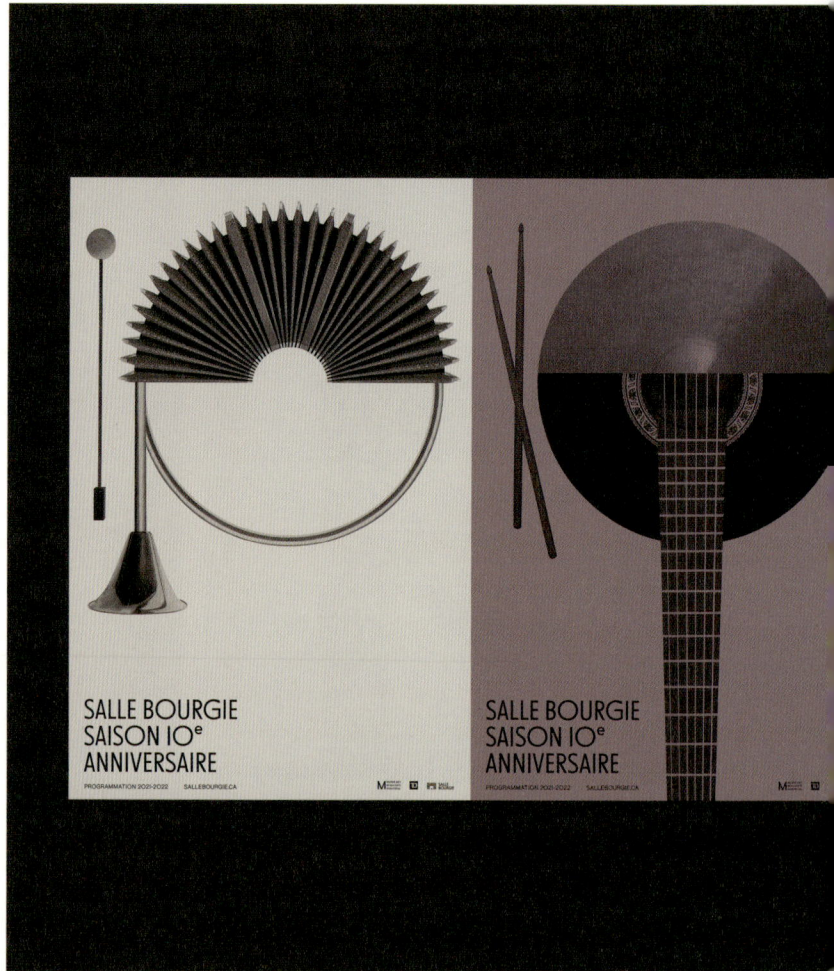

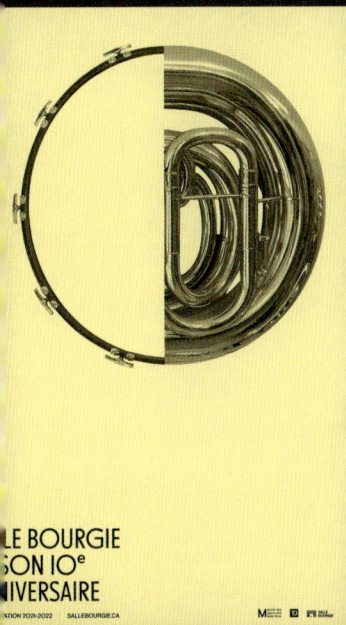
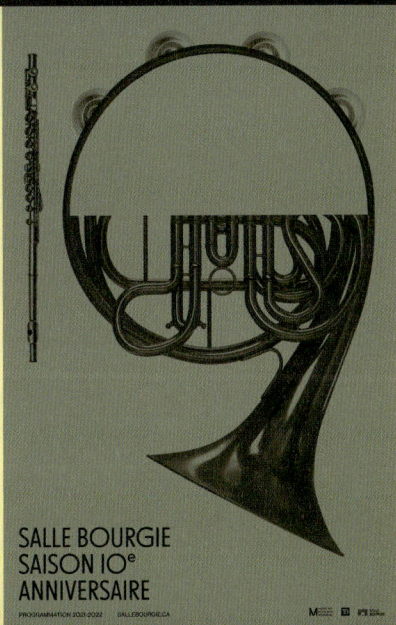

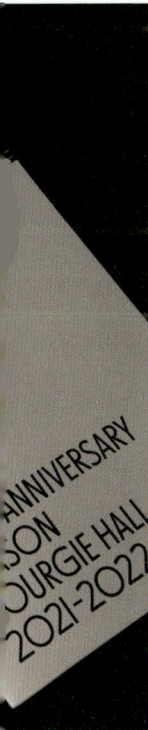
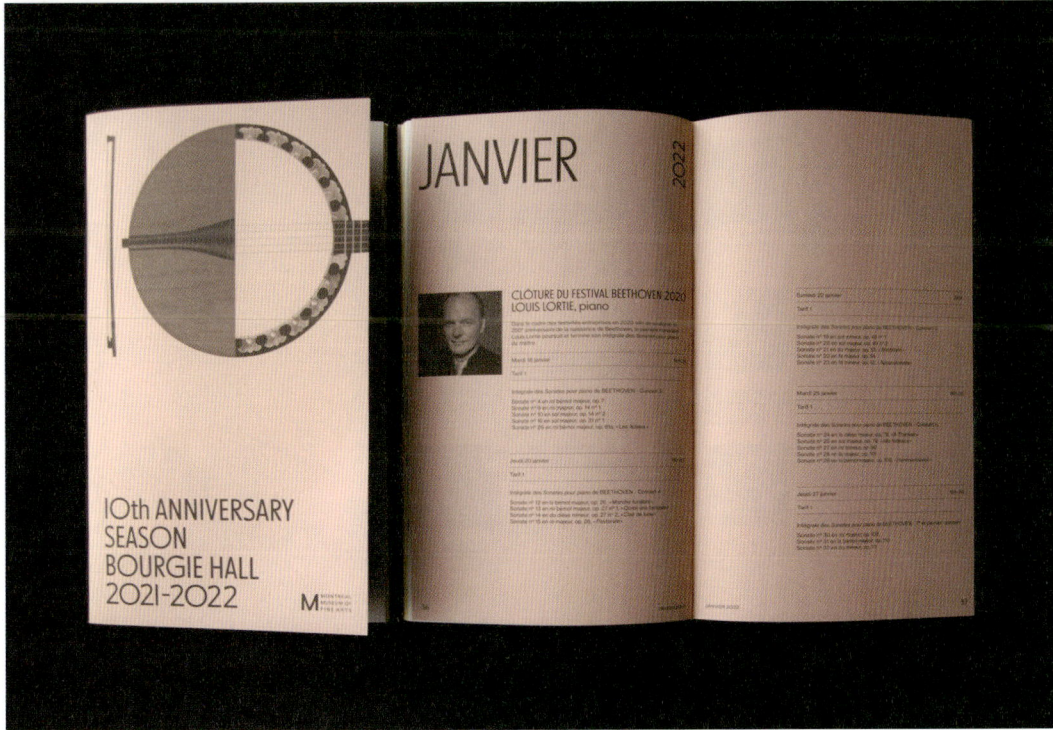

MAD HAUS (MALIQ & D'Essentials Studio)

Studio Woork collaborates with MALIQ & D'Essentials (a Jazz and Soul music-based band from Jakarta, Indonesia), Conture, Nouv, Dandy Darman Studio, and Andra Matin dan Roca Indonesia in Bintaro Design District.

Along with MALIQ & D'Essentials' two-decade-long musical harmony journey, MAD HAUS is aimed to be a calming (Teduh) home, with musicians, architects, and designers involved in its construction, and carrying light/hope (Pelita) as a way to show that collaboration gives an alternative to survive and be relevant in facing future uncertainties. The audience is invited to experience the holistic process of the creative industry through an atmosphere reminiscent of a collective studio.

Creative Direction
Studio Woork, Conture,
MALIQ & D'Essentials

Art Direction
Studio Woork

Client
MALIQ & D'Essentials

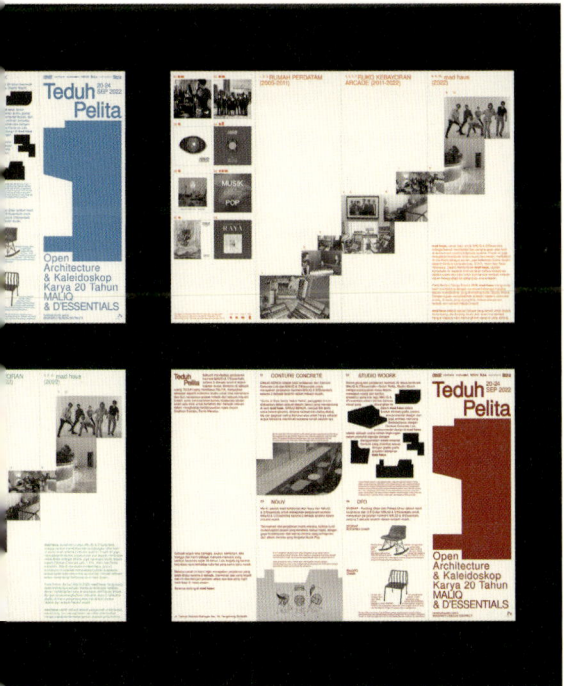

TRIDKINGDOM

TRIDKINGDOM is an educational institution that offers entrepreneurship programs for kids to discover problems by practices and develop core competence and thinking needed in the real world. When rebranding, designers keep the crown and the kingdom, which are two essential elements from the original logo representing not only the founder's very beginning mind but the linkage to existing customers. With the simplified graphs and elegant serif fonts, the brand is elevated to a fine and international level. Extended from the brand's name and spirits, designers use shields, flags, city gates, and gems to distinguish different education programs and textbooks. To solve the previous application problem of multiple colors, they use the bright royal yellow to build a warm and soft atmosphere that keeps the brand at an advanced level but attractive to all ages, so both parents and kids can understand the brand's core value and thus feel secure about their professional programs.

Design Studio
Triangler

Creative Direction
Chi Yao Tang

Art Direction
Chun Yao Huang

Design
Yi Wang, Wei Huang

Client
TRIDKINGDOM

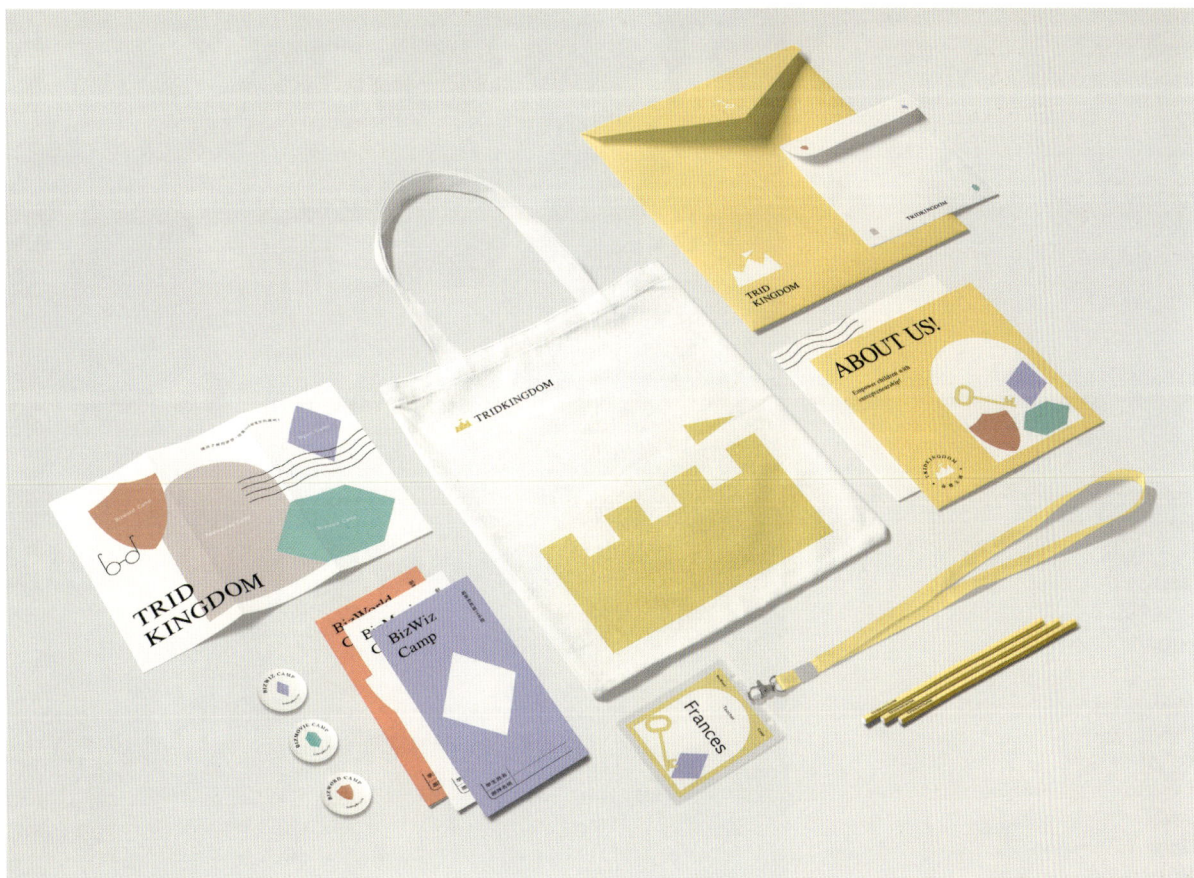

United Christian Music Kindergarten

United Christian Music Kindergarten (UCM) was envisioned as a nurturing ar supportive environment for children in Hong Kong, China, a place where learning and growth is backed the foundations of a unique music-focused curriculum.

The brand identity is accompanied by a series of supporting graphics in a vibrant palette applied across printed stationeries and collaterals. Building a playful graphic language, a set of icons was also designed for signage across the school campus.

Design Studio
Toby Ng Design

Creative Direction
Toby Ng

Design
**Toby Ng,
Banana Chan**

Illustration
**Hazel Chan,
Tony Leung**

Client
**United Christian
Music Kindergarten**

From Our Land to Your Table

Born out of love and appreciation of the land, this range of products shares the flavors and characters of all Sogrape terroirs.

"From Our Land to Your Table" was the motto chosen to unveil the unique characteristics of the product while positioning the product in the premium market segment. Based on the irregular contours created by using the chutneys and jams, designers have developed several shapes spread out on the entire packaging. Vivid and flashy colors, outstanding materials and superior finishes reflect the excellence of this remarkable product.

Design Studio
327 Creative Studio

Creative Direction
Mafalda Portal

Art Direction
Mafalda Portal

Design
Mafalda Portal,
Matilde Igreja

Client
Sogrape

Mockup&Co

Mockup&Co wanted to create a brand that illustrates flexibility and opportunity when using mockups. The brand mark focuses on an interchanging typeface, illustrating this versatility and making it the focal point of the brand identity. The color palette is purposely wide-ranging, for a fresh and optimistic brand. They use illustrated shapes to bring warmth and personality against the pared back simplicity of the branding.

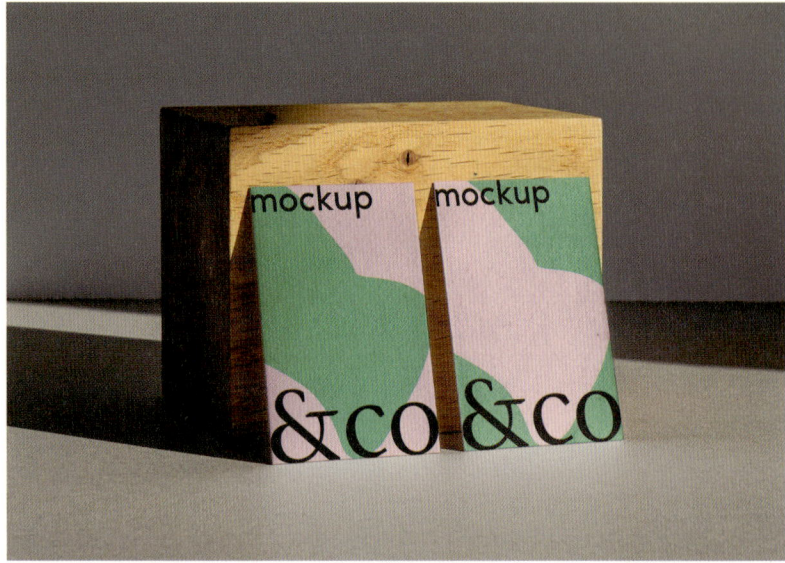

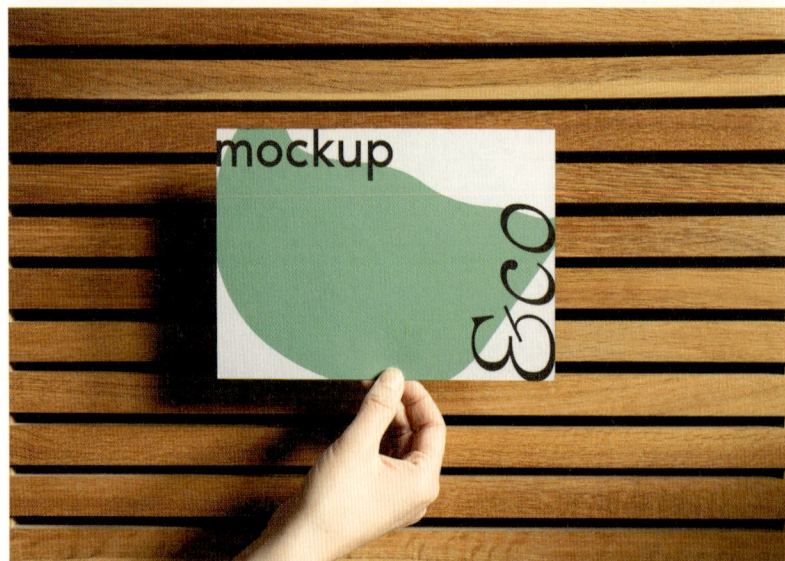

Design Studio
Mockup&Co

Design
Milla Adler & Ro Kealey

Client
Mockup&Co

Easy Fresh

Easy Fresh aims to enhance the food service market, by providing a refreshingly and deliciously healthy diet to the urban community, with fresh and nutritious ingredients in a quick and casual culinary concept.

Designer hopes to bring forward a healthier lifestyle to the public, especially young people, through fresh ingredients and raw materials. By adopting the current food trend, he intends to improve the existing fast food culture with healthier options.

The overall design based on the growth of vegetables to express the energy of health, balancing between form and irregularity with typography and organic illustrations. The design offers a casual, simple and romantic look into the brand.

Creative Direction
Au Chon Hin

Art Direction
Au Chon Hin

Design
**Untitled Macao,
Untitled Design Ltd.**

Photography
Rex Chang

Client
Easy Fresh

Venimos a Ver

"Venimos a Ver" ("We came to see" in English) is an art store and community in Cancun, Mexico. They curate local artists and also host foreign artists. They are known for being affordable for the buyer while providing fair pricing to the artist. For the graphic style designers proposed to create a fun, friendly, and colorful image to allude to the name and its personality.

Design
Wikka

Client
Venimos a Ver

Instant optimism/ Taresso Coffee Capsules

An original story that narrates the everyday power of coffee is depicted on the packaging of Taresso Artisan Coffee Roasters' coffee capsules. The illustrations showcase that combining moments from ordinary life with a cup of your favorite coffee can be a special and unique experience, while the pale pink color is illuminating the optimism that exudes from every single capsule.

Design Studio
Luminous Design

Client
Taresso

Taresso Capsules Packaging – Wired Up

Coffee is an electrifying daily experience. Its aficionados won't function until the first sip of their favorite blend makes them all wired up, and this is the story Luminous Design is narrating in the design of the packaging for the Taresso Artisan Coffee Roasters' capsule series. The capsules are turning into faces, just by adding them one specific feature: eyes that wide open that can be linked with the intense effect of a single coffee capsule. The illustrations are vivid and diverse, displaying the extraordinary yet unique influence which every capsule can have on coffee lovers.

Design Studio
Luminous Design

Client
Taresso

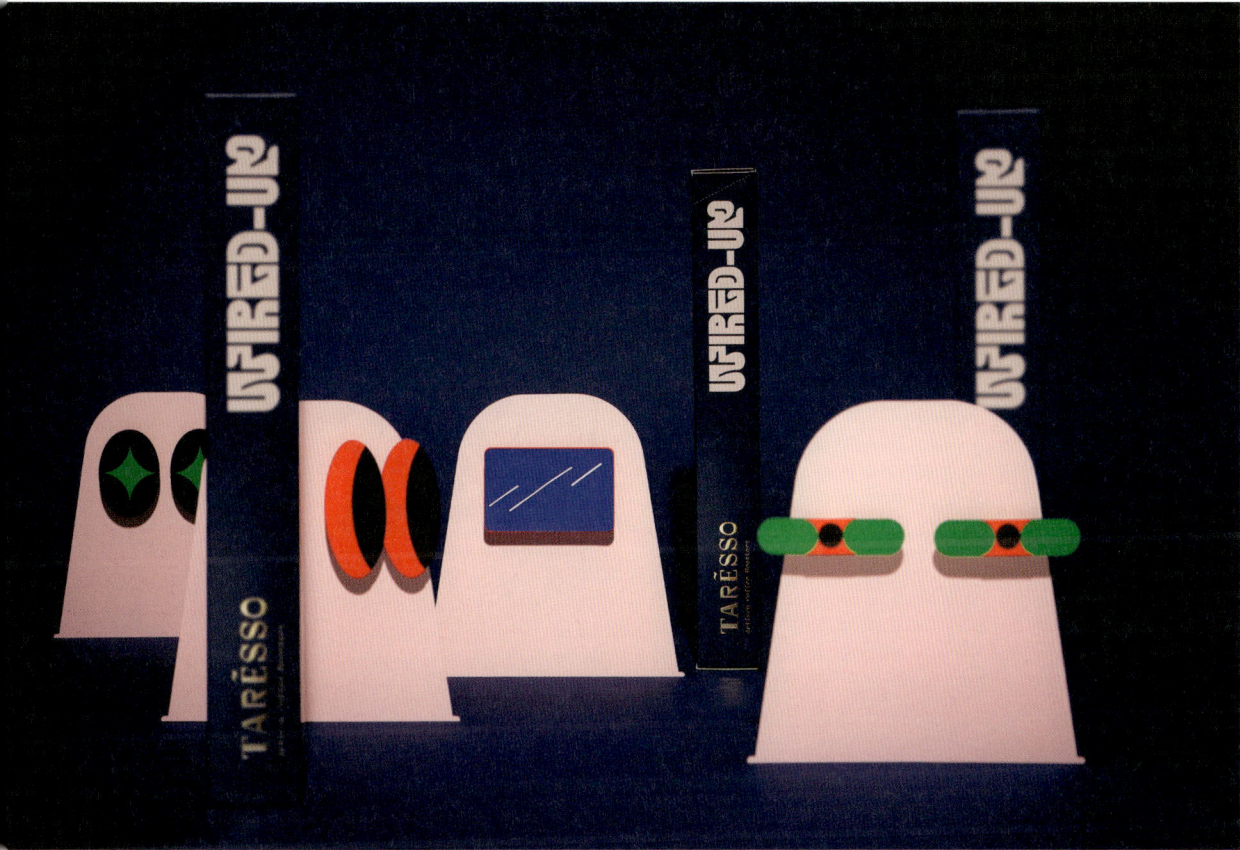

Coffee Roy

Coffee Roy is a stylish and sophisticated coffee shop located in Hungary, with a brand identity design that perfectly captures its retro minimalistic style. The design incorporates bold and striking typography with a vintage-inspired color palette. Also the design features a fun and quirky logo, which is created using the letters of the shop's name to form a whimsical face.

Design
Elena Yaremchuk

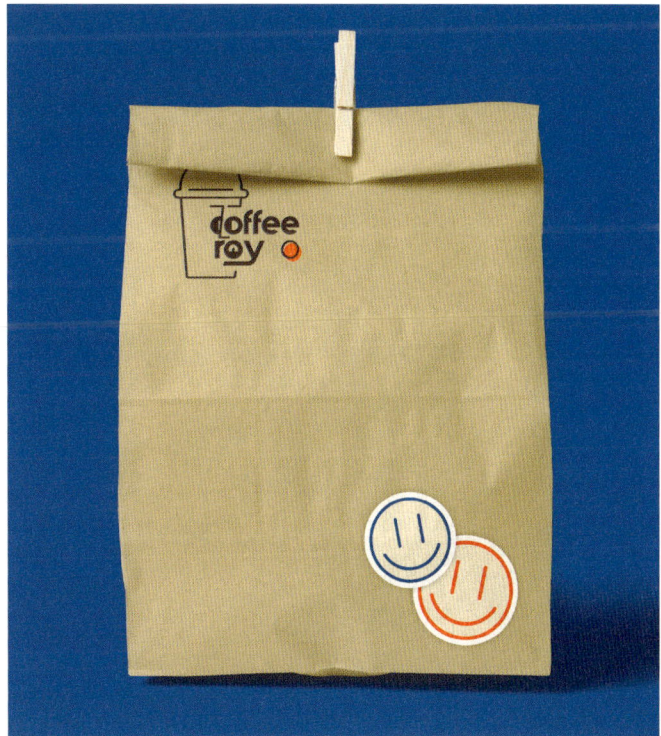

Bilbò Academy of English

Bilbò Academy is an English language school based in the city center of Bologna, Italy.

Designer's job was to create simple, understandable and playful graphic language for interior, exterior and online materials. Based on basic, geometric shapes and bright colors, she created happy and funny branding that connects the school with the streets of Bologna.

Dojo

Chit Chat Square

Rookie Island

Neptune Reef

Prodigy Bay

Ivy Peak

Design
AguWu

Client
Bilbò Academy

SPICCA IL VOLO CON L'INGLESE A BOLO!
Bilbò!
Via san Felice 18, Bologna www.bilboacademy.it
L'INGLESE PAR TÒT
Bilbò!
NON È SOLO INGLESE, È FUTURO.
Bilbò!
DUE MILIARDI DI PERSONE PARLANO INGLESE. E TU?
Bilbò!

SPICCA IL VOLO CON L'INGLESE A BOLO!
Bilbò!
Bilbò Academy è la nuova scuola di inglese nel centro di Bologna.
Prima lezione gratuita!
Company Courses
Conversation Club
one 2 one
Business
length of the lesson
frequency
beginning of classes
price
Certificate
lenght of the course
Lavoratori
Bambini
Ragazzi
Terza età
Adulti
Studenti
city camp
children summer camp
teenagers summer camp
Bilbò Academy Scuola di Inglese
Bilbò!

Figurative

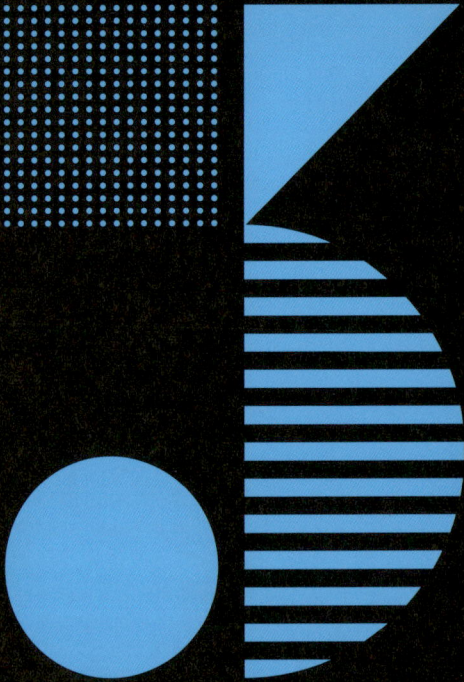

Shapes

Figurative shapes are the imitation of creatures and objects in the reality, often with designers' recreation. The images are always straightforward and easy to understand.

01. What role do you think graphics play in visual communication?

We believe graphics have the utmost potential when considering different elements for a brand or visual identity. They can be the starting point of a project, using an intrinsic style that begs you to look at them, but they also have the ability to transform and be highly malleable, adapting to the visual style and craft of an already defined branding. Their versatility makes a strong case for one of the essential elements of a visual identity, along with typography, color, and composition.

On the other hand, shapes tend to be virtually infinite. Unlike other elements in a visual identity, once a specific style is defined, we're able to create endless figures following the same principle and representing different things.

This idea does not apply to fonts or colors, which, in most cases, would harm the system while making it too complex. In comparison, additional shapes contribute to the system being thorough and versatile.

● **BACILE & La Libertad TNC**

Graphic is everywhere. Since we get up, until the night comes we are influenced by powerful graphics. The shampoo packaging, the instructions to make your coffee, the signage to take public transport or the menu of the restaurant in which you dine, are typical examples of the relevance of graphic design in everyday life. Visual communication requires design thinking that articulates ideas, sometimes it is enough to have a photograph as visual communication, sometimes a map solves the problem of visual communication; but most of the time, it is the thought of graphic design and its resources, which systematize the information and make everything more digestible for society.

● **Folk Estudio**

Graphics are a key part of visual communication, a bridge built between the audience and the work through the visual language of graphics, allowing audiences to communicate silently across geographical, contextual and cultural differences. At the same time, we can get the unique graphic art feeling and unique beauty feeling in the communication.

● **Chai Kunpeng**

It is the strawberry on the cake as a prominent visual focus, and it can also be the cake under the strawberry as a carrier for message organization and planning. It is also a common understanding across languages and regions to a certain extent, and anyone can intuitively interpret the message conveyed visually through graphics.

● **Chiang Lung-Hao**

Graphics, for us, are what reinforce the idea behind a brand. How we convey personality, attitude, and the vehicle that carries the message we want to communicate. It adds another layer of creativity and expression to something that may not absolutely need it but makes it unique.

At a functional level, it's a preview of what the customer can expect when first coming into contact with a brand. But for people in visual fields, it's also what makes our job fun, dynamic, and a challenge to overcome.

● **Heavy**

I haven't been able to verbalize into simple definition but below are my personal notes when using graphics: Graphics give a more approachability; Graphics are catchy; Graphics can be abstract or direct; Graphics can linger; Graphics convey nuances; Graphics are lingering imprints in minds, while typography echoes; Graphics are selectively informative; Graphics are representative.

Graphics tend to become a statement, and I avoid the usage when the item or brand needs a more subtlety to co-exist neutrally with something else. e.g. a jewelry brand that has the necessity to fit into your everyday lifestyle, or a gallery identity that acts as a white cube for artists.

● **Koyuki Inagaki**

Lisa: Graphics transfer the looks and feelings and sometimes even the values or manifesto of the brand in a very short amount of time. Nothing else does this job as fast and as good. Of course, it is not only about the graphics, but how everything works together: composition, colors, typography, etc.

Marina: Graphics attract the eye of the viewer and communicate information in a clear, concise, and engaging way, and include a wide range of visual elements, from illustrations to charts, diagrams, and photographs, all of which can be used to support and enhance a message or story.

● **Lisa Kuntysh & Marina Coll**

In visual communication, graphics are the "personification" of conceptual ideas. It is like the melody of music, which directly makes people feel the emotion of the content, and divides the corresponding crowd at the fastest speed.

● **ONNFF STUDIO**

For me graphics play a crucial role in visual communication. They are essential elements that serve to convey ideas in an easy and memorable way.

They are the best way to convey concepts, create emotional connections, and enhance the overall visual appeal of any communication.

● **Pao Bassol**

They are tangible representations of visual concept in a system. They have the role to inspire and to create an identity, they must make sure consistency and flexibility of usage for the branding.

● **Rebu**

Graphics can express information concisely and quickly in terms of visual communication. Moreover, graphics can overcome the language barrier to be presented according to how you maneuver humor or elegance by the way of making or coloring.

● **Sitoh inc.**

Graphics play an important role in visual communication, and I think that is because graphics are not as restraining as typography do, as it does not require a certain level of knowledge or limited by language barrier. Graphics communicate visually which welcome and convey to audiences efficiently from all different places.

● **Untitled Macao**

02. In what kind of project do you prefer to use figurative shapes?

As a studio, we primarily focus on branding projects and developing new visual identities, so we always feel inclined to use them in a project of those characteristics. The thing about figurative shapes is that they're evident and unavoidable, whereas their close-to-reality nature makes you recognize the object they're representing. This may come in handy when working with a brand or product that benefits from this quick recognition. In the case of Mercado San Antonio, we wanted people to know what it is about fast, and the shapes take you to the world of consumables in an instant.

● BACILE & La Libertad TNC

Whether or not figurative graphics are used is a matter of how well the designer understands the project. The graphic designer acts as a visual translator. Depending on the type of project, there will be different "sensory translations" and figurative graphics are just one of the many qualities conveyed.

● Chai Kunpeng

In fact, I don't consider whether to use graphics in the preliminary thinking. Graphics are more like "method" than "style" to me, a choice of design expression and concept output. But in terms of the conclusion, graphics can simplify the depth and breadth of the concept, concentrating it into a simple but not decreasing symbol, so the use of graphics in the design strategy has always been one of my preferred ways.

● Chiang Lung-Hao

At the studio, we love being open to different resources that allow us to strengthen graphic solutions: typography, photo retouching, illustration or geometric shapes, are some of the ingredients we use the most in Folk's creative kitchen. We use figurative forms and shapes for projects that require a greater impact than just specific information. Typography and editorial design is usually enough in most cases, but using geometric shapes, containers, symbols and figures helps to give dynamism to a project, to generate emotions and to create relevant and authentic graphic scenarios.

● Folk Estudio

It all depends on the concept and strategy behind the brand we're creating and how literal the understanding of the concepts we're trying to communicate should be.

For us, it makes more sense to think about style than how figurative a graphic should be. When working on a project, we're considering if the style fits the concept and personality regardless of how figurative or abstract those elements are.

● Heavy

If it's for an identity design, I tend to use it for projects that need more defined statements, or a touch of warmth. It really depends on the brand personality but I would typically avoid when building more timeless, classy brands that aim to fit into lifestyles of a wider audience over different generations.

I would also evaluate graphics if it was for short-spanned communications such as promotional posters — something that people would not lay their eyes for too long.

● **Koyuki Inagaki**

Lisa: To be honest, I just love figurative shapes, and love using it. They give space for imagination for both parties: the creator and the consumer.

Specifically in Kudos, it could be nothing else but figurative shapes, the most important part of the graphic concept. Through this approach we are trying to deliver an idea: there are no ugly shapes, they are all unique and beautiful. We don't want to promote it with food photography that is trying to make things look better, so we use shapes.

Marina: Figurative shapes are often used in projects that want to transmit a specific message or emotion, such as advertising campaigns, book covers, and movie posters. For example, a project that seeks to promote a particular product or service may use figurative shapes to ensure that the product is easy to identify or to create an emotional connection with the audience.

● **Lisa Kuntysh &Marina Coll**

Most people don't take much time seeing or recognizing the design itself, so figurative shapes are preferably chosen for identities or media in order to convey the purpose or ideas concisely and quickly.

● **Sitoh inc.**

For publicity-oriented, fast-moving consumer items, figurative shapes can express the content of the product more quickly, and give the customer the first impression of such products in the first place. Therefore, for this kind of more targeted projects or customer groups, I will tend to figurative shapes directly.

● **ONNFF STUDIO**

I find them particularly effective in projects that require a visual storytelling or communication of complex ideas.

The fact of including direct and easy-to-understand images makes a complex concept "visually digestible" and captivates the audience at the first impact.

● **Pao Bassol**

As a branding specialist, I personally prefer to use figurative shapes when a brand requires a straightforward and quick approach to resonate with consumers. However, it's important to note that a strong design identity can still be achieved without relying solely on figurative shapes. The identity element should be consistently present in every visual asset, extending beyond just illustrations. Focusing too heavily on a specific illustration style could lead to saturation and make it difficult to effectively apply the visual identity.

● **Rebu**

We seldom have a preference as in what kind of project requires shapes, that is because we do not want the project to be limited. Usually it depends on the ideas and preferences from clients, or the message and story they want to convey. We prefer to use figurative shapes when it is necessary.

● **Untitled Macao**

03. What will be your focus when creating shapes?

Shapes might be something of a double-edged sword. There's an irresistible urge to use them on plenty of projects, but as a studio, we have to be able to craft and construct them from a unique point of view. When searching for something distinctive, it's easy to fall for the trap of trends or inspiration coming from every angle. Given this, our focus usually relies on finding that distinctive element, discovering the unique style, but, on top of that, being able to combine that with the rest of the branding elements in a compelling way.

Sometimes, the secret to finding something innovative lies in trying to escape the pressure of discovering something great and enormous, but rather in paying attention to the details. Working out minimal variations and iterations that bring something to the table that no one had paid attention to.

● **BACILE & La Libertad TNC**

Creating shapes is creating sensations, when a project focuses on a graphic development with shapes, it usually is an impressive project. People tend to love the characteristics of a well-constructed typography, the orderliness of a well-developed editorial design, the sensitivity of a forceful illustration; however, it is in the system that articulates everything, in which shapes appear. The designer who breaks with the established and lets him/herself be carried away by exploration, by drawing, by art, by analogy, usually reaches powerful results that captivate the observer's gaze.

● **Folk Estudio**

We pay more attention to how we feel about the work when we see it from different perspectives, and understand what kind of creation is more fresh from the audience's perspective.

● **Chai Kunpeng**

If I choose to use graphics as the design expression, my focus will be on whether the graphics can convey the message that the product/artwork wants to convey well, followed by whether the work is "graphic" enough while respecting the subject matter and the design requirements.

● **Chiang Lung-Hao**

There are a couple of different layers of consideration that go into this. First, as we mentioned, much of the focus will be on ensuring the style is cohesive with the brand's strategy.

Then, after that, we think about the specifics of what that graphic should be trying to convey. Be it something physical, conceptual, or metaphorical, we make sure that it can be understood by the target audience.

And finally, we think about how it fits into the piece compositionally. That means considering where it should fit into the brand (a print piece, packaging, web, app, etc.) and making sure it physically adapts to the other design elements we're working with.

● **Heavy**

I treat the amount of ambiguity important. The exact amount of abstraction and literalness would depend on the need of the project, but it is important for me that graphics leave space for interpretations from the audience. I believe that the space for own interpretations leaves lingering impressions for those who see the graphics.

● Koyuki Inagaki

I care a lot about the relationship between figurative shapes and typography or branding. Figurative graphics are not only an image expression, but also establish a complete visual logic with the brand. They are very purposeful in typography and color use.

● ONNFF STUDIO

Lisa: I would say, no focus is the best approach! This way you can truly create unique shape. Have you seen fruit drawn by a little kid? That's the most beautiful ones!

Marina: When creating shapes, my focus is to ensure that they are visually appealing, easy to understand, and support the overall message and tone of the project. This may involve experimenting with different shapes, sizes, colors, and textures, as well as considering how the shapes will be used in conjunction with other visual elements, such as typography, layout or the support on which they are to be used.

● Lisa Kuntysh & Marina Coll

I am dedicated to illustrating for brands, therefore I always try to focus on the personality, values, motivations and concept of each brand when designing the figures. It is important that the brand is implicit even in the style of each graphic. That's why I'm a bit of a hater of following trends.

● Pao Bassol

While combining universal and simple shapes, the emphasis is on creating shapes with ideas and humor by making them look like some other motifs.

● Sitoh inc.

Always emotion and function.

● Rebu

When creating shapes, we tend to focus on uniqueness and balance. We try to bring in certain degree of abstract sense into our creations in order to allow imagination.

● Untitled Macao

04. How do you keep the graphics coordinated with the typography, layout, and color composition in your creations?

This question has a lot to do with the previous answer. It's always a challenge to find a working system that also feels like a novelty, so we must be ready to ditch the idea of shapes and graphics and look in different directions if it doesn't fit well with the brand.

Having said this, we feel this coordination is an exercise of compensating. Finding the role and strengths of each element, as in a football team. Shapes might be solid and straightforward when using them as backgrounds for a complex or detailed font to go on top. Or they can be detailed and full of different colors, using them as illustrations if the color palette of the identity is monochromatic. The challenge lies in finding that perfect balance and, therefore, synergy.

● **BACILE & La Libertad TNC**

It's all about balance, about equilibrium. In Folk we have understood with years of expertise, that everything is valid but everything must be coherent and consistent as well. We are in a good stage but we are not totally specialized in something specific and that's why we always like to learn from everyone around us.

When we start designing a proposal, we like to evaluate all the resources available to us, accepting explosions of color or gray scales, very irreverent fonts or very classic fonts, rebellious artistic manifestations or conservative layouts. We try not to limit ourselves so as not to slow down creativity, but always making sure that we do not lose focus on what the brand needs and that any graphic form that we deliver, is determined with the coherence that the brand has with its purpose.

● **Folk Estudio**

Graphic designers want to make a difference in their career path, I don't know if others believe in the law of 10,000 hours, but they may need to believe. When the accumulated experience reaches a stage when the content layout, color coordination of these issues, I believe will have a more correct judgment of these issues, "genes".

● **Chai Kunpeng**

Special attention will be paid to the contrast of strengths and weaknesses and the relationship between master and subordinate in the work. If the graphic is the main character, the design of the layout and arrangement of the message as the stage for the performance is to highlight the dramatic tension of the main character, with the graphic as the focus of development, complementary arrangement of other messages and color matching.

● **Chiang Lung-Hao**

While actually working on the visuals for a proposal, we work on most of the components including ideas fonts, colors, compositions, materials, graphics, patterns, and illustrations, always combining elements, taking a step back to look at them, and ensuring that everything makes sense. A big part of our process is to have an initial plan and modify and experiment with these elements along the way until we have something that we know will work. From there, we can create as much (or as little) as the project calls for and follow the rules we've intuitively set to make sure everything makes sense.

● **Heavy**

I believe it's very much up to personal preferences but I would pair loose graphics with serious-looking serif typefaces, and sharp graphics with typefaces of softer nuances. To me, these contrasting elements create more interesting, unexpected results.

As for the composition and colors—it again depends very much on the brand personality that I am designing for. Whether it should have a strong sense of typography for edginess or a more authentic, straight-forward layout to achieve sincerity. I believe it is about whom you are trying to communicate to, and determining what language you are using to best deliver.

● **Koyuki Inagaki**

Lisa: Apart from basics of composition, in Kudos case we were trying not to avoid the conflict between the shapes and everything else, and we use a lot of white space, quit classic compositions, and use the beautiful very well done Swiss typography Noi by Studio Feixen.

Marina: To keep the shapes coordinated with the typography, layout, and color composition we need to pay attention to the principles of design, such as balance, contrast, and hierarchy.

We can't forget the overall composition and how the various elements work together to create a cohesive and visually appealing design that at the same time is easy to understand and read.

● **Lisa Kuntysh & Marina Coll**

It helps me a lot to make a list of keywords with the main attributes that the brand I am working on should connote, I keep it in mind throughout the creation process, it is a very useful tool so that everything is consistent with the general concept and achieve effective communication.

● **Pao Bassol**

Among typography and color, shapes with generality should be the main ones. Don't over-emphasize their details, but use a concise and direct method to let them emphasize themselves in the brand. The shape itself needs to have its own memorable characteristics, and then designer can use these characteristics to program its position in the brand design.

● **ONNFF STUDIO**

It depends on the type of communication we need to design. It's always a matter of finding the right balance. For example, in a poster, graphics, typography, composition, and colors can work together to create a cohesive and customized composition.

However, in an identity system, elements need to be carefully considered both separately and as a whole. Graphics should provide inspiration and flexibility. They should be able to work and inspire in a simple manifestation, as well as in a more elaborate and complex manifestation, without losing the underlying concept and identity element.

● **Rebu**

Firstly, we ascertain the purpose or recognition of the visual communication, then arrange the elements in a hierarchy to design the layouts and coordination.

● **Sitoh inc.**

I think my way is to keep exploring. It is quite common when a shape does not fit with the rest of the elements such as typography, layout and colours, etc. However, my solution is to keep trying with different possibilities, eventually, I can get it right after many attempts.

● **Untitled Macao**

I (Eye) am MIKAN

This product was produced by focusing on the "eye-contact" with mandarin orange as communication. Eyes are an organ that expresses emotions, and those lines of sights are important elements that connect people's hearts. Therefore, this became a unique product differentiated it from competing products, that always keeps "eye-contact" with people and stays close to the feelings.

In order to bring out the individuality of various oranges such as taste and appearance, designers designed eye-shaped stickers and brought the oranges to life. The stickers also play a role of the quality proof recognized by the connoisseur. Moreover, by making the hole in the handle of the cardboard for transportation look like eyes, they aimed for an impact that would make the eyes meet the oranges.

Design Studio
MARU

Creative Direction
Koichi Sugiyama

Art Direction
Koichi Sugiyama

Design
Minako Endo

Client
Kadoya

STAY UPLINE

Upfield has always adhered to the concept of spreading premium coffee, selecting premium coffee beans from all over the world. Constantly breaking the routine, Upfield keeps up, breaks through its own top line, and presents a series of coffee with unique taste for each customer. It is a mental state that constantly reminds itself of touching the "top line". Not succumbing to the market and reality, it keeps the original intention, casual, and pursues an idealism of "emotional freedom".

Design Agency
Azu doesn't stop

Creative Direction
Azu

Art Direction
Azu

Design
Azu, 00 Su, Director Yang

Illustration
Azu

Client
STAY UPLINE

KOKOS

Each sweet and delicious in the iron box carries the desire to "take everyone to the Netherlands with taste buds". Eight kinds of cookies have different informations of provinces in the Netherlands, various festivals and a little history and culture. Although they are all made of cream, flour and sugar, they are more like an arbitrary door than a cookie gift box.

KOKOS is the meaning of coconut in the Dutch language. The two founders from the Netherlands and Taiwan, China hope to run a restaurant for the purpose of life and welcome everyone with delicious food and comfortable environment. Brand identity and gift box vision use coconut image as a role design, hoping to echo KOKOS's brand spirit of passion for food and land with a clean, interesting and more "human" visual feeling.

Design
Lung-Hao Chiang

Client
KOKOS

peekoo

This is about the brand image of peekoo, which is created around the concepts of coffee, orientalization and urban culture. The slogan of the brand is "Chill Out for A While", means stopping to feel life.
The mountains, are not only a scenery, but also a metaphor. "Chill out for a while", so that people can re-examine themselves and find the beauty of life, and implant the brand gene.

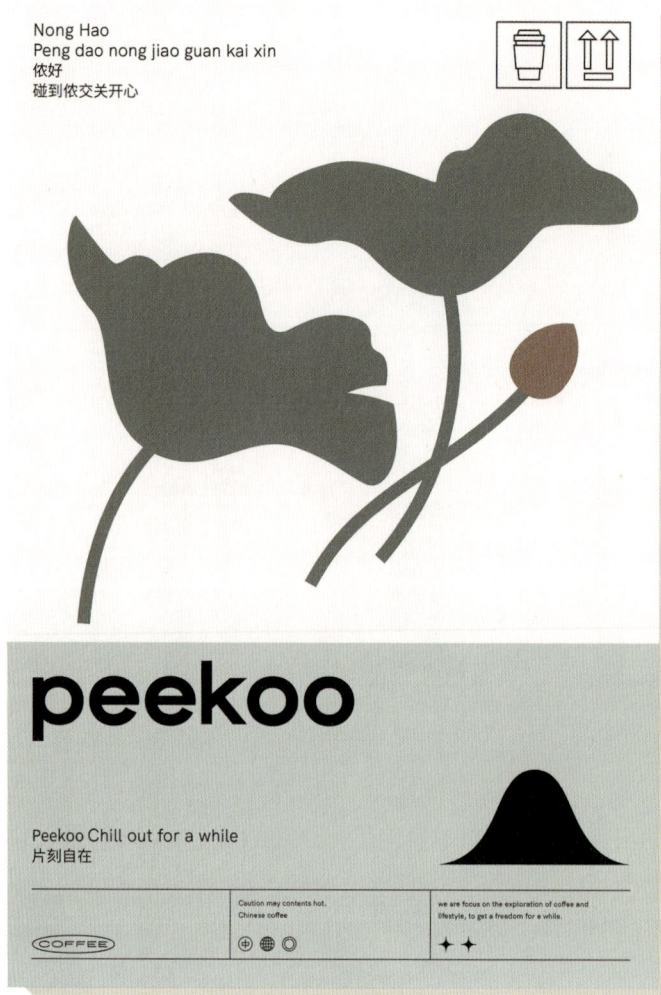

Nong Hao
Peng dao nong jiao guan kai xin
侬好
碰到侬交关开心

peekoo

Peekoo Chill out for a while
片刻自在

Caution may contents hot.
Chinese coffee

we are focus on the exploration of coffee and lifestyle, to get a freedom for a while.

COFFEE

Nong Hao
Peng dao nong
侬好
碰到侬交关开心

pe

Peekoo Chill ou
片刻自在

COFFEE

Design Studio
Batoer Studio

Creative Direction
batoer

Art Direction
batoer

Design
Dooaoki,batoer

Client
peekoo coffee

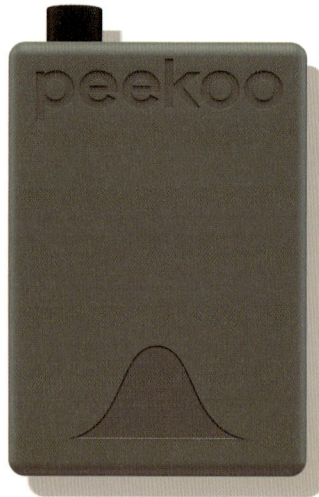

xin

Nong Hao
Peng dao nong jiao guan kai xin
侬好
碰到侬交关开心

peekoo

Peekoo Chill out for a while
片刻自在

Caution may contents hot.
Chinese coffee

we are focus on the exploration of coffee and
lifestyle, to get a freedom for a while.

COFFEE

Nong Hao
Peng dao nong jiao guan kai xin
侬好
碰到侬交关开心

City Series
城市系列

Caution may contents hot.
Chinese coffee

In City

上海

Shang Hai
上海

City Series
城市系列

peekoo

It's worth stopping for a moment
值得你停留片刻

Maca Baka

This is a brand identity made for a fashion brand Maca Baka.

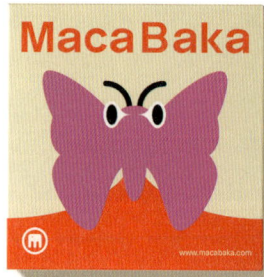

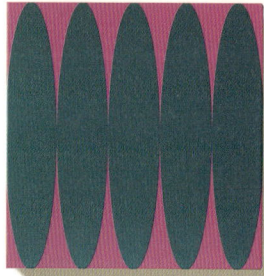

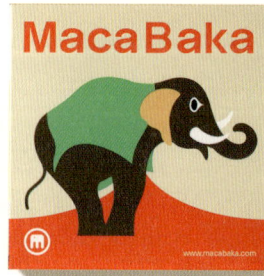

Design Studio
Batoer

Creative Direction
batoer

Art Direction
batoer

Design
Dooaoki, batoer

Client
Maca Baka (sweetheart)

Maca Baka
Outdoor playground

Mangaba

Mangaba means "good thing to eat". It names a surprisingly Brazilian restaurant. Rebu got inspired by its origin and legends, who turned into beautiful graphic expression and fantastic stories matching perfectly the warm and elegant colors. Rebu created naming, narrative, stories and visual language.

Design Studio
Rebu

Creative Direction
Pedro Mattos,
Fernando Andreazi

Art Direction
Pedro Mattos

Design
Joanna Dalleth, Regys Lima,
Thiago Siqueira, Pedro Mattos

Illustration
Thiago Siqueira, Pedro Mattos,
Joanna Dalleth

Copywriters
Fernando Andreazi,
Giovanna Marques,
Fernanda Damas

Client
Mangaba

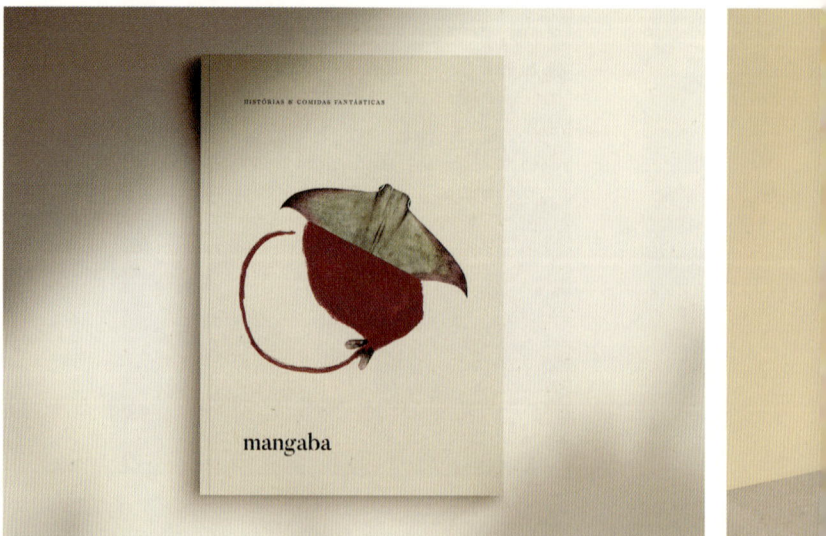

mangaba

mangaba
A calma do lago é tanta que, vez ou outra,
Pirarucu sai pra dar umas bandas.
Olá, tudo bem?
Você está convidado(a) a participar da
inauguração do Mangaba Restaurante!
14/02/2022
A partir das 12h
R. Canário, 1301
Moema, São Paulo - SP
HISTÓRIAS & COMIDAS FANTÁSTICAS
@mangabarestaurante

a do chef

pratos principais
Arroz Paraense
Paella caipira
53
79
CARNES | DA TERRA
Denver Steak ao chutney de figo
79
Rossini pantaneiro com piamontese
68
Ancho com pirão de leite de cabra
112
Filé ao molho de cerveja preta
48
bebidas
TAÇAS DE VINHO
De los Man Cabernet Sauvignon
22
Postales Roble Chardonnay
35
Postales Roble Chardonnay
18
mangaba

mangaba

Ishida Coffee
Packaging Design

It is a coffee package of Ishida coffee shop, a cafe located in a quiet residential area of Sapporo. Cats always know how to enjoy themselves and designers transformed the idea to present relaxing time at home like a cat and the coffee bean is designed as a curling-up cat image.

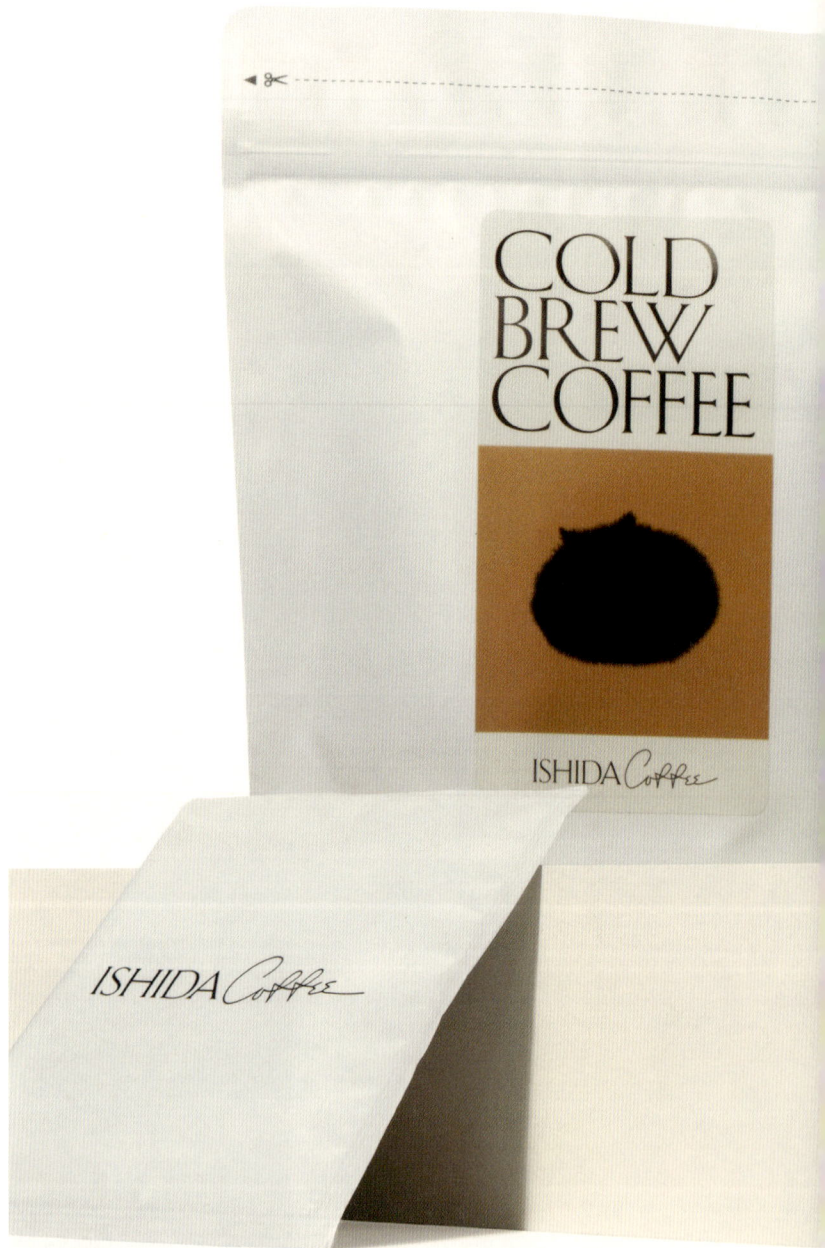

Design Studio
Sitoh inc.

Art Direction
Motoi Shito

Design
Motoi Shito

Illustration
Masanobu Ishii

Client
ISHIDA Coffee

ZIP

LATTE
BASE

ISHIDA Coffee

ICED
COFFEE

ISHIDA Coffee

Tridente

Tridente is a coffee brand from where the sea and the land meet. Its experience, from the design of the packaging to its flavor, will take people on a maritime expedition with new horizons to discover.

Inspired by a mythological story that designers made about coffee beans, explorers, and magic, Heavy created a brand that is reminiscent of Ancient Greece and its graphic imagery. Each illustration tells people parts of its story.

Design Studio
Heavy

Creative Direction
Lane Cope, Sofía Vargas

Art Direction
Lane Cope, Sofía Vargas

Design
**Lane Cope, Sofía Vargas,
Eduardo González,
Diego Rocha**

Illustration
Lane Cope, Diego Rocha

Photography
Ale Melo

Client
Sebastián Zepeda

DINO BURGER

This design emphasizes on the brand's think-out-of-the-box attitude and its innovative operating method. Therefore, designers break the stereotype of average burger shop and use the peculiar yet adventurous dinosaurs as the subject, while following it onto the path of looking for delicious burgers. The logo design is clean and concise by combining the brand's English name with the characteristics of dinosaur's feet. As for extended designs, plenty of creative illustrations are used to attract customers' attention in order to highlight the uniqueness of the brand.

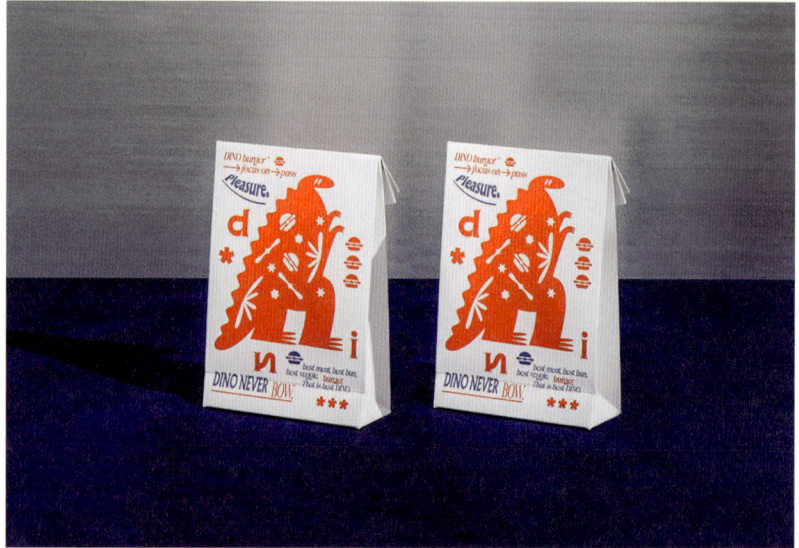

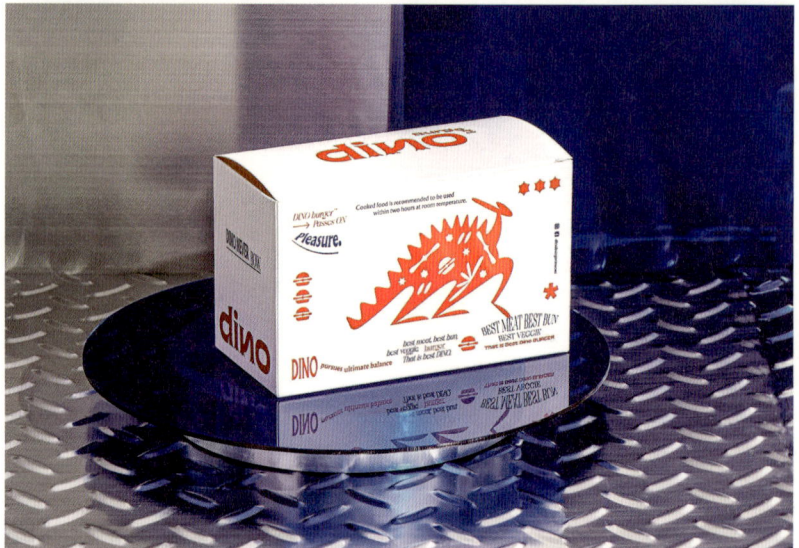

Creative Direction
Au Chon Hin

Art Direction
Au Chon Hin

Design
Untitled Macao,
Untitled Design Ltd.

Client
Dino Burger

Stickers for a Coffeeshop in Batumi, Georgia

"Kava ginda" means "Fancy a coffee?" in Georgian. This is also a small cozy coffee shop in Batumi. It's pet-friendly and actively supports dog shelters. The idea was to create illustrations reflecting the soul of this space. This is how yoga dogs were born. These adorable tails enjoy their moment with sweet treats in various asanas.

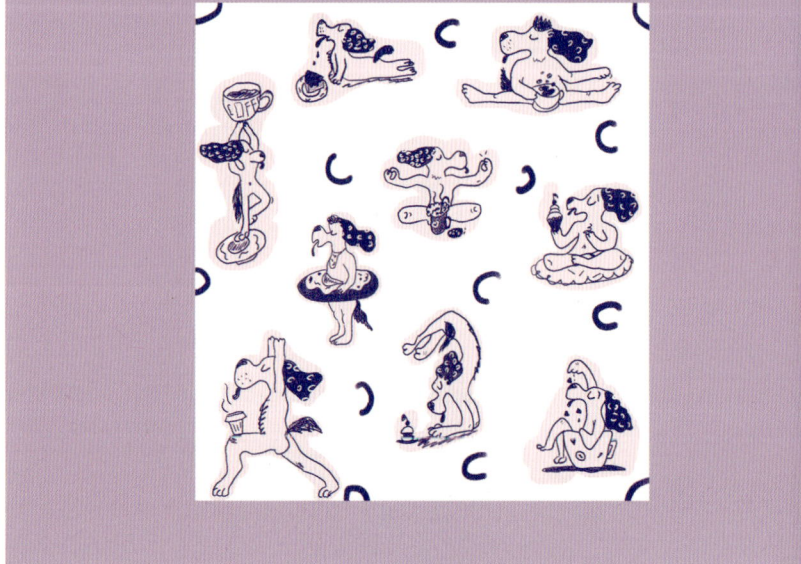

Design
Katsiaryna Stsiapanava

Client
Kava ginda

Lickabite

Lickabite is a signature ice cream brand located in Bangkok, Thailand, reaching Folk Estudio to design its entire brand identity. Both of them really enjoyed the whole process, with very different time schedules, three parallel languages and an amazing brand manifesto that empowers Thai women. The voice can be raised in a feminine and bold way through an authentic ice cream.

Creative Direction
Sebastián González

Art Direction
Laura Flórez

Design
Folk Estudio

Illustration
Johana Vargas

Photography
Studio Thaan

Client
Thititip Boon

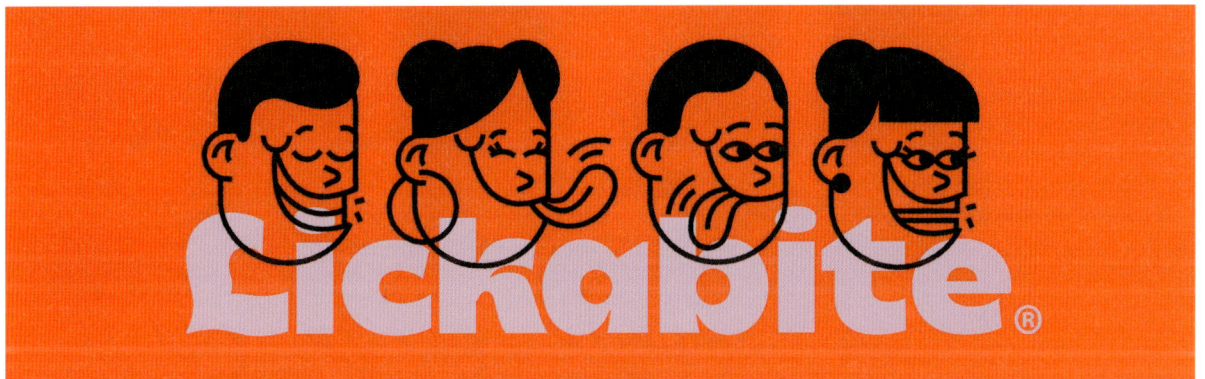

WIM

This is an identity design for WIM, a new daytime cafe by YOWIE in Philadelphia. The vision for WIM's identity was bold and welcoming, design-forward and approachable.

The result is a play of contrasts: graphic typography and bold color create a contemporary feel while playful illustrations keep it light-hearted. The ambigram-like logo highlights the flexibility of the space by being readable from different perspectives. The outlined illustrations were drawn imperfectly to contrast with clean graphic layouts and offset the heaviness of the logo. As a kit-of-parts, the WIM identity can be rearranged to suit the needs of such a transformative and connected space.

Creative Direction
Shannon Maldonado

Art Direction
Hanna Karraby

Illustration
James Paris

Photography
Breanne Furlong

Client
YOWIE

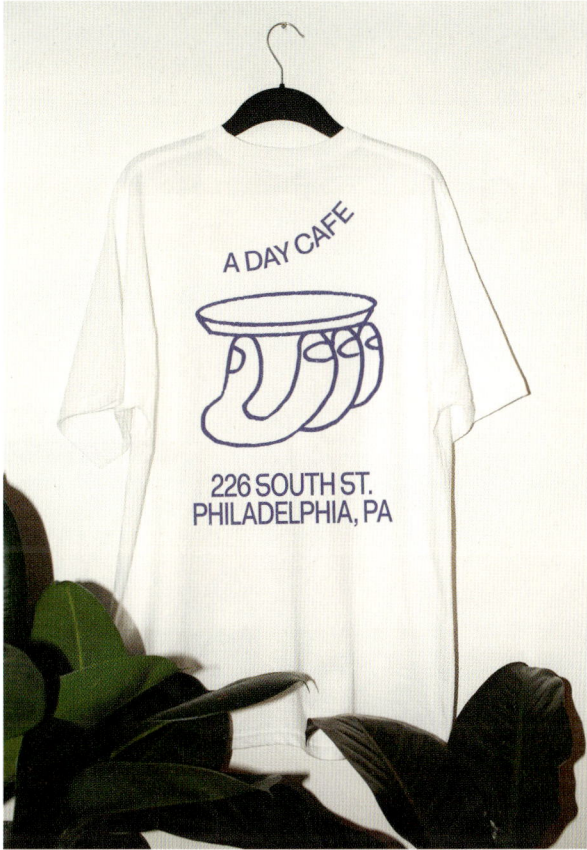

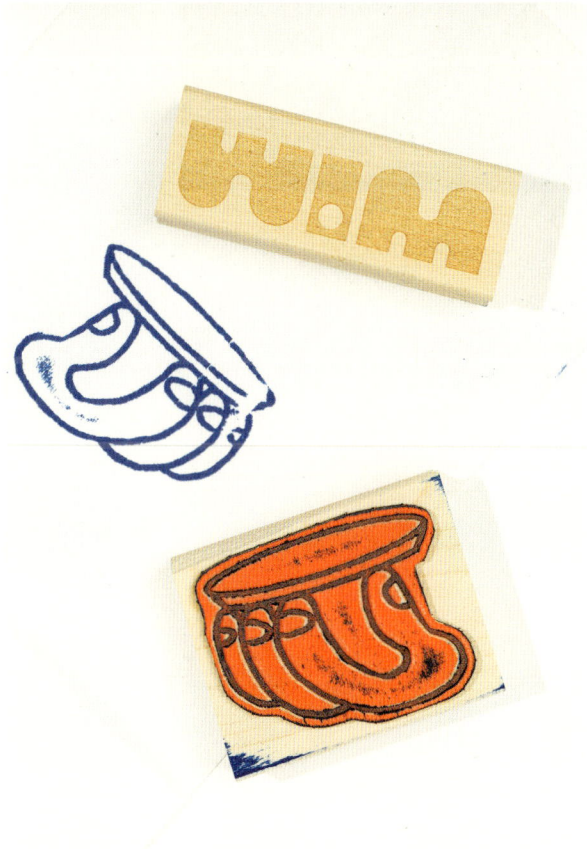

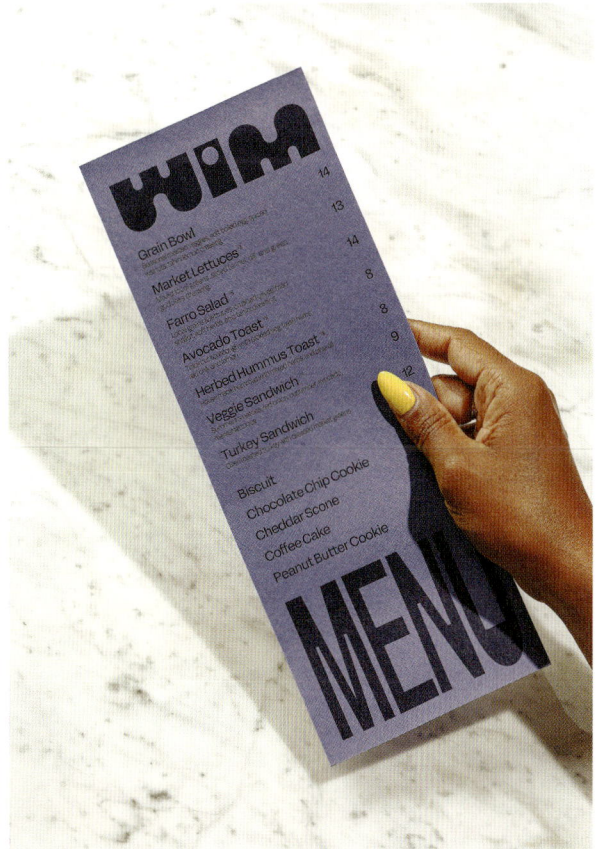

Nud

Nud is an artisanal bakery and coffee shop specialized in sourdough bread and gourmet coffee. It was designed as a place where only good things happen and life stops for a moment.

"Bread and coffee" is possibly the best combination that exists and some of the most enjoyable things in this world. Few things compare to the sensation of the first sip of a good cup of coffee or the first bite of a delicious bun; hence the concept of the brand is born. It all begins from that first sip or bite that makes you feel as if nothing existed, there is no rush, there are no troubles, neither people, it's just a person "nude" enjoying a brief moment of happiness.

For the visual identity designers designed a series of lovely characters that portray the love for coffee and bread and those pleasant sensations people feel when tasting them. The feeling of the brand is soft, cute and casual, it is a brand that communicates in diminutive, a peculiar manner of speaking in Mexico with the things people care and enjoy the most.

Design Studio
Maniac Studio

Creative Direction
Andrés Domínguez

Art Direction
Andrés Domínguez

Design
**Andrés Domínguez,
Andrea Flores**

Illustration
Andrés Domínguez

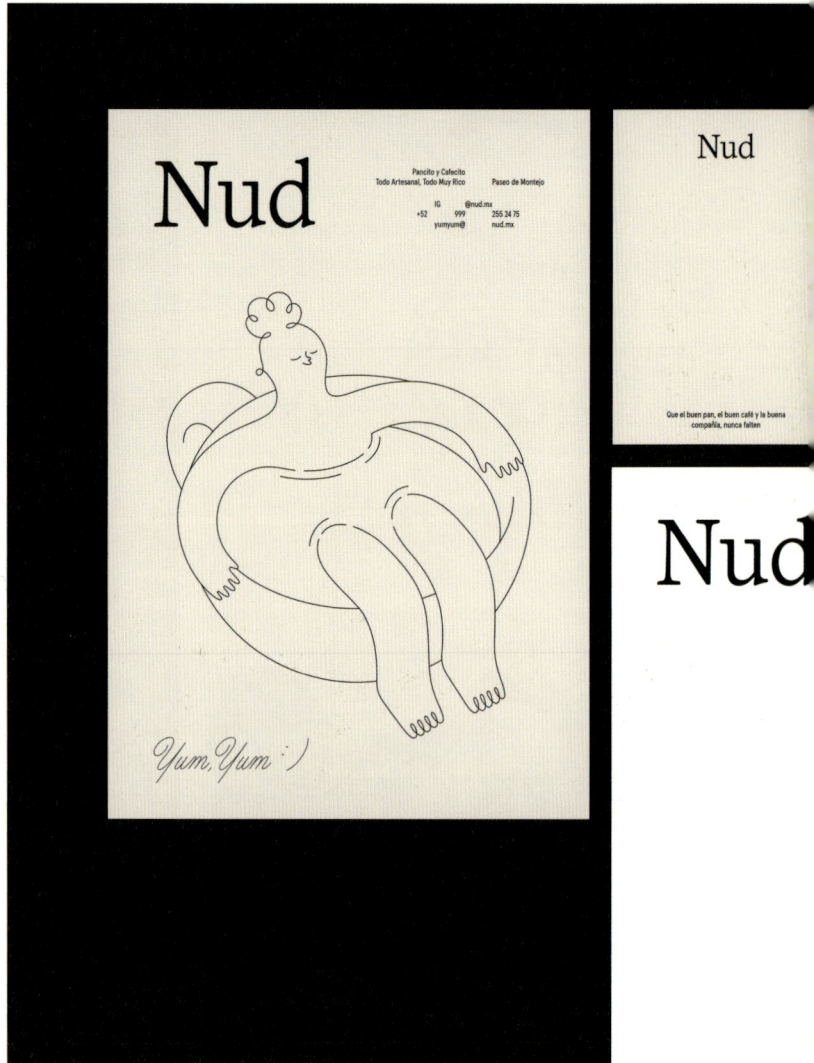

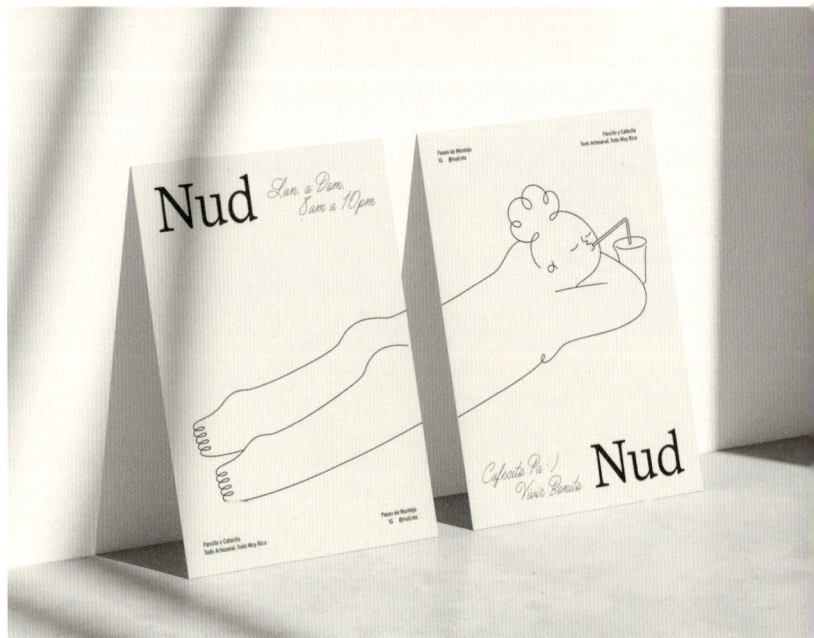

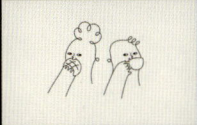

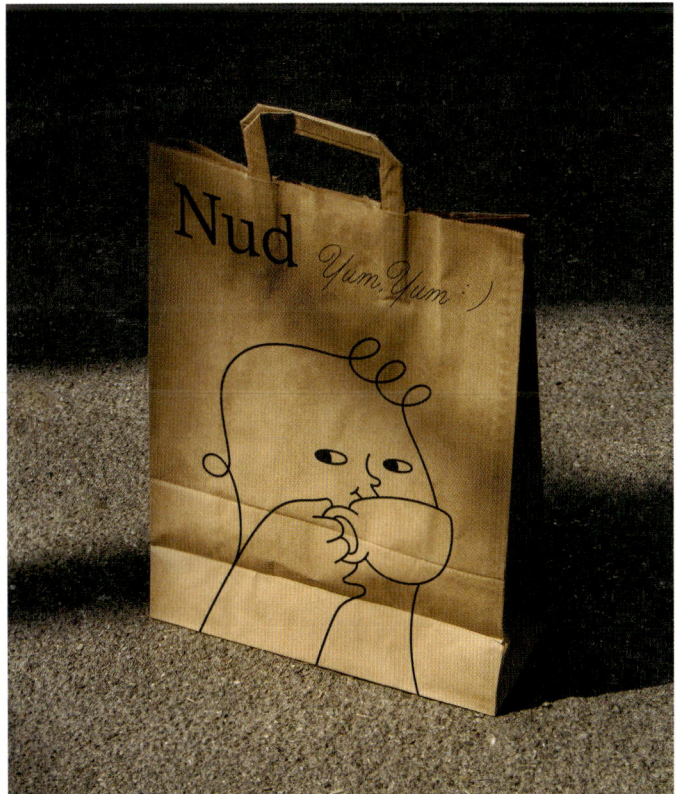

rang brunch

rang brunch as a "Mini-Expo" event on the theme of "Specialty Coffee", combined with entertainment activities and delicious food at an event space that is designed with creative atmosphere. Modern, bold "street brunch" but still shows the spirit of "minimalism" that rang rang coffee pursues.

   rang brunch is held throughout with activities revolving around corner: Expresso Bar, Coffee Roasting, Sandwich Food, DJ & Merchandising. Each zone will be led by talented artists, chefs, mixers and professional DJs to experience the wonderful flavors of instant roasted coffee along with different types of coffee. Besides attractive cocktails, attendees can understand more interesting information about coffee in many different ways.

Design Studio
InSpace Creative

Creative Direction
Sanh Nguyen

Design
Nhi Tuong, Duy Trinh,
Trung Chau, Phuong Vo

Illustration
Nhi Tuong, Phuong Vo

Project Manager
Trang Ho

Photography
rang rang coffee

Client
rang rang coffee

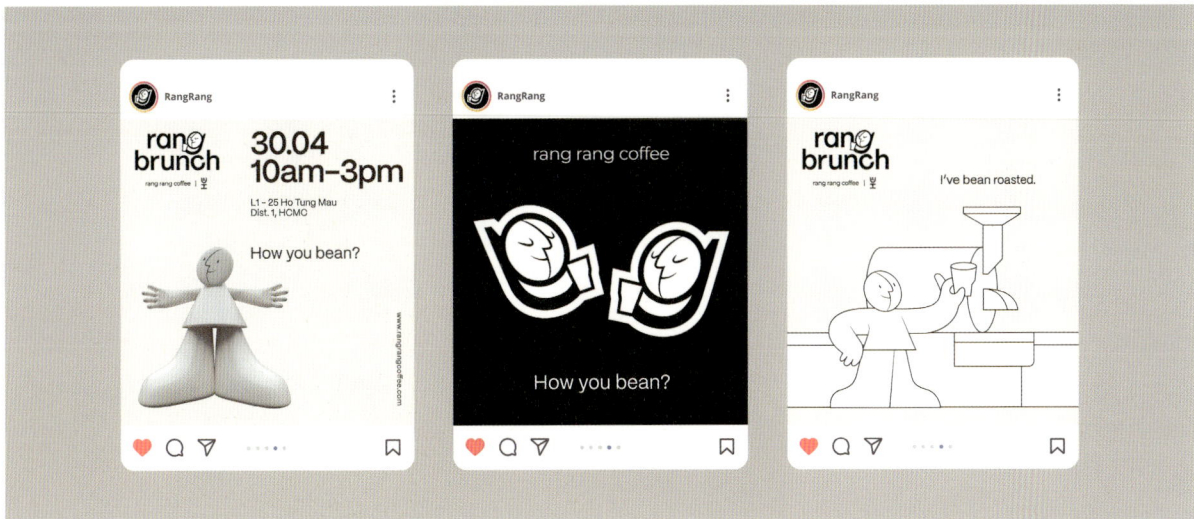

ÉCRU

It is a branding design for coffee and wine stand in Fukuoka. The branding comprises "stacked" coffee beans and grape berries. The elements, when stacked, form a new, accidental shapes—just like ÉCRU creating new chemical reactions by being a crossing point for coffee and wine drinkers.

Design
Koyuki Inagaki

Client
Ito Soken Co., Ltd.

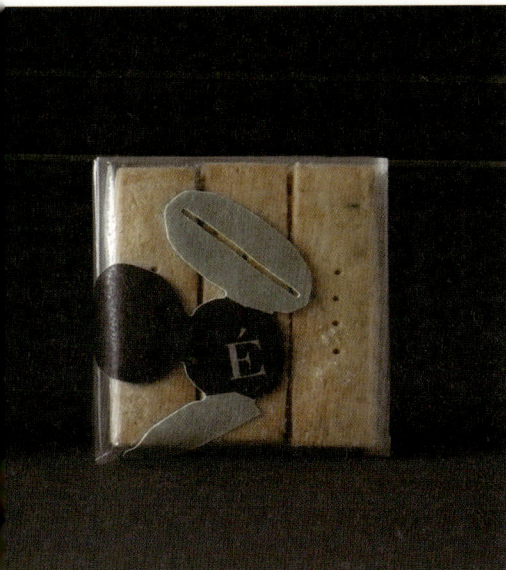

Quadraft Brewing

The work is a packaging design for a wine made from natural grapes, which are used as food for animals in nature. In order to interpret the method of making this wine, designer has tried to preserve the wild and rugged vitality of nature in the design, using a rugged animal silhouette approach as the main visual element and a straightforward black and white palette as the main color of the packaging. The typography, combined with the rugged illustrative images, is like a recreation of a natural garden world, conveying the concept of a product made from natural ingredients.

Design
Chai Kunpeng

Client
Quadraft Brewing

Langham Place
Say Cheese

2020 is the Year of the Rat. In this traditional festive season, the design team injects modern graphics and vibrant colors into the traditional red packet design. In order to match with the theme of Year of the Rat, inside the package there is a small gift together with the red packets, a handcrafted soap in cheese outlook.

Design Studio
llab design ltd

Creative Direction
Mike Wong

Art Direction
Yan Cheung

Printing
Champion Co.

Client
Langham Place

La Lune CNY Collection

This is a series of packaging design for Chinese New Year gift box of pastry products in the year of Tiger.

Design
Pengguin

Client
Patisserie La Lune

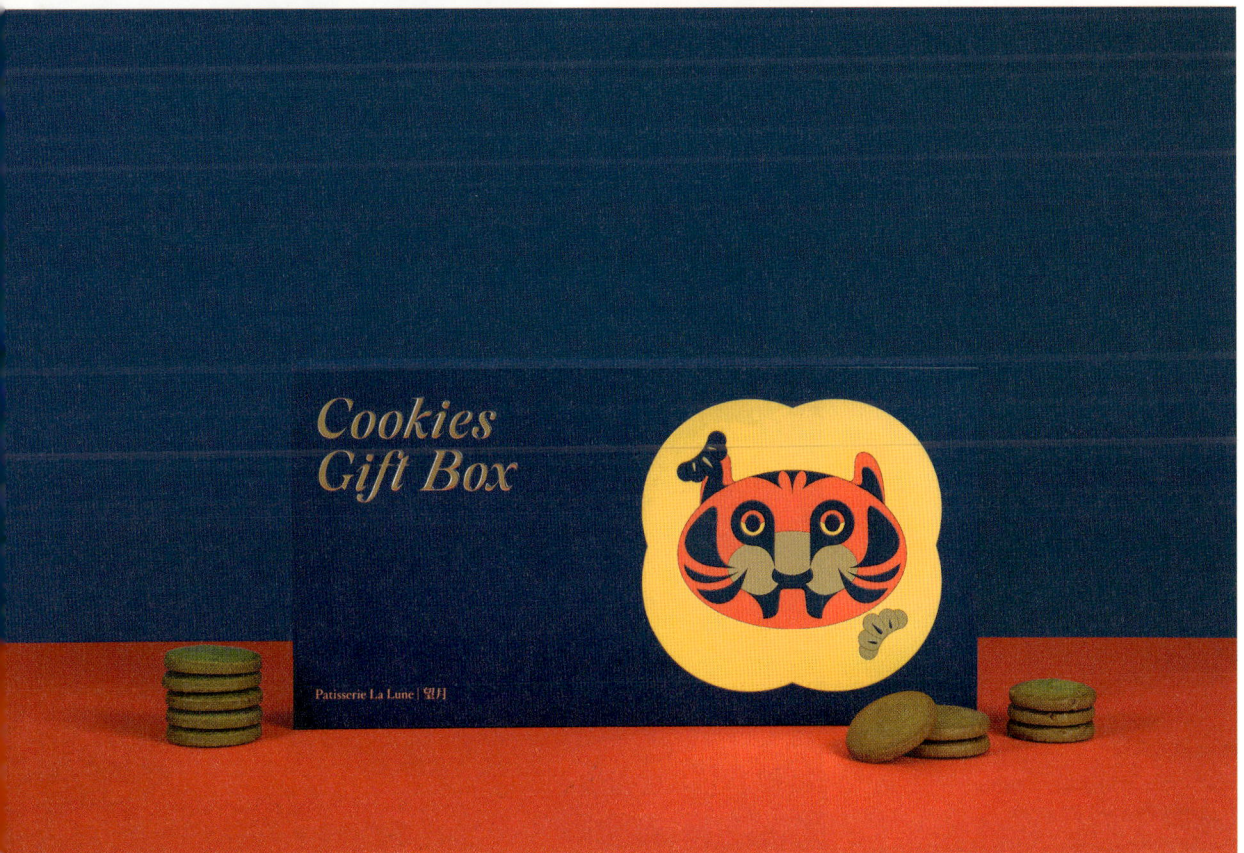

CDN—NDG

The Borough of CDN—NDG (Borough Côte-des-Neiges–Notre-Dame-de-Grâce) has to deal with the challenge of communicating with a diverse population, defined by different and at times opposing financial, family, linguistic and professional realities. Using various media, the campaign's objective was to start a conversation with residents about the future of the borough's parks. Through the friendly colorful characters, the campaign was meant to convey accessibility and optimism breaking away from traditional communications while engaging residents.

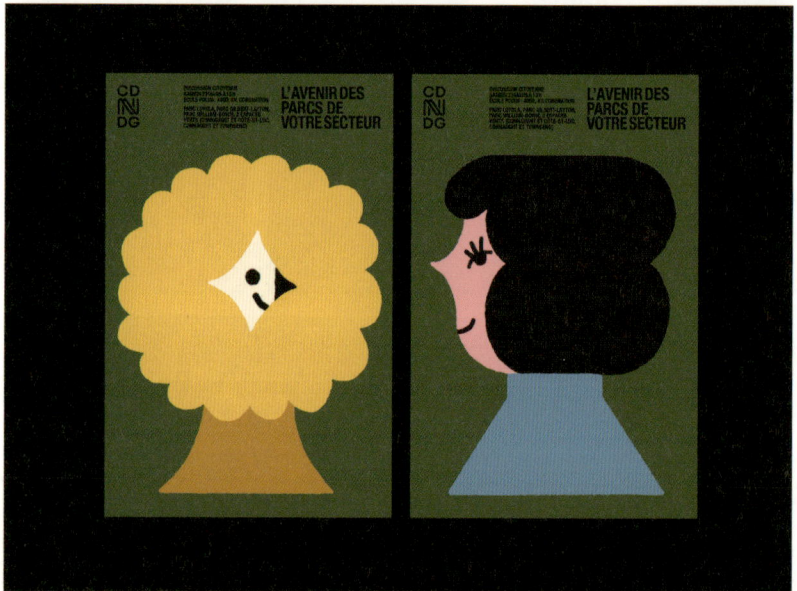

Design Studio
Paprika Design

Creative Direction
Louis Gagnon

Art Direction
Daniel Robitaille

Illustration
Mathieu Labrecque

Client
Borough Côte-des-Neiges–Notre-Dame-de-Grâce (CDN—NDG)

Nature Rules

In 2019 designer created two emblem stickers inspired by his hometown, Visaginas, Lithuaina. In 2020 it grew into a whole series inspired by the moments when nature meets urban life.

Design
Bogdan Katsuba

Aldea Venado

Aldea Venado is an eco-camping space located in Yucatan, Mexico that offers something different from a conventional camp site. It has ecological facilities, permaculture and a lot of cultural diversity where the experience of contact with nature is enriched and human relations are strengthened.

Design
Pao Bassol

Client
Gerardo Perez

Jockey Club Contemporary Art Literacy and Appreciation Programme

Jockey Club Contemporary Art Literacy and Appreciation Programme (JCCALAP) aims to popularise the knowledges of contemporary art appreciation in Hong Kong, China.

VINCDESIGN participated in the branding and visual identity design of the programme. To make the programme more lively and recognisable, they chose a little character for it, a snail. JCCALAP exactly wants everyone to learn from a snail, to enjoy and reflect on art slowly. Also, a snail leaves traces wherever it goes, just like JCCALAP walks through and leaves traces in the art learning journey. They used orange as the main color, which is energetic and also the representative colour of the organiser. Black, gray and white as supporting colors, representing different forms of arts. The visual identity is formed by random strokes and a clear lap, showing that with JCCALAP, everyone can find their own clear path in the seeming messy world of art.

Design Studio
Vincdesign Branding Co.

Creative Direction
Vince Cheung

Design
Kaman Kan

Photography
Vicky Ip

Client
1a Space

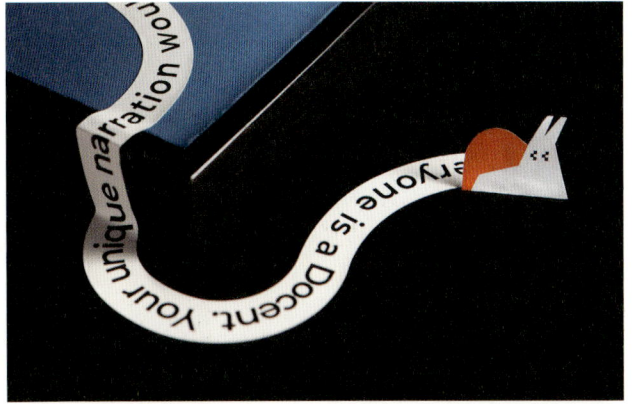

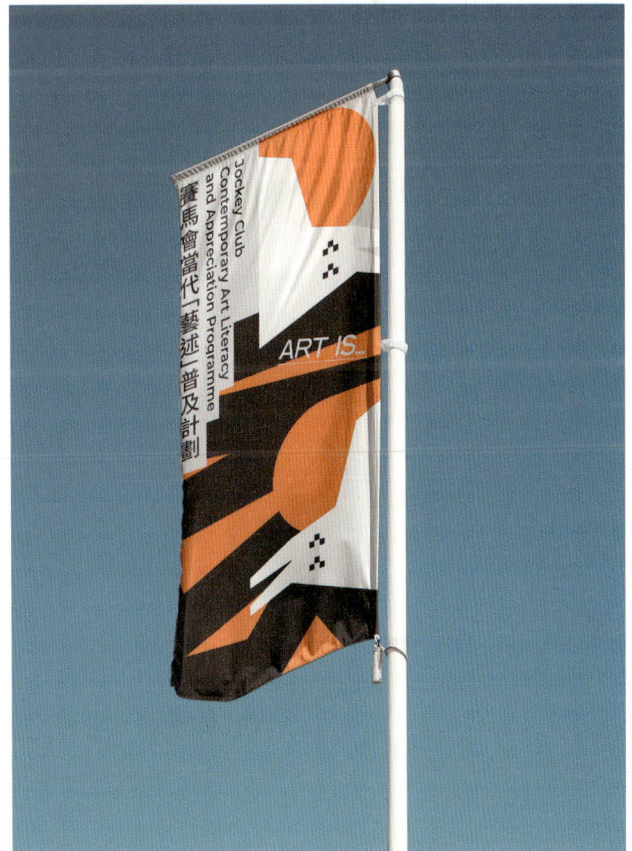

Mercado San Antonio

San Antonio is a market located in Villa Carlos Paz, Córdoba, Argentina. But far from being a market like any other, this place offers fresh, local, tasty food, promotes different experiences for its visitors, and invites them to be part of a new gastronomic community. That was the starting point for developing the brand concept and aesthetics.

Designer tried to convey the idea of being a large market with a wide variety of products, but at the same time, perceived as a small local market. The visual identity and its communication concept represent the idea of being a neighborhood market that knows each one of its customers. For this, a vibrant but classic color palette was used, along with traditional-modern typography and organic shapes and containers.

Design Studio
BACILE* & La Libertad TNC

Creative Direction
Santiago Guillamondegui,
Gonzalo Prunesti &
Nicolás Bacile

Design
Gonzalo Prunesti &
Nicolás Bacile

Copywriting
Santiago Guillamondegui

Client
Gustavo Bacile & Claudia Mulé

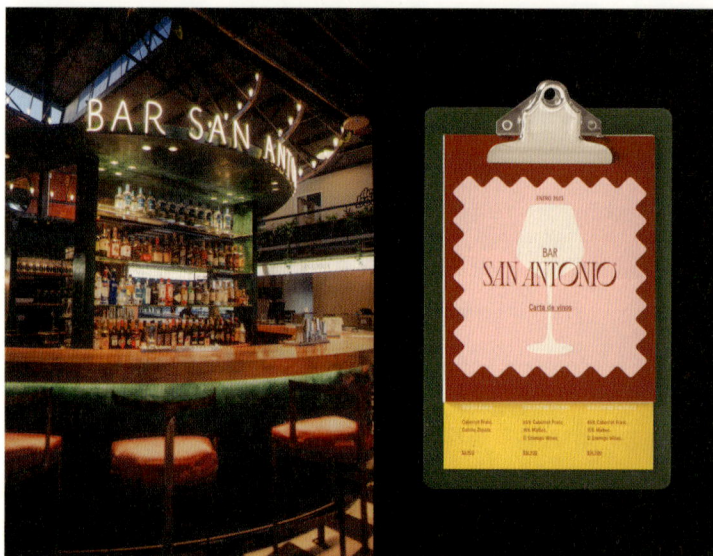

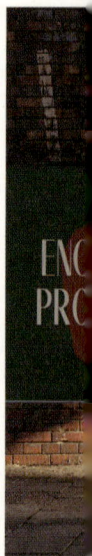

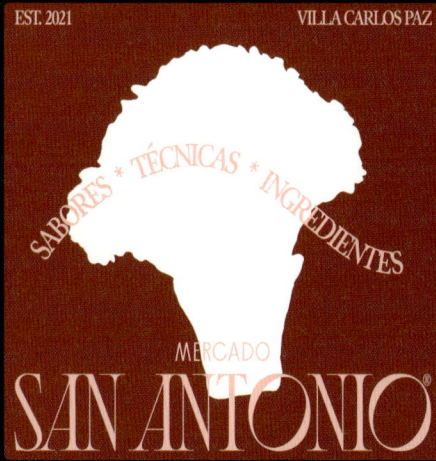

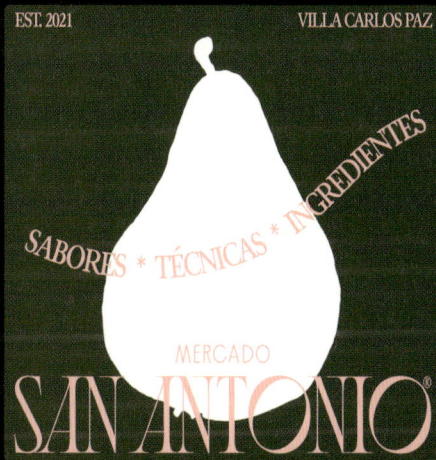

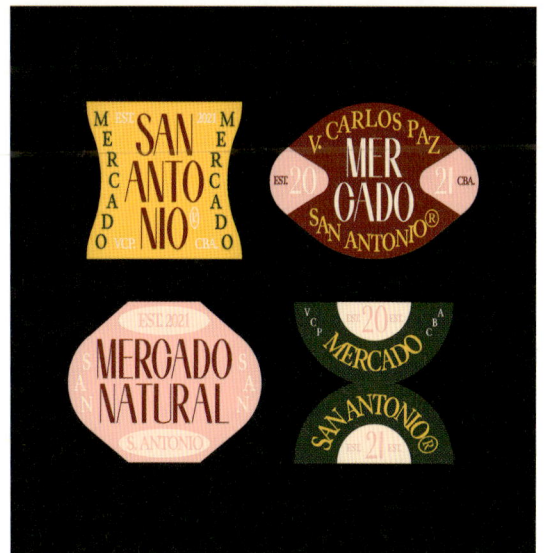

Bong Hoa Nho

Bong Hoa Nho's next chapter, titled "Burnt Out – Light Up the Burnt Out," began in summer 2023. This theme focuses on addressing burnout and rekindling the passion within artists. The project aims to provide support, resources, and a sense of community to help artists heal and reignite their creative flame.

Pixel Flowers is the concept of the first season of Bong Hoa Nho exhibition. This is an online exhibition on a digital platform. It is designed to display the illusions of judgments, where these illusions run after the ephemeral things, and unwittingly lose themselves. The exhibition aims to give viewers a profound insight into the negative effects of judgments, and negative thoughts that people impose on themselves, and how they affect people's lives.

Design Studio
Bapxao

Creative Direction
Vi Tuong Ngo

Art Direction
Vi Tuong Ngo

Design
Xuan Phan,
Minh Sang Nguyen,
Vi Tuong Ngo

Illustration
Xuan Phan

Project Manager
Maikhanh

Copywrite
Linh Polly

Branding Supervizor
Alex Dang

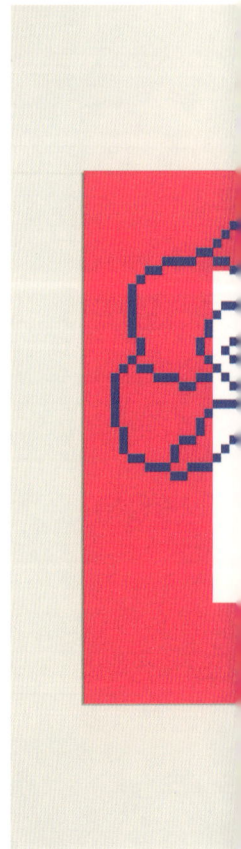

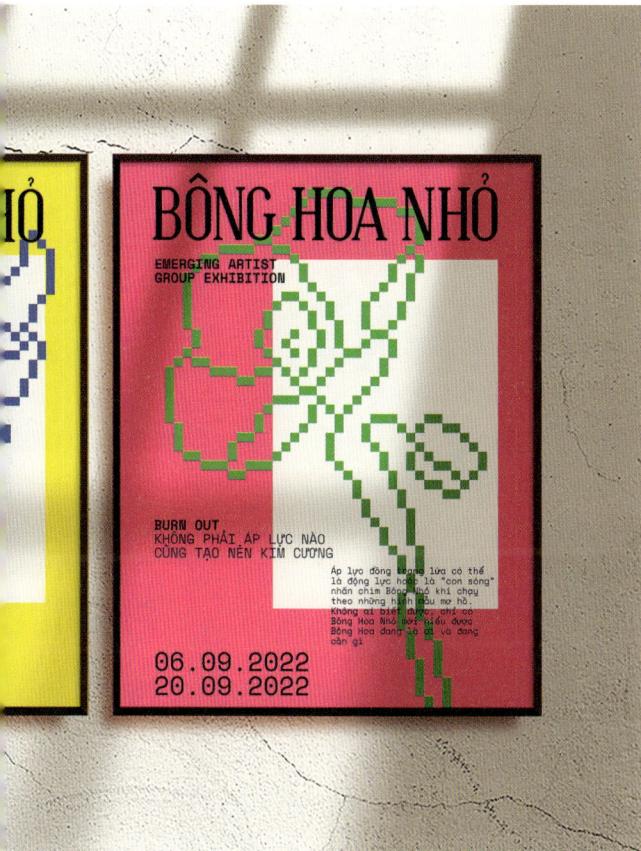

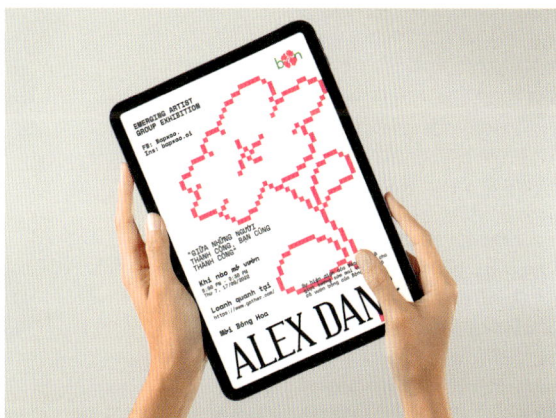

AMI AMI

AMI AMI is a brand founded in California by two friends who opted for boxed over bottles to minimize the carbon footprint by 50%.

    The main challenge was to overcome the lower-quality perceptions of boxed wine through high-quality design and packaging worthy of the MoMA store. Design team strategically defined and designed an approachable brand that invites people into a new way to wine and think outside the bottle. The box itself is a custom 1.5L design made to fit naturally on your counter or carry to the dinner party. The logo is designed specifically to fit the panel and incorporates half-circles or "cups" of wine. Ten half-circles fall across the packaging, indicating the number of glasses to enjoy. Playful illustrations bring the name to life (ami is "friend" in French) and create a spirited brand universe with a sense of quality and time. This is because they are directly inspired by Italian Futurist, Fortunato Depero's work, the artist known for iconic Campari advertising across the 1920s and 1930s.

Design
Wedge Studio

Client
AMI AMI

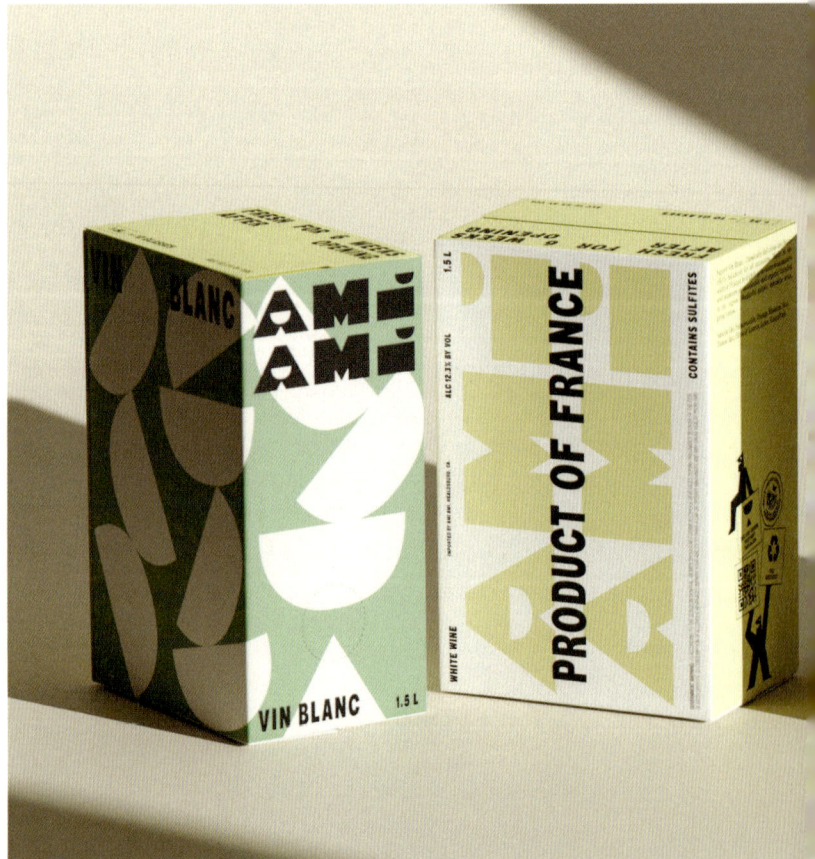

Kudos

Kudos is an honestly good supermarket that sells out-of-standard fruit and veggies, products with slightly damaged packaging, and juices & jams made from the unsold fruit. The project aims at the young cool kids who want to fight food waste.

"Kudos" means "thank you", and that is what the brand wants to say to people who change the way they consume in order to make the world a better place. Thinking about all the stages in the production cycle where food waste is created, they decide to tackle this with a inventive different solution.

After Kudos closes at midnight there might be some fruits and veggies left, so designer create juices and jams out of them. This way, the minimum amount of food is wasted. These juices and jams are the last opportunities these fruits and veggies have to be eaten. This is their last chance. As food waste is a huge world problem in general, at Kudos they wanted to educate about this topic in a playful and fun way, not to make this content even more sad or boring to consume.

Creative Direction
Anna Berbiela
(Pràctica Design)

Design
Lisa Kuntysh,
Marina Coll

Photography
Oriol Puchol

Mushroom Compadres

Mushroom Compadres is a project dedicated to the cultivation for sale of specialty and functional mushrooms for gastronomic and medicinal use in the West Algarve, Portugal. Its goal is to provide people with delicious, high-quality products for their consumption, helping their physical and mental well-being through nature. Initially, the mushroom farming project was part of the offerings of the parent company Fazenda Compadres, which is dedicated to regenerative agriculture in the southwest of Portugal.

The idea was to move away from the somewhat neutral and clean aesthetic of organic products and design an identity that was less conventional but more honest, fun, and quirky. The result combines the fresh, friendly, and fun vision of the founders with the natural and special character of their products in an authentic way.

Design Studio
Ochodias

Creative Direction
Manuel Vargas

Art Direction
Manuel Vargas

Design
Manuel Vargas,
Karla Márquez

Illustration
Manuel Vargas

Client
Mushroom Compadres

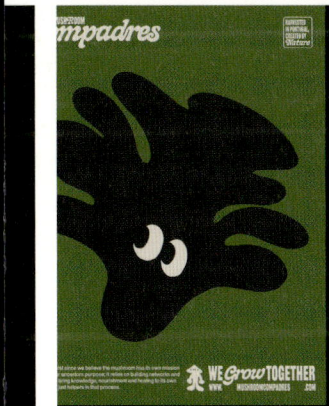
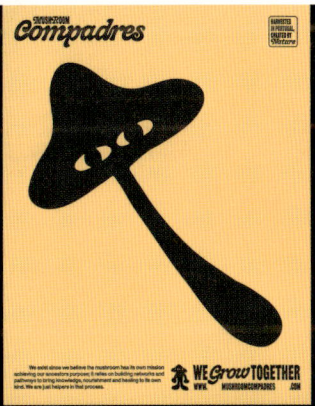

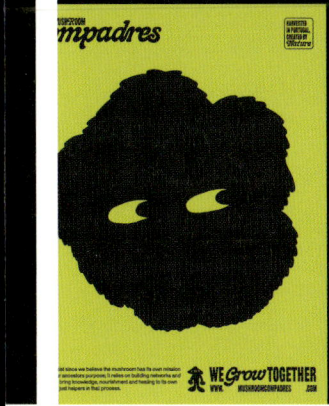

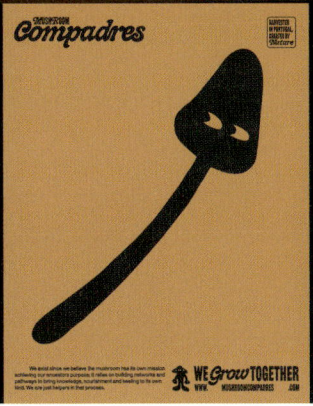
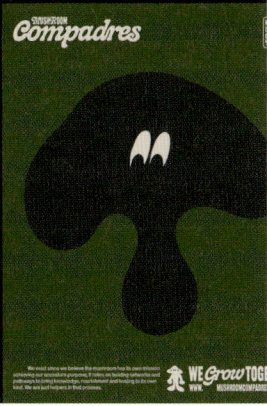

AICOKEN

Started from the perspective of children, and with the childishness and innocence of a child, AICOKEN connects the distance between children and clothing by the fabric temperature. Inspired by "stay curious" and based on the shape of a small bench, the brand design of AICOKEN symbolizes children stand on their tiptoes, grow, and explore with full of curiosity. ONNFF STUDIO chose the "A" of AICOKEN as the prototype to create a cartoon image with a vibrant "A" silhouette. It looks friendly, bold, brave, and energetic. They used it throughout the brand packaging, hoping to accompany children to experience the beauty of life together.

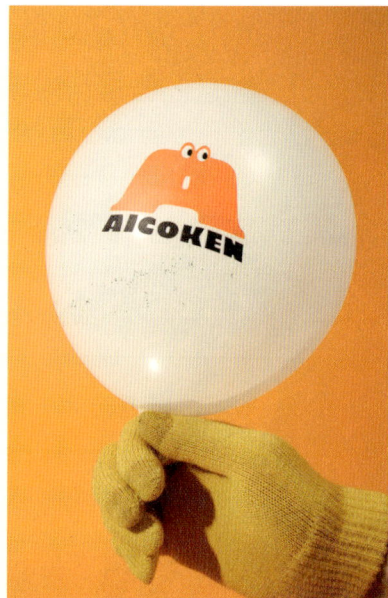

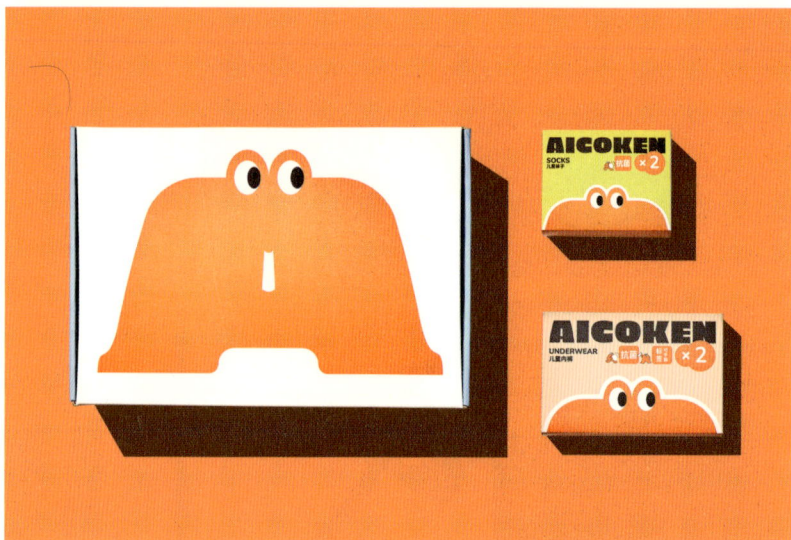

Design Studio
ONNFF STUDIO

Design
Hu Zhengrui@ONNFF

Photography
Chen Dazhi

Client
AICOKEN

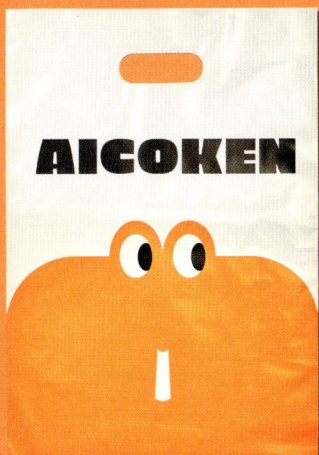
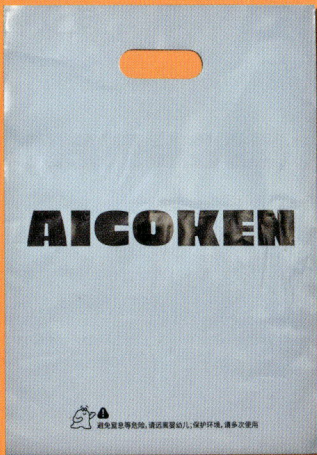

Sytnoe Mesto

Sytnoye Mesto means a nourishing place or place full of food. It is a family food store in a small town, whose specialization is sausages and cheese. The challenge was to stand out among the similar shops and create a unique friendly image of a "good neighbor". Designer made a naming, came up with friendly branding and a dynamic logo that turns into a funny character. Icons of products create a pattern and become a part of the interior. The name and slogan of the project contains an ironic play on words: the words "mesto" (place) and "vmeste" (together).

Сытное место

Design
Eugenia Maximova

Client
Sytnoe mesto

Открытие
магазина
15 июня

Сытное
место

Вместе
теплее

Doggll

Doggll is a pet store based in Surat, India. With a focus on providing personalized and knowledgeable customer service, Doggll is a trusted source for all things pet-related. The identity design was inspired by a fun and playful brand personality. Doggll celebrates the joy and companionship that come with being a pet owner.

Design
Elena Yaremchuk

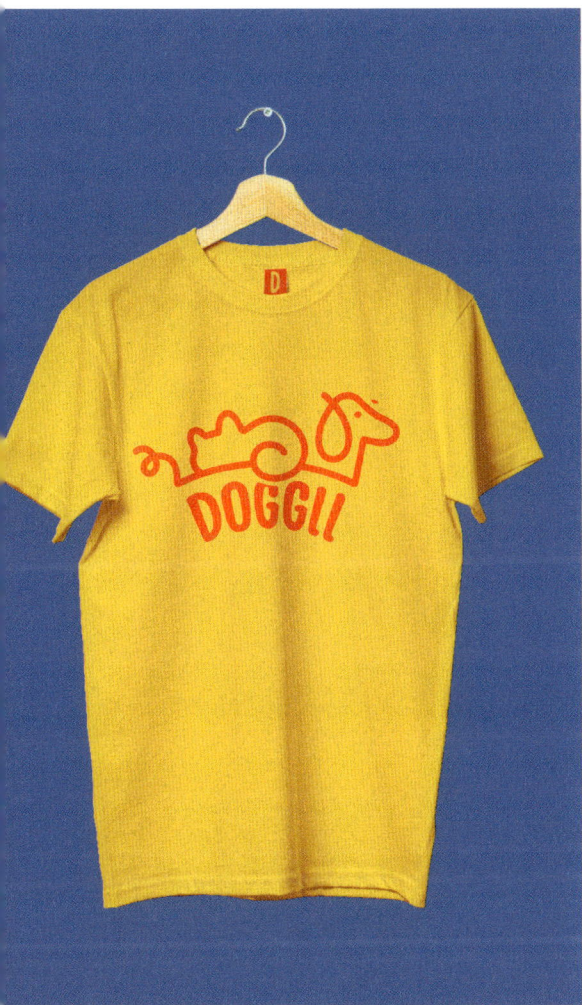

Veter

Veter is a veterinary center with focus on creating extraordinary truly experiences, reflected through fun and dynamic service.

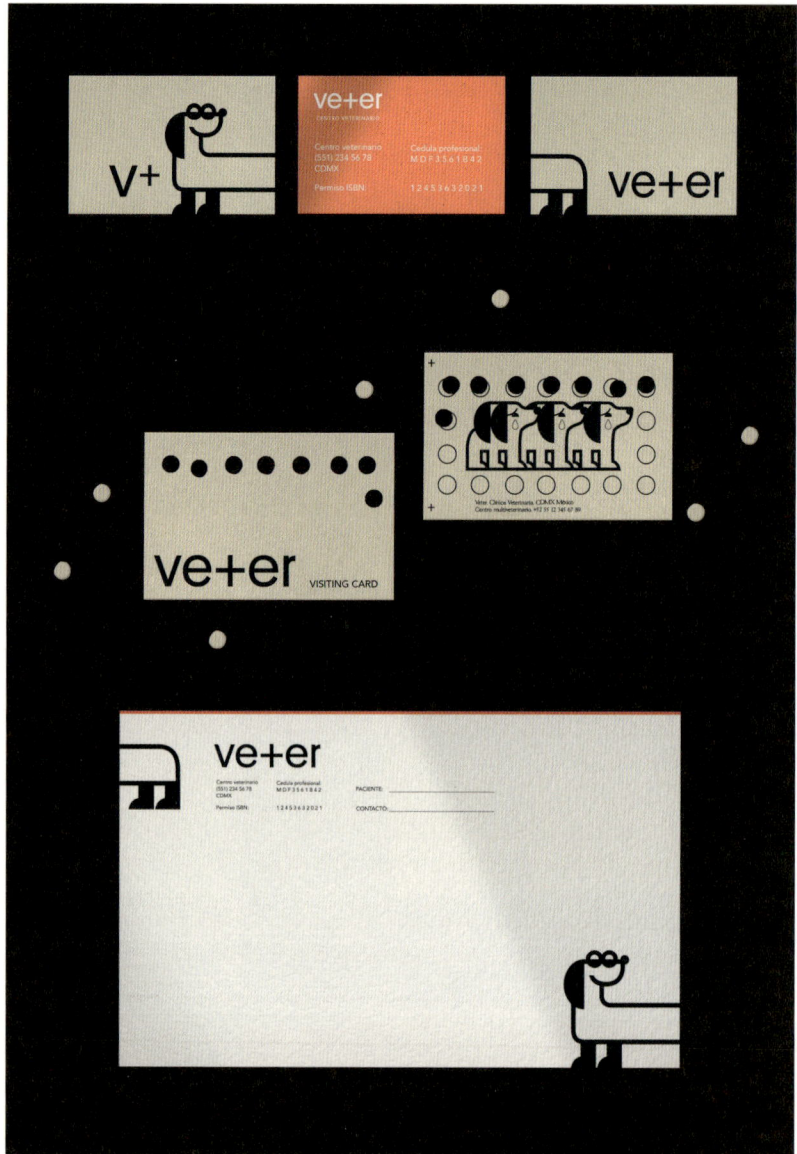

Design
Enrique Puerto

Others
Dimension studio

Photography
Tere Robledo

Café Fugaz

Café Fugaz is a specialty Mexican coffee brand, offering six experiences designed to elevate any kind of present, from the early morning to the dusk delight.

Menta designed a brand where each coffee features an illustration that communicates the time of day it represents. The moments that give meaning to daily life. The illustrations are vibrant with a color palette that synthesizes Mexican culture with a contemporary take. The logo is an honest wordmark, with character in its sans serif typeface. They created a complementary icon of a shooting star, which is falling and reminds people of how ephemeral life is. By placing this icon as the security label, it reinforces the meaning purposefully on the packaging: like a shooting star. The icon is designed with simplicity to create a contrast with the graphics on each packaging.

Design Studio
Menta

Creative Direction
Laura Méndez

Art Direction
Laura Méndez, Alhelí Águila

Design
Alhelí Águila

Illustration
Alhelí Aguila, Majo Corona

Photography
Liliana Barraza

Client
Café Fugaz

Pecks

It is designed by an e-commerce brand.

Design Studio
LovHer Studio

Design
**Livia Hermanny,
Kamila Lovo**

Index

Samsung and Sony Music has been awarded with 100+ awards including Cannes Lions, D&AD, One Show and Art Directors Club. Erik Herrström is now co-leading Studio Herrström as creative director.

P028

errorerror.studio®

www.errorerror.studio

errorerror.studio® is a Valencia-based creative studio working on brand identity, graphic design, typography, photography and communication campaign always from creative and art direction.

P046

Eugenia Maximova

www.behance.net/eugeniamax

Eugenia Maximova is a graphic designer and creator from Moscow. She creates ideas for brand identities, advertisign campaigns and packaging. She loves creating beautiful graphic story. Also she develop animation, advertisign video and photos for brands. Her goals is to evoke emotions in the viewer.

P240

Evgeniia Prokopeva

www.behance.net/mitrozhe

Evgeniia Prokopieva is a graphic designer from St. Petersburg, Russia.

P082

Folk Estudio

folk-estudio.com

Folk Estudio is a multidisciplinary design studio that seeks to add value to brands. Through creative, understandable and useful work, they develop customized projects and focus on design as a fundamental tool to help the positioning and growth of brands, companies and personal projects. Their work has been recognized by important design portals such as The Dieline, Behance, Morrre Design, etc.

P204

for&st

for-st.co

for&st is established with the moral "design for story", believing design is not just pure aesthetic but also to construct the experience. The name for&st extracted from "form & structure" and "forward & stand" and "for & story", they draft the aesthetic form and also the information hierarchy, and make ideas forward and stand with values that should treasure: to ask whom they are designing for and make the story behind to be heard, and at the end to grow together with all the partners like a forest.

P050

Han Gao

Workbyworks.nl

Han Gao, founder of Workbyworks, which offers creative direction, branding, web and graphic design. He has been working internationally with artists, musicians, fashion designers, programmers on various multi-field projects.

P030, P036

Hanna Karraby

hannakarraby.work

Hanna Karraby is a Philadelphia-based graphic designer working across branding, exhibition graphics, and editorial design. Her work is typographically-led and concept-centered. In addition to her independent practice, she is a senior graphic designer at the Philadelphia Museum of Art, where she specializes in designing visual identities for exhibitions.

P206

Heavy

heavy.mx

Heavy is a design studio based in Guadalajara, Mexico that focuses on branding and corporate identity. Heavy brands are created by building a narrative and core concept that the target can relate to, and hopefully, fall in love with. They perceive brands as people with character, taste and aspirations. Their method relies on a balance of emotional and aesthetic values that translates into strong positioning in a given market and recognition within the target audience.

P198

InFormat Design Curating

informat-design.com.tw

InFormat Design Curating is dedicated to renovate the process of design. The core value while dealing with projects are the spirit of curating and curating-oriented workflow.

   Within their former projects, InFormat Design Curating is aimed at seeking "the perfect" solution according to each case. Their preparation items include researching and analyzing the content, further developing working strategies. They integrate visual and interior teams through design planning, carrying their novel ideas and profession into a harmony — high quality works for customers.

P114

InSpace Creative

www.instagram.com/inspace_creative

Inspace Creative is a creative agency for brand identity and visual design in Ho Chi Minh City.

P210

Marina Coll, Lisa Kuntysh

marinacoll.com
lisakuntysh.com

Marina Coll and Lisa Kuntysh are graphic designers that are based in Barcelona, Spain. They met in Elisava while doing their Master degree in Visual Design in 2020 and ended up working together. Currently they are working for different design studios but always happy to reunion and work together on freelance projects.

P234

MARU

maruinc.net

Since 2013, Koichi Sugiyama has been developing a wide range of design activities from logos to packages and advertisements, aiming to create simple, powerful designs that convey as a good sign like "○" (maru, means "good" in Japanese) to everyone.

P185

maum studio

maumstudio.co.kr

maum studio is Seoul-based design studio. Their project starts with a story. In addition, they aim to deliver love and peace to projects such as graphics, space, and products that they are working on.

P066, P068

Menta

menta.is

Menta is a graphic design studio based in Guadalajara, Mexico, specializing in branding and packaging. Founded in 2008, Menta looks for inspiration in past decades and present times, to create meaningful brand identities that balance classic and contemporary aesthetics. Through clear concept definition and careful craftswoman-ship, they are passionate about the work they do for ethical, sustainable and conscious brands, with an ever-present focus on quality.

P246

Mockup&Co

mockupand.co

They are Milla & Ro, freelance designers making mockups so good, they don't look like mockups.

P160

Morcos Key

morcoskey.com

Morcos Key is a Brooklyn-based design studio collaborating with arts and cultural institutions, non-profits, and commercial enterprises in North America and the Middle East. They translate the clients' stories into visual systems that demonstrate how thoughtful conversation, and formal expression make for impactful design.

P076

My Creative

wearemycreative.com

My Creative is an independent design studio helping brands tell their story in the most memorable way. They help brands from all over the world communicate their story and work with people who have real passion for their product and for the people they want to engage with. They work with international large and small businesses, government and local agencies, non-profit organizations and even personal projects for individuals.

P104

NEON studio

neonstudio.cz

NEON studio is a graphic studio from Brno and they specialize in web projects and visual identities.

P042

nomo®creative

nomocreative.com

nomo®creative, a design studio from Taiwan, China. Founded in 2015, with different experienced people from various backgrounds, nomo®creative covered various industries includes fashion, art, entertainment and technology.

P054

Ochodias

www.behance.net/ochodias

Ochodias is a Latin-American creative studio in Mexico, a group of passionate people with curious spirits and strategic creative thinking. Ochodias helps build brand experiences through meaningful stories and powerful visual concepts that connects deeply with people. They like to re-imagine brands beyond convention. As artist, they are deeply moved to create culturally and artistically motivated initiatives.

P236

Omar H. Abdulqadir

www.behance.net/OmarHAbdulqadir

Omar H. Abdulqadir is a graphic designer from Al Khobar, Saudi Arabia.

P080

ONNFF STUDIO

www.instagram.com/onnffstudio

ONNFF STUDIO literally comes from "ON AND OFF" and represents two extreme states of things. They are keen to dig out the appearance of things themselves and hope to make thoughtful designs. The studio uses graphic design as the main means to discover the beauty of the details in life. They hope that every "extreme" treatment can infinitely collide with new ideas and inspiration.

P238

Pao Bassol

www.behance.net/paubassol

Pao Bassol is a graphic designer and illustrator based in Mérida, México. She has been around branding studios for more than nine years, who loves to use her skill in illustration bringing a certain human quality and personal touch to her designs. She loves exploiting her ability to develop different styles of illustration, this has made her give a different personality and style to all the illustrations for brands that she has developed.

P224

Paprika

paprika.com

Paprika creates functional and smart visual identities that propel brands to new heights. This assertive branding is also laced with emotion, to make it both more attractive and effective. Each brand identity is designed within established guidelines, to influence its era and stand the test of time.

P044, P150, P220

Pengguin

pengguin.hk

Pengguin is a multidisciplinary design studio based in Hong Kong, China. Found by the design duo – Todd and Soho, who believe in good design should always give a positive energy and visual satisfaction. They are also a storyteller, keening on sharing different story and concept by catching the chemistry between space and visual context.

P034, P118, P218

PG Brand Reforming Company

pg-branding.pl

PG Brand Reforming is an international strategic branding agency. They both create new brands and refresh existing brands based on current market needs. Every project has its own personalized insights and well thought out long term communication plan.

P058

Plácida

placida.es

Plácida is a graphic design studio based in Granada specialized in visual identity, editorial design, packaging and web design. They offer functional graphic solutions, associating concept and form, for an effective and contemporary communication of the company, brand or project.

Plácida uses graphic synthesis to face each project, which they understand as a more direct and effective form of communication, as well as a way to reach less obsolete solutions.

P056

Rebu

rebu.work

Rebu is an independent Brazilian studio and an acronym for revolutionary, elegant and unique.They make people's living through strategic thinking and experimental expression. They partner with non-conforming brands and people.

P194

Sakaria Studio

sakaria.se

Sakaria Studio designs artistic visual identities for brands, exhibitions and individuals.

Minna Sakaria is a graduate from the Royal College of Art in London. Besides running Sakaria Studio, she also works as lecturer in visual communication at Beckmans College of Design.

P136

Sitoh inc.

sitoh.co.jp

Sitoh inc. is a Tokyo-based design consulting firm that focuses on communication designs. They dedicate to extracting the context that maximizes a company's philosophy and principles and building up a corporate stance that embodies its worldview through creativity.

P112, P196

Sofia Noceti Studio

sofianoceti.com

sofianoceti (STUDIO) is the creative practice of Sofia Noceti, specialized in branding and graphic design. From a multi-disciplinary approach, they offer holistic solutions based on research and concepts that give life to visual identities. They believe that collaboration and a genuine interest on client's projects is the best way to create unique brands. For each project, they build bespoke teams with designers from different areas.

P142

Studio Woork

studiowoork.com

Studio Woork is a design studio based in Jakarta, Indonesia. Their services include branding, exhibition, print, product design, and also creative direction. With an independent mind, they constantly explore the boundaries of creativity in graphic design by creating a product with great value and concept. Through experimenting with things around, nature, humans, culture, and the environment, they believe design will be turned into something fresh, contemporary, and bold.

P152

Tangible

tangiblebd.com

Tangible is a creative agency where creates visual and verbal creativity for brands. Since 2013, it has been proposing a comprehensive branding solution ranging from brand concept, story, naming, brand identity, corporate identity, packaging, signage, and visual identity system. Tangible's mission is to maximize one's branding value by visualizing intangible corporate's philosophy to tangible.

P038

Tencent | FXD | :Daily Studio

:Daily studio is a studio within Tencent's FXD design team, mainly doing some independent researches and development projects, such as intangible cultural heritage or social welfare related projects.

P132

Tobias van der Valk

tobiasvandervalk.com

Tobias van der Valk is a graphic designer focused on visual identity, branding and motion design.

P032

Toby Ng Design

toby-ng.com

Toby Ng Design is an independent awards winning branding and design studio formed by creative communicators. They depict meaning from essence to generate value and impact for their partners, working closely with clients to find and amplify their voices, communicating with value and substance that places people first. They believe in the effectiveness of simplicity, they distill ideas to their essence, constructing compelling messages that endure.

P156

Triangler

triangler.com.tw

Triangler is a young design company composed of a group of design lovers based in Taipei. Triangler offers various design services, with the goal of delivering and creating the most suitable design service for every brand. They believe that good design is based on mutual trust and positive knowledge sharing. Triangler's main design services include brand and visual identity, graphic design, packaging design, web design and event hosting.

P154

Un Barco

unbarco.com

Un Barco is a creative studio based in Buenos Aires, Argentina, founded and led by Josefina Hernalz Boland and Tomás Fernandez Treviño since 2015. They create fresh brands, using a simple and direct language. They develop the whole branding process, from the first idea to its full implementation working closely with the clients, building strong relationships and taking care of every aspect of the design process. They do it all with passion and detail because they love what they do and they truly believe in the power of

visuals for changing things and accomplishing goals.

P100, P106, P108

Untitled Macao

untitledmacao.com

Untitled Macao, established in 2017, is a Macao based design studio. They are known for the professional, innovative, and progressive style of work. They strive to combine the power of strategic thinking, concepts, and creativity to bring the uniqueness of brands into our image design. Untitled Macao's services encompass the building of the brand image and visual identity, event promotion, and signage systems.

P126, P162, P200

VincDesign Branding Co.

vincdesign.com

VincDesign is a Hong Kong-based branding and design studio that specializes in creating visual identities and packaging. They believe that a brand is more than just a logo or a tagline. It's a representation of a company's values, mission, and personality. Their approach to branding is centered around a deep understanding of the clients' business goals, values, and aspirations. They work closely with the clients to develop custom branding solutions that are tailored to their specific needs.

P226

Wedge Studio

wedge.work

Wedge Studio joins clients to clarify and elevate their unique signature in the world. They work with a limited roster of clients each year. From legacies companies to up-and-coming icons, the goal is the same: ELEVATE POTENTIAL.

P232

Wikka

estudiowikka.com

Wikka is a creative studio that was born in a tiny corner of the Caribbean Sea. The headquarters are located in Barcelona and Cancun, but since 2016 they work with clients all over the world. They like great ideas, challenges, cool projects and good vibes.

Their goal is to create visual languages that communicate with impact, based on logical thinking, intuition, aesthetics and sensibility. That's why it is essential to always keep the minds and senses alert. They are passionate about building teams, shaping visions, innovating and transforming aims into new visual assets.

P164

Acknow-
ledgements

We would like to express our gratitude to all of the designers and agencies for their generous contribution of images, ideas and concepts. We are also very grateful to many other people whose names do not appear in the credits, but who have made specific contributions and provided support. Without them, the successful compilation of this book would not have been possible. Special thanks to all of the contributors for sharing their innovation and creativity with all of our readers around the world.